# FREE WILL AND THE
# CHRISTIAN FAITH

# FREE WILL AND THE CHRISTIAN FAITH

W. S. ANGLIN

CLARENDON PRESS · OXFORD

1990

Oxford University Press, Walton Street, Oxford OX2 6DP
Oxford New York Toronto
Delhi Bombay Calcutta Madras Karachi
Petaling Jaya Singapore Hong Kong Tokyo
Nairobi Dar es Salaam Cape Town
Melbourne Auckland
and associated companies in
Berlin Ibadan

Oxford is a trade mark of Oxford University Press

Published in the United States
by Oxford University Press, New York

© W. S. Anglin 1990

British Library Cataloguing in Publication Data
Anglin, W. S.
Free will and the Christian faith.
1. Christian doctrine. Free will
I. Title
234.9
ISBN 0–19–823936–X

Library of Congress Cataloging in Publication Data
Anglin, W. S.
Free will and the Christian faith/W. S. Anglin.
Includes bibliographical references and index.
1. Free will and determinism. 2. God—Will. 3. God—Omniscience.
4. God—Omnipotence. I. Title.
BJ1459.5A54    1990    233'.7—dc20    90–37548
ISBN 0–19–823936–X

Typeset by Cambrian Typesetters, Frimley, Surrey
Printed in Great Britain by
Bookcraft (Bath) Ltd
Midsomer Norton
Avon

*To Jesse*

# Preface

LIBERTARIANS such as J. R. Lucas have abandoned traditional Christian doctrines, such as the doctrine that God has complete foreknowledge, because they cannot reconcile them with the freedom of the will. Traditional Christian thinkers such as the later Augustine have repudiated libertarianism because they cannot fit it in with the dogmas of the Faith. What I hope to show in this book, however, is that it is possible to be both a libertarian and a traditional Christian. I believe there are other ways than mine of being both a libertarian and a traditional Christian, but I hope this work establishes the fact that there is at least one way.

In the first chapter I undertake to prove that we do have libertarian free will. To do this, I show that if we lack it then various awkward consequences follow, and these consequences are more awkward than those which follow on the opposite view.

In Chapter 2 I discuss God's existence and some of his attributes. I argue that God himself has libertarian free will, and I talk about how this relates to his uniqueness. Although proofs for God's existence or non-existence are not usually convincing, they do serve to bring out certain presuppositions about divine beings, and we therefore examine some of these proofs.

The third chapter looks at God's omnipotence. We give an improved version of Kenny's definition of this concept. We also answer the question, 'how can an omnipotent God lack the power to prevent someone from sinning?'

In Chapter 4 we uphold the view that, although our future choices are not determined, God has a complete knowledge of what they will be. To do this we employ not the notion of 'middle knowledge' but rather the idea of 'backwards causation'—which we defend against a number of objections in the literature.

Chapter 5 investigates God's goodness. How can God be good and still take the risk of creating a person who, on account of libertarian free will, might do evil? We do not give the usual utilitarian answer to this question but rather make use of the Principle of Double Effect.

In Chapter 6 our premiss that we have libertarian free will plays a crucial role. For it is here that we confront the problem of evil. We show how free will explains not only moral evil but many of its consequences as well, and we do not hesitate to attack the problem of natural evil.

Chapter 7 discusses immortality. The claim that we have libertarian free will is evoked in an argument designed to defend a mind-body dualism against Parfit's views. It is also evoked in the discussion of whether hell can coexist with a just God.

Chapter 8 assumes that there is a God who wishes to communicate with us. We address this question, 'how do we know which messages really do come from God?'

In summary, we shall treat just those topics found in almost any introduction to Philosophy of Religion. However, we shall defend a position on them which is at once libertarian and orthodox.

I wish to thank the many philosophers who have given me key insights and kind encouragement. In particular, I wish to thank Ray Salmon, Bruce Garside, Jim Lambek, Allistair McKinnon, Peter Timmons, Fergus O'Grady, John Lucas, Basil Mitchell, Alvin Plantinga, Thomas Flint, Thomas Morris, and Eleanore Stump.

I also wish to thank the Centre for Philosophy of Religion at the University of Notre Dame for its support in 1988–9, and the Social Sciences and Humanities Research Council of Canada for its support in 1989–90.

W. S. Anglin

*McGill University, 1990*

# Table of Contents

# I

# Free Will

OUR understanding of God is related to our understanding of the universe. If we think that the universe is a nasty, inescapable torture-machine, we shall probably not think that there is a good and all-powerful God. However, if we think that the universe is a beautifully arranged hierarchy with persons near the top, we shall be inclined to believe that there is a good, personal God at its upper limit. To get the right view of God, then, it is useful to start with the right view of the universe, and, in particular, the right view of human beings. Are we just nuts and bolts in some materialistic system which is, for all practical purposes, determined by arbitrary laws of nature? Are we, on the contrary, immortal souls, captains of our own eternal destiny, as necessary to creation as matter and energy? From someone's answers to such questions it would not be difficult to guess his answers to questions like 'what kind of God is there?' Our view of God reflects our view of man and vice versa. Indeed, some thinkers claim that doing theology is merely a backhanded way of doing anthropology. It is not that God makes us in his image but that we make God in ours.

In my Philosophy of Religion, the question of whether God is a person, the nature of his omnipotence, and the resolution of the problem of evil are all bound up with the premiss that human beings have libertarian free will. In this chapter, therefore, I try to argue for that premiss. Sometimes I shall talk about God in order to make certain points. However, except for some of my opponent's putative objections, nothing in this chapter depends on the assumption that there is a God. It is only in the next chapter that we shall ask whether God actually exists. In this chapter we confine ourselves to a discussion of human decision making.

The argument in this chapter may be summarized as follows:

> If human beings do not have a libertarian free will which includes the possibility of choosing evil then eight 'unacceptable' conclusions follow. Hence human beings do have a

libertarian free will which includes the possibility of choosing evil.

This chapter is divided into four sections. In the first, I discuss the concept of 'unacceptable' conclusions. In the second, I define libertarian free will. In the third, I give eight arguments with eight unacceptable conclusions. In the fourth, I answer an objection to the effect that my position, no less than its negation, also leads to eight unacceptable conclusions.


I


In mathematics there is the *reductio ad absurdum*. If *p* then *q*. If *q* then 2 + 2 = 3. But this is absurd. Thus not-*p*. In philosophy there is also another sort of *reductio*. If *p* then *q*. If *q* then babies should be boiled alive. Thus not-*p*.

Let us call a statement 'unacceptable' if (1) it is not known to be true, and (2) its truth would contradict assumptions and attitudes which go deep in our lives, and (3) it would contradict them in such a way that life would become, not just miserable or pessimistic, but unthinkable. For example, the statement

> Hitler killed six million Jews

is in this sense acceptable (because it is true) but the statement

> Babies should be boiled alive

is not. Other examples of unacceptable statements are:

> Everything is ultimately meaningless.

> All great art is repugnant.

> It would be all right to destroy the human race for the fun of it.

> Women are no better than dogs.

The fact that a statement is 'unacceptable' does not imply that it is false. None the less, it does imply that it would be perverse not to reject it. This is because the acceptance of such a statement would undermine life in general, and reason in particular. A person who rejects 'unacceptable' statements is not a naïve optimist: he is simply choosing to think like a sane, functioning member of the human community.

Take, for example, the idea that everything is ultimately meaningless. It is perverse not to reject this idea, because its truth would contradict our view that certain kinds of work are ultimately meaningful, and our view that it is not ultimately meaningless to be kind to others.

In any case, if a philosopher succeeds in showing that a premiss leads to a conclusion which, although it cannot be ruled out as factually false, is none the less unacceptable in the above sense, then he has dealt that premiss a solid blow. For example, against utilitarianism one tries to show that it implies that sometimes innocent people ought to be hanged. Against Christianity one tries to show that it implies that women are no better than dogs. If one succeeds in such an argument, one may not be able to claim that the known facts imply the falsity of the premiss, but one can claim that it would be highly inappropriate or infelicitous to accept such a premiss.

I do not think that we have any way of knowing whether we have what philosophers call libertarian free will. Certainly, psychologists have not yet given us this delicate information. It does not come from quantum mechanics or astrophysics. Even theologians are no better able to tell us. For although some of them believe that God's omnipotence requires that there be no free will (at least not in the strong, libertarian sense we shall define below), others hold that the fact of moral evil cannot be explained without it. God himself (assuming for a moment that he exists) has not thought it worthwhile to utter a proclamation that would settle the issue. He does have his prophets bring messages about individual responsibility and the importance of choosing virtue over vice but he never gets them to define the terms in such a way that a philosopher could know that the freedom involved was 'incompatibilist' as opposed to 'soft determinist'. Might one conclude from God's silence that this precise bit of information is neither necessary to our salvation nor sufficient to set us at odds with each other?

As a two-value logic realist, I assume that the proposition 'human beings have libertarian free will' has exactly one of those two truth values. It is either true or false. In this chapter I am going to argue that if it is false then eight unacceptable conclusions follow. This will not prove absolutely that we have libertarian free will but it will allow us to chide our opponents for their melancholy, repugnant, and 'unthinkable' picture of the world.

## II

We begin by setting up some terminology. Roughly speaking, an event, act, or state of affairs *e* is *determined* in a possible world *W* if and only if there is no possible world *W'* such that (1) *W'* does not contain *e* and (2) *W'* is the same as *W* (having the same natural laws, for example) except that it does not contain *e* or the consequences (in *W*) of *e*. If we let *S* be that part of *W* which includes everything except *e* and its consequences then we can rephrase this definition as follows: an event, act, or state of affairs *e* is determined in a possible world *W* if and only if it is not possible to have *S* without *e*. The event, act, or state of affairs *e* is said to be determined by *S*.

(We could make this definition more precise by saying some things about what it is to be a consequence, about events which turn on something's *not* being the case, about the possibility of the same state of affairs occurring at two different times, once deterministically and once indeterministically, and so on. The extra punctiliousness would not affect our arguments. However, the reader should note that our definition does *not* imply that an event is determined merely by the past.)

As an example, suppose Professor Smith throws a book out the library window. It is determined that the book hit the ground (as it actually does) if and only if there is no possible world like this one (except for the book's hitting the ground and its consequences) in which the book does not hit the ground. The book's hitting the ground is determined, if it is, by the general situation consisting of the nature of the book, the law of gravity, and, indeed, everything except the book's hitting the ground and its consequences.

As a second example, suppose that God has irrevocably decided that at eight o'clock Professor Smith shall decide to go to church and repent. Either Smith will make this decision on his own or else, failing that, God will intervene to make him make this decision. Then, given this initial situation, it is not possible that Smith not decide to go to church—and this is true even if, in fact, God does not have to intervene.

If *e* is determined by *S* then if *e* were not to occur, *S* would not occur either. There are a number of possible reasons why if *e* were not to occur, *S* would not occur either. If *e*'s not occurring together with *S*'s occurring would imply a breach of natural laws or the failure of some object to act in accordance with its nature, then *e* is *nomologically* determined by *S*. For example, the book's hitting the ground would be nomologically determined by the situation sketched above. If *e*'s not occurring together with *S*'s occurring would involve countermanding an irrevocable divine decision, then *e* is *deistically* determined by *S*. For example, Smith's deciding to go to church would be deistically determined if God had irrevocably decided that Smith would decide to go to church. Note that if God has complete control over the laws of nature then nomological determinism is merely a species of deistic determinism. If, in either of the above senses, *e* is determined by *S* then *S* is said to be a *sufficient cause* of *e*, and *e* an *inevitable outcome* of *S*.

Note that a human action, even if it is not determined, is not in any sense 'random'. For the person is typically aware of what he is doing, and he is doing it because he wants to. What he does, determined or not, does not 'happen to him': on the contrary, it is a bit of conscious and purposeful behaviour. Often, too, there is a specific reason for the action which, even though it does not determine the action, makes it perfectly intelligible. For example, suppose Professor Smith decides to go to London in order to buy books. This decision is certainly not a random event, nor does it become one if we somehow discover that his decision was not determined, that, in exactly the same circumstances *S*, Smith could equally well have decided to go to New York to buy books. Thus someone like Galen Strawson is completely off-track if he describes Smith's decision as an 'entirely non-rational ... flip-flop of the soul'.[1]

Let *Z* be a person and let *p* be a proposition which *Z* believes is not (yet) true. We say that *Z* *wills* that *p* if and only if *Z* decides to bring it about that *p* is the case (if he can). The proposition *p* might have the form '*Z* does the dishes', in which case '*Z* wills that *p*' is usually rendered '*Z* decides to do the dishes'. Since deciding is much like willing, this definition might be accused of circularity. However, we can supplement it with some axioms to help give it

---

[1] Galen Strawson, *Freedom and Belief* (Oxford: Clarendon Press, 1986), 53–4.

content. Where $Dp$ is intended to mean 'Z decides to bring it about that $p$ (if he can)', we could have

    1. If $D(\neg p)$ then $\neg Dp$
    2. If both $D(\neg p)$ and $D(p$ or $q)$ then $Dq$
    3. If $D(p \ \& \ q)$ then $Dp$ and $Dq$[2]

Let us consider these axioms in turn. The first axiom is

    1. If $D(\neg p)$ then $\neg Dp$

which is meant to be read: if Z decides to bring it about that $p$ is not the case (if he can) then he does not also decide to bring it about that $p$ be the case (if he can). For example, if Maid Marilyn decides not to seduce Professor Smith then she does not, at the same time, decide to seduce him. (She may *want* to seduce him but she wills otherwise.)

The second axiom is

    2. If both $D(\neg p)$ and $D(p$ or $q)$ then $Dq$

which is meant to be read: if Z decides to bring it about that $p$ is not the case (if he can), and he also decides to bring it about that at least one of $p$ and $q$ is true (if he can) then he decides to bring it about that $q$ is the case (if he can). For example, if Wily William decides not to seduce Maid Marilyn and also decides to seduce at least one of the two young ladies, Maid Marilyn and Mary Jane, then he is, in effect, deciding to seduce Mary Jane.

The third axiom is

    3. If $D(p \ \& \ q)$ then $Dp$ and $Dq$

In other words, if someone decides to bring it about that both $p$ and $q$ be the case (if he can) then he decides to bring it about that $p$ is the case (if he can), and he also decides to bring it about that $q$ is the case (if he can).

In discussing God's choices, Zeis and Jacobs claim that choosing two things together does not mean choosing each individually.[3] For someone might choose to have two kinds of food together but not choose to have the first kind alone. Suppose that Smith decides to

---

[2] Jaakko Hintikka, *Knowledge and Belief* (Ithaca: Cornell University Press, 1962) contains a discussion of such axioms.

[3] John Zeis and J. Jacobs, 'Omnipotence and Concurrence', *International Journal for Philosophy of Religion*, 14 (1983), 17–24.

have pork and apple sauce but then learns that there is no apple sauce left. Does his decision commit him to have pork without apple sauce? It seems not.

To this I reply that when someone decides to bring something about he assumes that it is in some sense possible. When Smith learns that there is no apple sauce left he can no longer choose to have pork and apple sauce because, short of going to another restaurant, he cannot have pork and apple sauce. He must change his mind. During the time he wills to have pork and apple sauce he does will to have pork, but as soon as he learns this is not possible he ceases both to will to have pork and also to will to have pork and apple sauce. Thus the counterexample proposed by Zeis and Jacobs does not defeat the above axiom.

Furthermore, on the view Zeis and Jacobs put forward, if Maid Marilyn decided, for example, to rob the poor and give to the rich, it would not necessarily follow that she had decided to rob the poor. And if she had never decided to rob the poor, how could she be held responsible for having robbed them? Zeis and Jacobs wish to exonerate God for choosing to create a universe containing both good and evil. However, if they do this by denying that he willed the evil then they may end up exonerating all those criminals who have any good mixed in with their evil designs.

We might want to add a fourth axiom to our system:

4. If $Dp$ then $DDp$

This is meant to be read: if Z decides to bring it about that $p$ then he also decides to bring it about (if he can) that he decides to bring $p$ about. For example, if Professor Smith decides to pay the blackmailer then he is deciding to decide to pay the blackmailer. This fourth axiom attempts to express the idea that if someone wills something then he does so willingly.

In certain cases this fourth axiom is false. Suppose Marilyn is struggling against the temptation to seduce Professor Smith. She decides that she shall not decide to seduce him and hence (by the first axiom) it is not the case that she decides to decide to seduce him. None the less, at the same time, she does decide to seduce him. She wills to seduce him but, perhaps because of her conscience, she does not will this willingly. Thus we should not add the fourth axiom to our list.

In this connection, it may be claimed that, although we cannot always put our decisions into effect, at least we can implement decisions about what we shall decide or not decide. Thus the following should be axioms:

5. If $DDp$ then $Dp$

and

6. If $D(\neg Dp)$ then $\neg Dp$

To this I reply that we are not always masters of our own wills. Just as one can have false beliefs about what one believes—Marilyn says she believes she will go to heaven but she none the less has a morbid fear of death—so one can fail in implementing decisions about one's decisions. For example, I can decide that I shall decide to treat my wife better but fail to make that latter decision because I am confronted by her spitefulness. Again, a sick person might decide to get better and therefore decide to decide to eat but still not succeed in deciding to eat. It is therefore appropriate that the above statements are not axioms on our list.[4]

We say something *makes* Z will that $p$ if there is some identifiable factor in Z's environment, his mind or his brain which causes him to will that $p$, in a way that precludes all other alternatives. Stock examples are: Z is drugged, brainwashed, addicted, hypnotized, mad, senile, or threatened. Note that nothing is said about determinism here. If Z decides to open the safe under threat of death, we can quite happily say that Z was made to do this, even if we think that it was not determined that he not choose death instead. Again, suppose that, unknown to Z, he is given a drug which, in 99 out of 100 cases, causes a person to decide to seek a new wife. Suppose, moreover, that, as a result of being given this drug, Z does decide to seek a new wife. Even though there is no strict deterministic link between the drug and the decision, we still say that the drug made him decide to seek a new wife. The issue of determinism does not come in when we talk about 'free will' merely in the crude sense that a decision taken under the influence of a drug is not free. Whether one is a determinist or not, one will agree that freedom is lacking when, in the above sense, something makes the agent decide as he does.

Determinism does come in when we want to differentiate

---

[4] See Romans 7: 14–25 and also A. Van den Beld, 'Romans 7: 14–25 and the Problem of Akrasia', *Religious Studies*, 21 (1985), 513.

'libertarian free will' from the very broad notion of free will which is at stake in the above examples. A *libertarian* is one who holds that human beings sometimes have free will in the following sense:

> A person Z freely wills that $p$
> if and only if
> Z wills that $p$
>> and nothing makes Z will that $p$
>> and it is not determined that Z will that $p$.

We say that

> A person Z has libertarian free will
> if and only if
> Z has the ability or capacity to will freely in the libertarian sense.

Let us consider an objection to the libertarian's definition of free will. Suppose that Z wills that $p$ and the only reason he does not freely will that $p$ (in the libertarian sense) is that, unknown to him, there is some 'barrier' which, without actually having any effect on Z, precludes the possibility of his not willing that $p$. For example, suppose there is some brain malfunction or some decision of God's which, in the circumstances, is sufficient to ensure that Z does not fail to will that $p$, and suppose, moreover, that it does not, in fact, come into play because, all on his own, Z goes ahead and wills that $p$.[5] In such a case there seems to be no psychological difference between what Z does and what he would do if this hidden barrier were not there. Because it happens that Z picks the alternative open to him—and he picks it in the normal way—the barrier never shows itself, and Z's willing is no different from what it would be were the barrier absent. Thus we cannot say that in the two cases the willing is different. Hence there is no distinction between libertarian and nonlibertarian free will.

In answer to this I say that two acts can differ simply because they occur under different circumstances. It is one thing to stay at home to read when you could go out, and quite another thing to stay at home to read when, unknown to you, you have been locked in your house in such a way that you cannot get out. The 'freedom' of your staying at home depends not only on your psychology but

---

[5] Such an example is due to Harry Frankfurt. See, for example, John Martin Fischer (ed.), *Moral Responsibility* (Ithaca: Cornell University Press, 1986), 146.

on the circumstances as a whole. For a libertarian the will is not free unless it is free to make a difference to the sequence of events—and this difference must be more than the mere fact that something is willed indeterministically rather than deterministically. If the same things are going to happen regardless then, even if the local causal history of a choice is indeterministic, the choice itself is no more significant than some flimsy epiphenomenon. Whether the determinism works through the agent's will to produce the uniquely determined outcome or whether it merely stands by to ensure that the uniquely determined outcome is produced, it still precludes what a libertarian calls a free choice.

We say that $Z$ has libertarian free will which *extends to evil* if for some proposition $p$ which describes a state of affairs believed by $Z$ to be on the whole bad, $Z$ has the power freely to will that $p$ (in the libertarian sense). In the next section we argue that normal human beings are finite or limited in certain ways such that, if they have libertarian free will, then it does extend to evil. We shall ignore peculiar cases such as human beings who think everything is, on the whole, good, or human beings who are in heaven. What we argue is that if normal human beings have libertarian free will then they can do evil.

### III

Consider the premiss that human beings do not have libertarian free will which extends to evil. In this section we argue that this premiss leads to the following unacceptable conclusions:

(1) Human beings are not truly rational;
(2) Human beings do not have any real artistic creativity;
(3) Human beings are not fully responsible for good and evil in a way that really makes a difference;
(4) Human beings cannot really choose their values;
(5) There is no genuine co-operation among human beings;
(6) There is no true love among human beings;
(7) Human beings cannot love unconditionally;
(8) Human beings cannot really make promises.

I do not think that in a deterministic universe human beings (or the nearest equivalent) cannot reason, create, love, and so on—if you are willing to adopt some watered-down versions of these concepts. However, as the reader will have noticed, words such as 'true' and 'genuine' appear in the above list. Thus true rationality, I claim, does presuppose libertarian free will. In what follows, I say, in each case, what I mean by the 'genuine' version of the ability or capacity in question. I hope it will be evident that the genuine article is a desirable thing. I then argue that having this genuine version entails that human beings have libertarian free will which extends to evil.

## (1) Rationality

What do we mean by 'true rationality'? True rationality is not a mere capacity to do logical deductions (although it includes this), nor a mere capacity to adapt to the environment, but a capacity to weigh or evaluate reasons in such a manner as to get at the actual, objective truth of things. A rational person evaluates different possibilities in such a way as to arrive at the objective truth. He chooses which reasons he shall consider important and which he shall lay aside. He decides which of a number of explanations, all compatible with the available evidence, is actually true. Rationality includes logical computation and it serves a pragmatic purpose but it also does more: it reveals the way things really are.[6]

Does reasoning, seen in this light, presuppose libertarian free will? Yes, for if reasoning were deterministic then, even if it yielded true conclusions by means of applying valid argument forms, it would still be more an instance of a system getting results than of a person deciding what was true. In order to reason about something, we must, as it were, stand back from the world and observe it objectively. Hence we cannot ourselves be part of some deterministic system which, although it might bring it about that we came to the correct conclusion, might also bring it about that we came to an incorrect conclusion (say, for some temporary pragmatic reason). If it is *we* who are to do the reasoning then there cannot be some deterministic system reasoning through us. On the contrary, we must ourselves be the ultimate judges of the data, the ultimate arbitrators of the various reasons and explanations put forth to

[6] This argument does, of course, presuppose a realist view of the world.

throw light on the matter in question. If we are to reason our way through to the objective truth then we—and not some factors extraneous to us—must have the ultimate control over the reasoning. Hence our reasoning cannot be determined. The choices involved in it must be free in the libertarian sense.

Note that this does not mean that to arrive at truth we must be 'free' to deduce not-$q$ from $p$ and $p$ entails $q$. The freedom comes in in evaluating the premises or in evaluating arguments that cannot easily be translated into logical symbolism because, for example, they involve subtle modalities or probabilities. It also comes in in deciding when to rely on principles such as 'the simplest explanation is the truest'.

To take an example, suppose the universe is in a state such that it follows by the laws of nature that in ten years there will be a configuration of human bodies and sound waves that can be described by saying 'Professor Smith is lecturing on his reasons for his recent conversion to Islam'. Is this compatible with Smith's reasoning his way to Islam? No doubt Smith will be embracing Islam for the reasons he will give in his lecture. However, if his considering those reasons to be important rather than some other reasons is merely a complicated but uniquely determined function of a previous state of the universe, then there is no reason for us or for Smith to think that the reasons are decisive from the point of view of objective truth. To reason is not just to work out syllogisms but also to evaluate reasons and, to do that, we must respond to them in an undetermined manner. We must stand apart from our wants, vested interests, and any other possibly determining factors, nomological or deistic, and accept or reject reasons on their own merits. When we accept certain reasons for embracing a doctrine, we do so, we hope, not merely because it is useful or convenient to do so but because we judge that they tell in favour of the objective truth of the doctrine. Indeed, it is only if our acceptance of reasons is not deterministic that we say that we are judging them in a truly rational manner and are thereby coming to know the truth. Thus there is the *ad hominen* argument against determinism that its proponents hold it to be true only because it is determined that they do so.[7]

[7] A much more subtle and sustained argument to the effect that reasoning is incompatible with determinism is found in J. R. Lucas, *The Freedom of the Will* (Oxford: Clarendon Press, 1970). A number of other authors draw attention to the

Given, then, that true reasoning does require libertarian free will—so that one can stand back from the world, free of distorting influences, judging the premisses and their interconnections in a wholly objective manner—is it necessary that the scope of this free will extend to evil? In the case of God (and of the saints who, by their free choice, are now in heaven), the answer is no. God can reason—using libertarian free will—but there is no possibility that in so doing he reject a reason he ought, morally, to accept, or accept one he ought, morally, to reject. He cannot choose to behave in an irrational manner because he is by nature good. In the case of finite, fallible beings such as ourselves, however, the situation is different. Because we are human (and not in heaven), the fact that we reason, and hence have libertarian free will, does imply that we have the power to act irrationally. We can, for example, decide to reject someone's argument, not because it is a bad argument, but because we have decided to maintain our own, opposing argument at all costs. Moreover, acting irrationally in this manner is a moral evil. It is a kind of wilful ignorance. Thus the existence of rationality in human persons implies the possibility of moral evil. Such persons are capable of making not only honest but also deliberate mistakes in reasoning. As another example, if we decide with libertarian free will whether to accept or reject explanations of people's conduct, we are in a position to put a better or worse interpretation on it. Sometimes the right interpretation is the bad one, but if we always chose the worse interpretation, that would be an evil. Yet because we are free to choose a good or bad interpretation, we are free always to choose a bad one. The freedom entailed by our rationality—assuming we are rational in the above sense—makes it possible for us to do evil.

What if we lacked rationality in the above sense? I claim that the assertion that we cannot reason in the above sense is an unacceptable assertion. This is because its truth would mean that we could not rely on our reasoning to arrive at the truth. Belief in such an assertion would undermine the human quest for knowledge. It would leave us with an enfeebling scepticism.

same point: Joseph M. Boyle *et al.*, *Free Choice* (Notre Dame: University of Notre Dame Press, 1976), 40–7 and 144–7; John Hick, *Death and Eternal Life* (Glasgow: William Collins Sons, 1976), 116–19; D. J. O'Connor, *Free Will* (London: Macmillan, 1971), 35 and 47–8; Edgar Wilson, *The Mental as Physical* (London: Routledge and Kegan Paul, 1979), 262–3.

## (2) Creativity

Does artistic creativity presuppose libertarian free will? A compatibilist would say it does not. According to him, there would be nothing wrong in saying that the state of the universe was such in 1000 BC that, precisely when he did compose it, Beethoven would compose his Fifth Symphony. Moreover, if we gave someone the same mental state as Beethoven and put that person in a situation similar to that in which Beethoven composed the Fifth Symphony then that person would automatically go ahead and write down the Fifth Symphony. This, according to someone who thinks that free will is compatible with determinism, is artistic creativity: being in such a state of mind and in such circumstances that one produces a work which is uniquely determined by that state of mind and those circumstances. One's 'creation' is a complex but necessary outworking of one's total situation.

The more exalted view of what it is to create, however, is the view that one brings forth something that is not implicit in the past. The circumstances of the artist influence him, of course, but they do not supply that particular vision or insight which becomes the work of art. It is not nature nor God but simply the composer who creates the symphony. One need not expect there to be a situation such that any person in that situation—with his character and musical abilities and so on similar to those of Beethoven—would write down exactly the same notes as Beethoven wrote down. Beethoven himself, in that situation, might well have composed a different symphony or even no symphony at all. What he did was not determined and, if it had been determined, then it would not have been a case of creativity. On one view of creativity, then, it does presuppose the exercise of libertarian free will.

Assuming that artistic creativity presupposes libertarian free will, does this free will have to include the power to do evil? In the case of ordinary human beings, the answer is yes. The artist, when given a choice between something less beautiful and something more beautiful, or between something less edifying and something more edifying, may well be right to choose the inferior. This might, for example, increase the beauty of the total composition. Given the libertarian free will necessary to his creating, the artist is thus in a position always to choose the inferior. The artist, because he can idealise, can also distort. Because he can bring out the divine aspect of things, he can also deliberately conceal it. Love poetry, for example, can lead the soul to God but it can also lead the soul to some merely finite order of being. Thus, although God can never misuse his creative powers (because he is by nature good), finite human beings, in being free to create works of art, are also free to create needlessly inferior works of art, to emphasise the creature rather than giving glory to the creator. Given the power to create, we are free to glamorise cigarettes instead of health, to fashion idols instead of icons.

Is the statement that we lack genuine creativity an unacceptable statement? Yes, for if we lack genuine creativity we can only produce what we are made to produce, or what it is determined that we produce. The 'genius' of the artist is reduced to a mere outworking of factors in the distant past. The artist becomes a messenger rather than a creator.

## (3) Reponsibility

As Frankfurt has pointed out, there is a sense of 'responsible' in which one can be responsible for the fact that one wills that $p$ even though one does not freely will that $p$ in the libertarian sense.[8] It is not the case that every kind of responsibility presupposes an exercise of libertarian free will. For example, suppose that Marilyn is deliberating about whether she should say yes or no to Smith. Unknown to her, God has set up some sort of barrier which makes it impossible for her to decide that she will say yes. Marilyn goes through her deliberations in the usual way and, in the usual way, decides that she will say no. The hidden barrier never comes into play. Since her deciding is just like the normal case of deciding—where there are no hidden barriers—she is responsible for her decision in the normal way. However, she did not decide freely in the libertarian sense since it was determined that she decide to say no to Smith.

What is peculiar about Marilyn's responsibility in the above example is that it is not a responsibility for anything that would have made a real difference. If the barrier had come into play (and if God rather than Marilyn had been responsible for the decision)

---

[8] Frankfurt, in *Moral Responsibility*, p. 146.

then Marilyn would still have decided to say no. Marilyn made a choice but she lacked the power to bring about a different situation. It was as if she was fated to decide against Smith's proposition.

Let *e* be a morally significant event. For example, *e* might be choosing to resist a temptation to commit adultery. Let us say that a person Z is *ultimately responsible* for *e* if (1) Z is responsible for it; (2) Z does not share this responsibility with any other person or thing; and (3) it is false that *e* would have occurred in any case, even if Z had not chosen it in the normal way. If a person is responsible in this sense for bringing something about then he alone deserves the credit or blame for having brought it about, and he alone has determined that it should be so. His is the dignity of being the sole originator of the event, the one master and cause of it. Thus a universe containing persons who have this sort of responsibility is better than one in which persons have only a partial, derived, or fated responsibility for their deeds. In particular, if these persons are ultimately responsible for doing good or evil then they can be described as the sole masters of their moral destiny—a glorious title indeed.

If Marilyn is ultimately responsible for some decision then it is not the case that part of the responsibility belongs to prior factors not dependent on Marilyn. Thus it is not the case that her decision is a mere outworking of some past state of the universe. Furthermore, it is not the case that God or nature has arranged matters so that, in one way or another, it will inevitably come about that she make that decision. Clearly, then, if Marilyn is ultimately responsible for some decision then she has libertarian free will.

To say that one has ultimate responsibility for one's decisions is not to imply that these decisions might be evil. God, for example, has ultimate responsibility for his decisions but there is no chance that they might be evil—for God is by nature good. However, in the case of finite, human beings with imperfect knowledge, there is the occasion not only for honest mistakes but also for morally evil choices. If Adam has libertarian free will in connection with morally significant alternatives then, since he lacks perfect knowledge, he may well do evil. Not being fully aware of the consequences of his decisions, he may choose to do evil in the hope of furthering his personal happiness. If human beings have ultimate responsibility for doing morally good things then they are able to do morally evil things as well.

Is the assertion that human beings lack ultimate responsibility an unacceptable assertion? Yes, for its truth would undermine statements like 'I'm sorry, I should have avoided it' or 'you did well, you deserve full credit for extraordinary honesty'. If we believed we lacked ultimate responsibility then we would believe that we ourselves could not make any real moral difference to the world. The effect would be a feeling of impotence and despair. If we lacked ultimate responsibility, it would be misguided rather than noble to 'accept full responsibility' for one's mistake; it would be naïve rather than generous to praise an enemy for 'unnecessary kindness'.

## (4) Choices of values

The ability to choose values is the ability not of doing what you think you ought to do but choosing which things you will henceforth think you ought to do. For example, you might decide that henceforth you will value God more than money, or your spouse more than your academic career. You decide that, in situations of conflict, you will take it that what you ought to do is put God ahead of money, or your spouse ahead of the academe. Compatibilists are sometimes given to praising the freedom of doing what you want, but occasionally we stand back from our various desires and decide which ones we shall renounce and which ones we shall encourage. We are then choosing what we shall value, making 'metachoices' which will affect our more ordinary choices.

In the examples of the previous paragraph, the choice seems to be between placing the higher value on the more valuable thing (e.g. God), or placing the higher value on the less valuable thing (e.g. money). There may, however, be cases in which it is not true that one thing is really more valuable than another. For example, cultural prejudices aside, it may be that polygamy is no more or less good than monogamy. In choosing values, one might choose to value polygamy at the expense of monogamy, and one might do so in such a way that one was thereby really happier with polygamy. If, as Paul asserts, a Christian is really 'released from the Law' then presumably God himself would accept such a choice and help the Christian find happiness in polygamy.

Does the ability to choose values presuppose libertarian free will?

A compatibilist may urge that 'metachoices' no less than other choices can be seen as based on psychological needs or other determining factors. Choosing values is just choosing to have some different 'lower-order' desires on account of having certain 'higher-order' desires. However, if the choice of values is determined, it will be determined in conjunction with existing values and will thus be a mere outworking of these existing values. The person will not be picking new values so much as merely expressing in a new way values already there. Against the compatibilist suggestion, there is the view that to choose a set of values is to act autonomously, detached from the past and even from God. Choosing values is a matter of transcending one's previous values, culture, and any other determining factors. One thinks of Camus's 'Outsider' who does not begin to be free until, faced with death, he stops valuing the things he was determined by society to value, and decides of his own accord to value the beauties of nature. To choose values is to 'come out' from one's previous culture, morality, and so on, and, in spite of such influences, embark on a course that is really one's own. In this sense, the choice of values does presuppose libertarian free will.

Since God is omniscient and wholly good, he cannot place a high value on inferior things.[9] However, in the case of human beings, the power to choose values does not imply that its possessor will always use it to value the things he believes he ought to value. I may know perfectly well that my spouse is more important than the television and yet decide to put the television first. This is simply the phenomenon of *akrasia*. Thus, in the case of human beings, the ability to choose values implies the possibility of its misuse.

One might object that, surely, God could create human beings who could choose their values but never in a way that was wrong. Their freedom would be bound by goodness.

I reply that God could not do this without giving these 'human beings' the property of necessary goodness. Now necessary goodness is a divine attribute which, as we shall see in subsequent chapters, is closely tied to other divine attributes, such as omniscience and omnipotence. It can be argued that no one is necessarily good unless he is preserved from evil by a vast knowledge, and it can be argued that no one has a vast knowledge,

---

[9] I am assuming that, in some cases, goodness is an objective matter. For a defence of this, see Richard Swinburne, *The Coherence of Theism* (Oxford: Oxford University Press, 1977), 183–203.

in this sense, unless he can translate that knowledge into powerful deeds. Thus if we are talking about beings who are necessarily good then we are not talking about human beings as we know them. A human being is something quite distinct from God. In particular, if a human being has libertarian free will then it is normally possible that, at least once during his existence, he give priority to something which he believes he ought to put in second place.

Is the assertion that we cannot really choose our values an unacceptable assertion? Yes, for our whole dignity as individuals depends on our ability to assert our own personal values in a way that is not determined by our environment. If we could not really choose our own values then, when we considered something to be important, we would do so only because our past or our culture brought it about that we did so. A person's priorities would not be in his own hands, and his identity would be fixed by factors alien to him.

## (5) Co-operation

Does genuine co-operation presuppose the existence of libertarian free will? Consider the following example. A clever speaker manipulates a crowd in such a way as to raise money. He appeals to people's guilt and they give large sums. Later, however, they regret having done so. This is a kind of co-operation with the speaker but not genuine co-operation. Similarly, God might have arranged things so that we went along with his perfect will, always doing what was right, but that would not involve genuine co-operation with him. The source of genuine co-operation has to be only the person who co-operates. The co-operation cannot be genuine if it has a sufficient cause external to the person. There has to be an exercise of libertarian free will.

Does the libertarian free will required for co-operation include evil in its scope? Human beings find themselves not alone in the universe but with other beings (e.g. God) with whom they may or may not co-operate. If this co-operation is to be genuine, moreover, there is implied the possibility of not co-operating, and that might be evil. If it lies entirely in Adam's power whether he will co-operate with God or not, then, since Adam is not by nature good or omniscient, he has the opportunity to refuse. There is the possibility of evil. Furthermore, if Adam has the power of genuine co-operation, he may use it to co-operate with, say, the devil.

Is the statement that we are incapable of genuine co-operation an unacceptable statement? Yes, for just as a denial of an individual's ability really to choose values undermines his dignity as an individual, so a denial of a group's ability to be based on genuine co-operation undermines its dignity as a truly human group.

## (6) Love

Sometimes we may wish we could just press a button and thereby make someone love us. Suppose we did. That person would then perhaps show us great signs of affection and admiration but would they really love us? There is a chance that they might have decided to love us even if we had not pressed the button but, as long as they behave as they do because we did press the button, they do not love us with a genuine love. We have not a lover but a sort of sophisticated appliance whose behaviour resembles that of a lover. The love is not 'true love' if the lover is made to love the beloved. Moreover, even if the sufficient cause of the 'love' is not something easily identifiable like button-pressing but something more subtly embedded in the causal structure of the world, it still seems that the love is not authentic. Suppose a mother 'loves' her baby merely because there is a biological mechanism which brings this about. Other mothers love their babies not only because of the biological attraction but also because they have made a mature decision to work for the good of their babies. This mother, however, is moved only by the biological attraction. Her 'love' depends on the attraction and will cease if the attraction ceases. She is acting out a biological pattern rather, I would claim, than really loving her baby.

God might have created us in such a way that it was pre-arranged that we 'love' both him and each other. This would not really be love. For no one can love truly unless, at some time or other, he is free not to love, and in a sense which precludes any arrangement which would be a sufficient cause of love-like behaviour. If love is ensured or made necessary, whether by the press of a button or by a natural law or by a possible direct intervention by God, then it is not true love but mere love-behaviour. To have real love between persons, we must have libertarian free will.

To this it might be objected that the saints in heaven have genuine love for each other although they can no longer not love each other. I reply that, at one point in time, they did have the chance not to love each other. Genuine love does not require the continued possibility of not loving but it does require libertarian free will at some stage. Moreover, it is only because they freely chose to become fixed in their love that the saints in heaven can no longer not love each other.

Again, it might be objected that God could have created, say, an angel with the intention of making that angel love him if the angel were not going to decide on its own to love him. In such a case it would be determined that the angel love God but, if the angel decided on its own to love God, that love would be genuine. Thus it is possible that love be both determined and genuine. I reply that it makes no sense to say that God might make an angel love him. If God makes someone 'love' him then that 'love' is not authentic. At most, God can arrange for love-like behaviour. Hence it is not possible that it be determined that the angel love God. Furthermore, if God made an angel love him, God would thereby undermine the dignity of the angel and it is not possible for a loving God to do such a thing. To make a person 'love' you is to exploit that person.

If God is not going to love someone he simply does not create them. There is no possibility that he both create someone and not love them. However, in the case of finite beings, if their love is an exercise of libertarian free will, then they do have the power to refuse to love. Hence they may abuse the power to love, refusing to return God's love or the love of some other person. If human beings love with libertarian free will then it lies in their power to do evil.

The statement that we are incapable of genuine love is an unacceptable statement. It is an essential part of our most intimate relationships that we view our love as a 'freely given gift'. If I learn that my spouse loves me only because this 'love' is the inevitable product of some childhood experience then the whole relationship takes on a strange and dark colour.

## (7) Unconditional love

To love unconditionally is to continue to love not on account of the circumstances (with their various determining factors) but regardless of them. If it is possible that the context or circumstances of my love are such that I must cease to love then I lack the ability to love unconditionally. Hence it is only if I have an indeterministic power of choice, one that is not always exercised in harmony with past influences or present temptations, that I have the ability to love unconditionally. Unconditional love presupposes a power to transcend the context of the love. It presupposes the existence of libertarian free will and, in the case of ordinary human beings, this libertarian free will may be misused. We have the power to cease loving.

Harré and Madden introduce the concept of a 'pure agent'.

Being of a certain nature endows a thing or material with the power to manifest itself in certain ways, or to behave in certain ways, in the appropriate circumstances. In the extreme cases of the pure agent, it is to do something, or to be capable of doing something, whatever the circumstances, i.e. to be the initiator of an act. A pure agent is that thing or material in which a causal chain terminates, be it the resolute gardener or a radium atom.[10]

The resolute gardener continues to garden no matter what the soil and the weather are like, and the radium atom decays when it does without regard, as far as the timing of the decay is concerned, to its surroundings. The exercise of these powers is not tied in a deterministic fashion to the conditions in which they are exercised The powers do not have to be exercised and they do not have to remain unexercised. Harré and Madden are 'doubtful whether there are really any pure agents' but, if there is to be a resolute lover—someone whose love does not depend on the circumstances— then there has to be a pure agent, someone in whom a causal chain terminates. His exercise of the power of love is not determined but is the terminus of the causal chain leading out from it. The pure agent chooses to love whatever the conditions. It is he or she, not some deterministic process, who is the initiator of the act of love. The decision to love is thus free in the libertarian sense. Moreover, he or she is also free to cease loving and hence has the power to do evil.

[10]  R. Harré and E. H. Madden, *Causal Powers* (Oxford: Basil Blackwell, 1975), 91.

It is part of the human conception of love that it is unconditional. If two people marry, they do so in the belief that they have the power to go on loving each other even if one of them becomes ill and irritable. We feel that love is a decision wholly within our control, and we reassure ourselves in this feeling by meditating on the lives of saints who loved those who persecuted them. The statement that human beings never love unconditionally is indeed unacceptable.

## (8) Promising

Does promising presuppose libertarian free will? Suppose I promise to deliver the goods on Thursday. On Wednesday, however, I choose to take a holiday in France and, by Friday, the promise is broken. On a deterministic view of the matter, my promise was only one of many factors influencing the future. It was not, as events proved, sufficient to bring it about that the promise was kept. On the contrary, at the time at which I promised, the situation was such that it was nomologically or in some other way necessary that I not keep the promise. Indeed, it was foolish of me to make the promise without realising that circumstances might well bring it about that I be on the beach in France on Thursday. For a determinist, there is nothing illogical about hedging a promise with a 'provided it is not determined that I do otherwise'. Yet, precisely, a promise is not merely a device for making the circumstances more likely to produce the thing promised but a device for committing oneself to keep the promise in spite of all but the most extraordinary circumstances to the contrary. Promising presupposes an ability *not* to do what one might otherwise be determined to do, but to carry out the promise instead. Promising therefore presupposes the libertarian free will with which we can detach ourselves from factors which might prevent us from keeping the promise, and keep it regardless. We transcend causality and do what we said we would do.

When I make a promise, I am deciding to take control of the situation in such a way that what I have promised will come about. This presupposes that, barring catastrophes, it is up to me what happens. Yet if I am part of some deterministic system, I do not have the kind of independent control presupposed by the promising.

In some sense of 'can', I can keep the promise—for example, I have the power to do the sort of thing in question—but in the actual circumstances, it may be nomologically or deistically impossible for me to keep it. If I am part of a deterministic system then I keep the promise if and only if it is determined that I keep the promise. My promise is as good as that but no better. Precisely, however, we think of promising as a method of transcending the circumstances, of ignoring all factors except the intention to keep the promise, and doing what was promised regardless. A human being is not capable of promising in this sense if his will is determined. He must be free—in the libertarian sense—to decide to keep his promise. Furthermore, he must be free to decide not to keep it. Hence if human beings do not have libertarian free will which extends to evil then they cannot really make promises.

Finally, the statement that human beings cannot make promises is an unacceptable statement. Its truth would be at odds with our conception of our whole way of life.

Let us summarise this section. We have argued that if it is not the case that human beings have a libertarian free will which extends to evil then

(1) they lack true rationality;
(2) they lack genuine artistic creativity;
(3) they lack a significant moral responsibility;
(4) they cannot choose values;
(5) they cannot really co-operate with each other;
(6) they lack the power to love;
(7) they lack the power to love unconditionally; and
(8) they cannot make promises in a meaningful way.

Since these conclusions are unacceptable—and, certainly, their conjunction is unacceptable—we are entitled to conclude that human beings do have libertarian free will which extends to evil. Moreover, many of our arguments apply in the case of any finite (non-divine) creature. We may thus conclude, for example, that if there are any finite persons (not necessarily human) who lack libertarian free will extending to evil then they also lack good things such as true rationality and genuine love.

## IV

One can imagine the following objection. Even if I have shown that the premiss that human beings do not have libertarian free will (extending to evil) leads to eight unacceptable conclusions, I have not shown that the contrary premiss does not lead to equally repugnant conclusions. If human beings do have libertarian free will, one might argue, then we are stuck with the following eight unacceptable conclusions:

(1) Psychology neither is nor even can be a science with laws like the laws of Newtonian Physics;

(2) Many events in history are intrinsically inaccessible to human understanding;

(3) People can be held to be ultimately responsible for certain dreadful evils;

(4) People who regret their choices cannot always correctly maintain that they did the best they could in the circumstances;

(5) One cannot count on another person's love since, at any moment, they can choose to stop loving;

(6) God does not have complete control over the universe;

(7) There is no substantial difference between God and man;

(8) One's fate or salvation lies not in the hands of a providential order but in the hands of one's own fallible decision-making powers.

A libertarian may have some other arguments for his position which are not of the unacceptable conclusion type. For example, he may hold that there is libertarian free will simply because it provides a free will defence in theodicy. However, if the libertarian wants to base himself on an unacceptable conclusion *reductio*, he must say something about arguments which, from the opposite premiss, lead to results which might seem equally unacceptable. If the libertarian cannot say why the conclusions drawn from his own position are not as bad as those which follow from his opponent's position, he is at best in a stalemate. He is in what Kant calls the 'Third Conflict of the Transcendental Ideas' where, from one point of view, there is free will, and yet, from another point of view, there is not.[11] Kant gives reasons of apparently equal strength for both sides of the question. Thesis and antithesis grin at each other from their respective sides of the page and nothing is resolved.

To this objection, I reply that my opponent's allegedly unacceptable conclusions are objectionable only if you presuppose that human beings are not at all God-like. However, if you hold the view that we are exalted beings, made in God's image, then none of my opponent's conclusions seems the least bit unhappy. In any case, none of them is unacceptable in the strong sense of 'unacceptable' we defined above.

1. In so far as we are like God, there is no reason to be disappointed that no set of deterministic psychological laws can reach up to capture our behaviour. Moreover, having libertarian free will does not mean that it is always being exercised in surprising ways. Thus a Psychology with statistical laws—like those of contemporary Physics—could describe the behaviour of persons with libertarian free will.

2. In so far as we are 'transfigured in a new creation' (to look at it from a Christian point of view), there is nothing untoward about concluding that history contains mysteries which, in some sense, put it beyond knowledge. Besides, even if an act is performed freely in the libertarian sense, this does not mean that it is performed without a reason. A history book which, like most history books, offers reasons for the decisions of great men and women—rather than determinstic explanations—is perfectly compatible with our having libertarian free will.

3. In so far as we are like God rather than the lower animals, we do have the dignity of being held fully responsible for certain acts. If a dog does something wrong then it should be retrained, muzzled, or put away. It suffices to alter the dog's behaviour. However, it would cut against our dignity if that was all that was necessary in the case of human beings. Although it is unpleasant to admit guilt and ask forgiveness, it is even more unpleasant to be treated as if one were an animal with a behaviour problem.

4. In so far as we are like God, we can think in terms of doing well next time. Although it may be reassuring in one sense to say

---

[11] Immanuel Kant, *Critique of Pure Reason*, trans. Norman Kemp Smith (London: Macmillan, 1929), B472–B479

that one could not have done better in those circumstances, it is not reassuring to say that one will never be able to do better in the same circumstances. An excuse for the past is an acceptance of defeat for the future. One therefore would not want to maintain in every case that he did the best he could in the circumstances. Thus the statement that people who regret their choices cannot always correctly maintain that they did the best they could in the circumstances is not an unacceptable statement.

5. In so far as we are like God, we can and will love each other with constancy. Sometimes it does happen that someone suddenly ceases to love another person. However, this does not happen more often if there is libertarian free will. The fact that a person is in a position to stop loving does not mean that he is unresponsive to his conscience, his habits, or the social context in which he lives. Usually, therefore, he will not make unpredictable decisions. If he loves, then, other things being equal, he will probably go on loving. On the other hand, there are logically possible deterministic universes where sudden cessation of love is in every case inevitable.

6. In so far as we were made to work with God, as 'co-creators' of his universe, there is nothing unacceptable about saying that we share in the control of it. This does not imply that the universe is, in any sense, out of control for, if he chose, God could at any time exert complete deterministic mastery over it. Furthermore, God can arrange matters so that, even though we are free in the libertarian sense to do what we like, there will in the end be perfect justice for all our deeds. We shall be exploring the relationship between omnipotence and libertarian free will in Chapter 3.

7. In so far as we share in the divine (this, as Christians believe, through God's grace), there is nothing but praise for God in the assertion that he intended us for this highest of ends.[12] We are called to be one with God, and this fact is not made less glorious by the fact that the power to answer this call comes only from God. We were made in his image, and those who do not resist his love will be his 'bride'.[13]

8. In so far as God gives us the grace to be like him, we may be confident that, although we have the power to fall back into sin, we also have the power to persevere. Our 'assurance' is not that it is

---

[12] See 2 Peter 1: 4 and Revelation 1: 5.
[13] See Genesis 1: 27; Isaiah 62: 5; John 17: 21–3; and Revelation 3: 20–1 and 21: 9–10.

determined that we always love God but that we alone are the masters of our fate. Nothing but our own decision can separate us from the love of God. Moreover, with his grace, we shall be in an excellent position not to decide to renounce God. He will give us every incentive to choose to remain with him, and, if we do sin, he will do his utmost to encourage us to repent.

My opponent perhaps prefers the security of deterministic order to the unpredictableness of sharing a divine destiny. However, he is going too far if he maintains that assertions to the effect that we lack this security are 'unacceptable' in the strong sense defined at the beginning of this chapter.

# 2

# God's Existence

IN this chapter we define the notion of a divine being and we prove that there is at least one such. Then, using a libertarian approach, we argue for the traditional Christian belief that there is exactly one divine being. As the Athanasian Creed proclaims, 'there are not three gods, but one God'.[1]

## I

There are so many religions, both public and private, that the question, 'what do you mean by "God"?' is a pressing one indeed, and this is made even more evident by the fact that some people claim that the notion of 'God' is logically incoherent. One of the fundamental tasks of a Philosophy of Religion, then, is to give a definition of God. A key notion in many concepts of God is the notion of contingency. In this section, therefore, I give an account of this notion. Like Aquinas, I want to say that God is a noncontingent being who has the power to create or destroy any contingent being.[2] However, what do I mean by 'contingent'?

A statement or proposition is *logically contingent* (or *contingent*) if and only if it is logically possible that it be true and also logically possible that it be false. That is, a statement is contingent if and only if there is a possible world (i.e. possible universe) in which it is true and a possible world in which it is false. Hence a proposition is contingent just in case it is neither logically impossible nor logically necessary. For example, 'I saw a tree' is a logically contingent statement. Statements which are not contingent are called *non-contingent*. For example, 'all married persons have spouses' and

---

[1] See also Augustine, *The Trinity*, trans. Stephen McKenna (Washington: Catholic University of America Press, 1963), 243.

[2] Aquinas, *Summa Contra Gentiles*, book I, ch. 15, sect. 5, and *Summa Theologiae*, 1a.2 art. 3.

'2 + 2 = 57' are both noncontingent statements. The first is noncontingent because it is necessarily true, and the second is noncontingent because it is necessarily false (i.e. logically impossible). By extension, the notion of logical contingency can be applied to events or things. An event is logically contingent if and only if the statement 'that event occurs' is logically contingent. A substance or object is contingent if and only if the statement 'that thing exists' is contingent. For example, I am a contingent being because, although I do exist, it is possible that I not exist. In the actual universe I do exist but in some other possible worlds I am nowhere to be found.

Let *Ex* be the statement '*x* exists'. To say that an object *x* is noncontingent is just to say that the statement *Ex* is not contingent, that is,

$$\neg\, (\lozenge\, Ex\ \&\ \lozenge\, \neg\, Ex)$$

and this is equivalent to

$$\square\, \neg Ex\quad \text{or}\quad \square\, Ex.$$

From this it follows that a noncontingent entity exists if and only if it is possible that it exist, and a noncontingent entity fails to exist if and only if it is possible that it not exist.

## II

In order to evaluate religions which identify God and matter, and in order to know whether God creates matter, we must find out whether matter is contingent. In this section, we give three arguments to the effect that it is.

### (1) Antimatter argument

Physicists maintain that in the actual universe the total amount of mass-energy in any interaction does in fact remain constant. However, the theories which they advance to describe how this happens often posit the annihilation or creation of particles. According to one theory, moreover, any particle whatsoever will be annihilated by being brought into contact with the corresponding antiparticle. Thus fundamental particles are contingent and, indeed, the universe as a whole is contingent.

## (2) Counterfactual thought experiment

Suppose you are out studying the stars. You reflect that if Arcturus did not exist, we would have connected the other stars in the Herdsman to the stars in Gemma and made some different constellation instead. In so reflecting, you are assuming that the star Arcturus is contingent. You can imagine the particles which compose Arcturus going into a number of other stars, and you can also imagine that those particles simply do not exist. Moreover, if, for any set of particles, you can imagine that they do not exist, you can imagine that the whole physical universe does not exist. You can imagine a possible world with no matter at all. You can think of it as containing only spirits or numbers, or you can think of it as a kind of empty set. Of course, what we conceive or imagine is not always logically possible. None the less, the fact that we conceive or imagine something does give us a valid reason for thinking that it is possible.

## (3) Argument from the structure of elementary particles

No matter can exist unless it have a certain form or order. To be a quark, for example, a thing must have certain physical properties. It must instantiate certain configurations. Now since, by its nature, matter interacts with matter, these forms and configurations are subject to change. Furthermore, at the subatomic level, particles have such simple forms or structures that any change means that the particle ceases to exist. A gold atom remains a gold atom if you pluck off one of its electrons because a gold atom is what it is according to the number of protons it has. Over and above its 'defining properties', it has some other structural properties, and hence it can change without being annihilated. However, with very simple particles this cannot happen. If, for example, the structure of a certain kind of quark is changed in any way at all then it becomes a different sort of sub-atomic particle. The old quark is replaced by a new entity. Hence we may conclude that every true elementary particle is contingent. Moreover, at any given moment, the existence or nonexistence of one elementary particle is independent of the existence or nonexistence of any others. The existence of quark $q$ at time $t$ does not depend on the existence of quarks $q'$ and $q''$ at time $t$. Thus from the fact that any one elementary particle might not exist, we may conclude that the whole physical universe might not exist. Hence all matter is contingent.

For those who like formal arguments, we might summarise the above as follows. Let

$P$ = physical objects are either elementary bits of matter or compounds of elementary bits of matter

$C$ = all physical objects are liable to change

$C_1$ = each elementary bit of matter is liable to change

$S$ = elementary bits of matter are (by definition) very simple

$C_2$ = each elementary bit of matter can cease to exist

$C_3$ = each elementary bit of matter is contingent;

$I$ = the existence of any one elementary bit of matter at time $t$ does not depend on the existence of any other elementary bit of matter at time $t$

$C_4$ = all matter is contingent.

The following is a valid inference.

$$P \ \& \ C \ \& \ S \ \& \ I$$
$$C \Rightarrow C_1$$
$$C_1 \ \& \ S \Rightarrow C_2$$
$$C_2 \Rightarrow C_3$$
$$C_3 \ \& \ P \ \& \ I \Rightarrow C_4$$
$$\overline{\phantom{C_3 \ \& \ P \ \& \ I \Rightarrow C_4}}$$
$$C_4$$

If matter is contingent, it makes sense to ask questions like 'why are there any physical objects?' If the material universe might not exist, one can ask how it is that the opposite possibility is, in fact, realised. Moreover, one can ask why there is as much matter as there actually is. Suppose the universe contains $K$ kilograms of mass-energy. Why does it not contain twice that much? Human beings have often answered such questions by saying that there is a God who created the physical universe and who decided just how it should be. Of course, this is not much of an answer if God, too, is contingent. Hence God is often seen as the non-contingent creator of the contingent universe.

## III

Is it possible that God exist? This question may seem silly because so many people have a distinct idea of God. Since God is conceivable, surely his existence is at least possible. None the less, it sometimes happens that an idea which many people take for granted turns out to be incapable of instantiation. For example, prior to the discovery of the Russell Paradox, some mathematicians believed that the notion of a set was a perfectly clear and coherent one, so clear and coherent, indeed, that the whole of mathematics could safely rest on it. A set, they said, is simply a collection of things, and for any property $P$ there is a set whose members are just the things with that property. What could be simpler or more obvious? However, said Russell, consider the set $S$ whose members are just those sets which are not members of themselves. Is $S$ a member of $S$? If $S$ is a member of $S$ then, according to the defining property of $S$, $S$ is not a member of $S$. However, if $S$ is not a member of $S$ then, according to the defining property, $S$ is a member of $S$. This is a contradiction. The idea of such a set is incoherent, and the idea that sets can be defined in terms of any property whatsoever is shown to contain a logical inconsistency. A great deal of twentieth-century set theory, in fact, consists in trying to substitute for the naïve notion of 'set' one that is logically coherent.

On some naïve notion of God, therefore, or on some careless definition of God, it may be that the notion of God is logically incoherent. For example, God might be thought of as being so merciful as to allow no room for justice and, at the same time, as being so just as to allow no room for mercy. Again, he might be (mistakenly) thought of as so powerful that he can make $2 + 2 = 1000$. It is not, of course, possible that such a God exist. However, this does not imply that the core concept of God cannot be instantiated. It may be that a particular idea of God has to be revised or refined before it becomes coherent but, just as in set theory it is clear that something like a 'set' is logically possible, so in

Philosophy it is clear that something like a 'god' is logically possible. The fact that so mảny people have thought about God is reason enough to conclude that, with some refinement if necessary, the concept of God is coherent, and it is at least logically possible that God exist. It may be that some clever philosopher will show that the definition which I give of God is somehow self-inconsistent but that, of course, will not prove that there can be no God. All it will mean is that my definition needs to be revised. Drawing on the many ideas which people have about God, moreover, it will no doubt be easy enough to suggest sensible ways of revising it. There is a core notion of the divine which, however much it may elude precision, is as real a part of our cultural and intellectual heritage as notions like 'force', 'justice' or 'set'. All these notions are difficult to define and all these notions are liable to be understood in a naïve manner which imports some contradiction into them. None the less, no one should doubt that they are meaningful, and no one should say that, properly understood, they cannot possibly be instantiated.[3]

## IV

In Section I we defined the notion of contingency which, as we shall see in this section, plays a key role in certain arguments for God's existence. In Section III we argued that it is at least logically possible that there be a god. In this section we look at some standard proofs for the existence of God. These may not make anyone change their mind on the issue but they do help clarify the idea of God. *What* we are proving the existence of is closely related to the premisses of the arguments we are using.

(1) The physical universe is contingent.
  If the physical universe is contingent then its existence is explained only by postulating a noncontingent creator of it.
  The existence of the physical universe does have an explanation.
  Therefore there is a noncontingently existing creator.[4]

---

[3] Aquinas claimed that God was 'above' definition. See, for example, *Summa Contra Gentiles*, book I, ch. 25, sect. 7.

[4] This is a version of Aquinas's Third Way. See the *Summa Theologiae*, 1a.2 art. 3.

(2) The universe is more or less good and beautiful.
If there were no God to keep it that way, the universe would not be more or less good and beautiful.
Thus there is a God to keep it that way.

(3) If there are miracles there is a God.
If everyday, all over the world, living, breathing, healthy babies are born then there are miracles.
Thus there is a God.

(4) It is a noble thing to believe in God.
If it is a noble thing to believe something then that thing is true.
Thus God exists.

(5) If you are using the word 'God' correctly then God is as great a being as possible.
If God merely exists in the human imagination he is not as great as he would be if he really existed.
If God is not as great as he would be if he really existed then God is not as great a being as possible.
Hence if you are using the word 'God' correctly, God does not merely exist in the human imagination.[5]

(6) Everyone will get their just deserts.
Not everyone will get their just deserts unless there is a God to raise people from the dead and send them to heaven or hell.
Thus there is a God to raise people from the dead and send them to heaven or hell.[6]

(7) If anyone seriously implies that he is God then either he is mad or he is a liar or he is God.
If anyone is wise and virtuous he is neither mad nor a liar.
Jesus was wise and virtuous, and Jesus seriously implied that he was God.
Therefore there is a God, namely, Jesus.

(8) It is at least logically possible that God exist.
God is such that if he does not exist, it is impossible that he exist.
Thus God exists.[7]

---

[5] This is a version of Anselm's Ontological Argument, found in his *Proslogion*. A very sophisticated version of this argument is found in Alvin Plantinga, *The Nature of Necessity* (Oxford: Oxford University Press, 1974).

[6] Kant has a more subtle version of this argument in section 87 of the *Critique of Judgement*.          [7] See n. 5.

(9) It is at least logically possible that God exist. If God exists then it is necessary that he exist. Thus, using modal logic S5, God exists.[8]

(10) For this argument we need some terminology. Let

$Exy$ = the existence of $x$ can be explained in terms of the existence of $y$

$E'xy$ = there is a finite sequence of entities $x = x_1, x_2, \ldots, x_{n-1}, x_n = y$ such that $Ex_1x_2$, $Ex_2x_3$, $\ldots$, and $Ex_{n-1}x_n$.

If $E'xy$ we say there is a *chain of explanation* for $x$, namely, the sequence $x, x_2, \ldots, y$. If $E'xy$ and there is no entity $z$ such that $Eyz$ then we say that $x$ has a *finite chain of explanation*. We now have the following argument.

There is a contingent entity whose existence has a complete explanation.
Nothing has a complete explanation unless it has a finite chain of explanation.
The existence of a contingent entity is always explained in terms of the existence of some other entity.
Thus there is a non-contingent entity.[9]

We can express this in terms of formal logic. Let

$Cx$ = $x$ is a contingent entity
$Px$ = $x$'s existence has a complete explanation
$Fx$ = $x$ has a finite chain of explanation.

Then the argument is the following:

$\exists x(Cx \ \& \ Px)$
$\forall x(Px \Rightarrow Fx)$
$\forall x(Fx \Rightarrow \exists y \ \forall z(\neg Eyz))$
$\forall y(Cy \Rightarrow \exists z(z \neq y \ \& \ Eyz))$
_____
$\exists y(\neg Cy)$

Proofs for the non-existence of God tell us something about the nature of God too.

[8] See n. 5.
[9] See Aquinas, *Summa Contra Gentiles*, book I, ch. 15, sect. 5, and *Summa Theologiae*, 1a.2 art. 3. Also see Kant, *Critique of Pure Reason*, B480–9 (the Fourth Conflict of the Transcendental Ideas).

(11) If there is a God, he can do away with evil, he wants to do away with evil, and he has no overriding reason not to do away with evil.

If God can do away with evil, and wants to do away with evil, and has no overriding reason not to do away with evil, then he does do away with evil.

However, God does not do away with evil.

Hence there is no God.

(12) It is at least logically possible that there be no God.
If God exists then it is necessary that he exist.
Thus God does not exist.

(13) God is a completely unchanging entity.
God interacts with human beings.
Anything which interacts with human beings changes.
Therefore God does not exist.

There are many other arguments dealing with God's existence. Some of them are simplistic (e.g. the argument from the premiss that twelve fishermen changed world history) but others are deep and subtle (e.g. Swinburne's probabilistic argument).[10] All these arguments are useful for meditating on the nature of God—and for studying language and logic. Few of these arguments, however, are very good at making people change their minds. One can always find something to say against some premiss. Of course, whatever is said against that premiss can be countered by something else and the game can—and does—continue until it is as complicated as a book of chess openings. The theist, however, fails to win over the atheist as much as the atheist fails to win over the theist. In Section VII of this chapter we give an argument for God's existence which is convincing.

## V

One recurring feature of the above arguments is that God is seen to be in some sense noncontingent. Some of the arguments tie the

---

[10] Richard Swinburne, *The Existence of God* (Oxford: Clarendon Press, 1979).

notion of God to a specific tradition but the 'noncontingency arguments' embody a more general notion of the divine. It is an idea very basic to mankind that things which can exist or not need some sort of explaining in terms of something which is either self-explanatory or beyond the need for explanation. God's existence is just the way he is, and it makes no more sense to ask why God exists than to ask why dogs are animals. (What else could they be?) God is a being whose existence forms, as it were, part of his nature.

A second recurring feature of the above arguments is that God is seen as having power over the universe. He preserves it—or ought to—in beauty and justice. God is not an isolated noncontingency but a watcher and protector of the contingent. The universe is subject to his providence.

In harmony with the above arguments, then, my own definition of 'god' combines his noncontingency with his mastery over the contingent. Where $x$ is a single individual, we shall say that

> $x$ is a divine being
> if and only if
> $x$ is a non-contingent being
> and, necessarily, $x$ has the power to create or destroy any
>     contingent being.

This definition is not complete without a few explanations. Why, for example, do I say 'where $x$ is a single individual'? The answer is that I wish to block the possibility of a divine being being a group of gods. On some versions of the 'social view of the Trinity', for example, God is actually a committee whose members are three distinct divinities.[11] This committee is noncontingent and it has the power to create or destroy any contingent being. However, I would not choose to call it a 'divine being': it is rather a committee of three divine beings. Note that I am not trying to rule out the social view of the Trinity by means of a mere definition. I am just stating how I am going to use the expression 'divine being'. In my terminology, the social view of the Trinity is the view that (1) there are three divine beings, all in perfect harmony, and (2) when the Bible says there is one God, it is referring to this group as a whole. In Section

---

[11] Thomas V. Morris, *Anselmian Explorations* (Notre Dame: University of Notre Dame Press, 1987), 140–2.

VIII I prove that there is at most one divine being and thus refute the social view of the Trinity.

Another question one might ask is why I insert a 'necessarily' before the clause '$x$ has the power to create or destroy any contingent being'. The answer is that I wish to block the possibility of a divine being ceasing to be divine. Suppose there were two non-contingent beings, Zeus and Cronus. Suppose that in odd-numbered years Zeus had the power to create or destroy any contingent being but in even-numbered years he did not. Suppose, moreover, that Cronus had this power just when Zeus did not have it. Then, without the 'necessarily', it would follow from my definition that Zeus and Cronus took turns being divine. Our pre-analytic idea of a divine being, however, is such that this seems absurd. A divine being is a kind of fixed point in terms of which we give an ultimate explanation for the changing universe. A divine being would, however, itself need explanation if it sometimes ceased to be divine. Thus I stipulate that if $Z$ is a divine being then he *has* to possess the defining power.

Suppose

$Dx$ = $x$ is a divine being
$Ex$ = $x$ exists
$Px$ = $x$ has the power to create or destroy any contingent being.

Then from what we said about contingency in the first section of this chapter, it follows that our definition can be symbolized as

$$Dx \Leftrightarrow \neg (\Diamond\, Ex\ \&\ \Diamond\ \neg Ex)\ \&\ \Box\, Px$$

From this it follows (in S5 modal logic) that

$$Dx \Leftrightarrow \Box\, Dx$$

In other words, something is divine only if it is necessarily divine.

The expression 'power to create' also needs some explanation. By 'creating' I do not mean mere bringing into existence *ex nihilo*, for a being might have that power without even being aware of it. By 'creating', I understand an activity that involves conscious planning, aesthetic evaluation, and scientific knowledge. A being who creates in this sense is fully aware of what it is doing and how its creation will work. I also take 'creating' to mean sustaining in existence. To create is not merely to bring something into existence and then, if this were possible, to leave it alone. It is rather to bring it into existence and then maintain or preserve it in existence.

If a divine being has the power to create in the above sense then it has the power to make rational decisions. It is therefore a thinking, willing being—a person.[12] Moreover, he is a person with great knowledge and power.[13] Since he can knowingly create a universe such as ours, he has amazing scientific and mathematical talent. Since he can maintain physical objects in existence at any number of locations, he has the attribute of omnipresence. Since he can preserve an axehead in existence at the surface of the Jordan, he can make an axehead float.[14] Since he can sustain atoms in existence anywhere he likes, he can reassemble the atoms of a decayed corpse in such a manner as to make a living human body and, in this sense, raise the dead. Since he is a person, he can value the things he creates, and he can love those contingent beings who are persons. Indeed, why would he create, say, a human being unless he were going to love that human being?

To make it clearer what we mean by a divine being, let us give a second definition which spells out some of the implications of the first.

> $x$ is a divine being
> if and only if
> $x$ is a non-contingent being
> and, necessarily, $x$ is a person who has the power knowingly to create (*ex nihilo*) or destroy any contingent being.

Note that this definition does not presuppose that there actually are any contingent beings. We could have a universe whose only inhabitants were necessarily existing entities. If there were a divine being in such a universe then the fact that there were no contingent beings would be due to his not exercising his power to create some. The relative emptiness of this universe would depend on the divine being.

Note also how both halves of the definition play their part. If we omitted the second condition then necessarily existing entities like

[12] This does not exclude the possibility that it also be three 'persons' in the trinitarian sense.

[13] The use of the pronoun 'he' does not imply that the divine being should be identified with the male sex. It is simply a fact about the English language that if a person is not known to be a woman (or girl), you can use 'he' to make the wanted references.

[14] 2 Kings 6: 6.

numbers (on a Platonic view) and impossible entities like wholly good sinners would qualify as divine beings. If we omitted the first condition then we would leave open the possibility that a divine being cease to exist (perhaps by committing suicide). That would not be faithful to the idea of God as the permanent, underlying substance, as the one who simply is. When God appeared to Moses in the blazing bush, God did not say, 'I am he who is here today and gone tomorrow.' On the contrary, he proclaimed, 'I am he who is.'[15] To John, God describes himself thus:

I am the Alpha and the Omega, who is, who was, and who is to come, the Almighty.[16]

The title 'Almighty' suggests that God can create or destroy any contingent thing, and the title 'Alpha and Omega' suggests that God is not a mere contingent thing himself.

Given what we said in Section III, we may assume that it is logically possible that at least one divine being exist. In Section VII, I try to show that this possibility is realised. First, however, we need to consider the question of whether divine beings have libertarian free will.


# VI

In commenting on our definition, we noted that a divine being is a person—that is, something which is normally conscious, intelligent, and capable of making decisions. From the fact that a divine being is a person it does not, however, immediately follow that he has libertarian free will. For this conclusion we need some further argumentation. In this section, then, we argue that divine beings do have libertarian free will.

The first argument turns on the premiss that among contingent beings are persons with libertarian free will. These beings are more exalted than non-persons and, as we argued in the first chapter, they are more exalted than persons without libertarian free will. If a divine being were more like, say, a force than a person, or if he were more like, say, a robot than a person with libertarian free will, then

---

[15] Exodus 3: 14.
[16] Revelation 1: 8.

that divine being would be inferior to persons with libertarian free will. He would be inferior to something he could create. However, it is absurd to think that the creature can surpass the creator.

The second argument for the conclusion that divine beings have libertarian free will turns on the premiss that, whatever a divine being is, the contingent things he creates find their ultimate explanation in him. In answer to the question, 'why do these things exist?' we say, 'because a divine being chose to create them'. Now if the divine being lacks libertarian free will, that answer does not suffice. For even if we know his reasons for his creation, there still remains the question, 'but how was it that it was determined that he produce just those things and not others?'. It is only if the divine being has libertarian free will that our answer is ultimately satisfying.

In a deterministic scheme there is always some sufficient cause behind a choice but, on a libertarian view, a choice is a natural terminus both of causation and explanation. Thus we can give an ultimate explanation for something in terms of the purposes and goals of a divine being if and only if that divine being has libertarian free will. To a question like, 'Why does Shaun exist?' we can answer, 'Because God wants to love her for ever and ever' but this is the ultimate answer only if God has libertarian free will.

If a divine being has libertarian free will, it is natural to interpret his power to create in terms of the genuine artistic creativity discussed in Section III of the previous chapter. Indeed, it is natural from the start to suppose that a divine being's power to create is a power to bring forth things not implicit in his circumstances. For a divine being, precisely, is an absolute beginning of contingent things. We should therefore refine our definition as follows.

> $x$ is a divine being
> if and only if
> $x$ is a non-contingent being
> and, necessarily, $x$ is a person with libertarian free will who has the power knowingly to create (*ex nihilo*) or destroy any contingent being, and whose exercise of this power is a genuine artistic activity.

Note that it still follows that $x$ is a divine being if and only if $x$ is necessarily a divine being.

## VII

In this section I show that there is at least one divine being. I do this beginning with the premiss that human beings, like the physical universe, are contingent, and arguing that, without a divine being, the universe is meaningless. There is no point to it unless it is created.

The mathematician J. Lambek once told me that he would be very disappointed to find out that God existed. He did not like the idea of a superior being who might interfere with his plans. He wished, he said, to decide his own destiny. To this I replied that he would not have much of a destiny if there were no God.

If there were no God then there is no real reason why there is something rather than nothing. In particular, there is no real reason why I exist. I just happen to be here and, very probably, I shall no longer be part of the universe in a hundred years time. There are, of course, partial statistical explanations in terms of genetics and so forth as to why I exist but, ultimately, it is just some brute, inexplicable fact. If there is no God then the contingent universe just happens to exist and I just happen to exist as something that happens to be for a little while a part of it. If there is a God then it makes sense to say that he wills that I exist. He created me and he intends me for some special purpose, if not in this life then in another. If there is no God, however, it does not make sense to say these things. If there is no God then we cannot really talk about the purpose of the universe. An individual person is just something which, thanks to various accidents such as the timing of copulation, happens to exist. Someone else might have existed instead—or there might not have been any persons at all. It would be all the same in a universe which did not have a divine being. Without a God, then, there would be no answer to our ultimate 'why?' and those who hold that, in the end, existence is meaningless would be right.

I agree that if there were no God there is a sense in which one could none the less inject a certain amount of meaning into one's life. One could fashion one's destiny by setting out various goals (for example, writing a book on mathematics) and then achieving those goals. However, what does that amount to? Someone else might just as well achieve those goals. Within a few thousand years almost every trace of those achievements will be gone. The universe itself may cease to exist. Lambek's destiny begins as an arbitrary goal imposed on a meaningless universe and, quickly enough, ends in nothingness.

Assume that there is no divine being and no contingent universe either. We have, as it were, the 'empty universe'. This unverse is not completely empty because it contains necessarily existing objects (other than divine beings). For example, if numbers are necessarily existing non-divine beings, it contains numbers. It is even conceivable that it contain a noncontingent but mindless manufacturing device capable of pumping out matter in some random fashion but not, in fact, doing so. Of course, the empty universe does not contain the many beautiful contingent things which we find in the actual universe. There are no stars, no planets, no human beings—and no God.

Now if our actual contingent universe just happens to exist, it may just happen to cease to exist. If there is no divine being then the only thing which distinguishes the actual universe from the empty universe is that, for no reason at all, it happens to have something contingent in it—at least for the moment. This basic, brute fact makes it more interesting than the empty universe but it does not add any meaning.

Perhaps our universe once was an empty universe. Perhaps the matter in our universe just suddenly appeared. If we do not want to posit a divine being then we may as well say this was what happened. However, what is the point of this arbitrary universe? Its existence or non-existence is like the smile of a capricious child. For no particular reason she frowns—and then she smiles. If there is no divine being, there is no ultimate explanation for the existence of contingent things. There is no ultimate meaning or purpose for my own existence. The universe is like a story with no point to it. It is a nihility. It may well collapse into the empty universe and it may as well collapse into the empty universe.

We may summarise the above by a short argument for God's existence. Like our arguments in Chapter 1, it turns on an 'unacceptable' statement.

> Contingent things, such as human beings, are either created by a divine being, or else they arise as a result of some ultimately random process.

If the latter, there is no ultimate explanation for them, and the contingent universe is ultimately meaningless.

It is unbearable to think that the contingent universe is ultimately meaningless.

Thus there is a divine being who creates us.


# VIII

In this section we assume that there is at least one divine being, and we argue that there is at most one divine being. We give three arguments. The first two are found wanting. The third, however, does establish the fact that there is at most one divine being. This third argument turns on the premiss that divine beings have libertarian free will. It is this premiss which allows us to demonstrate the traditional Christian doctrine that God is unique.


## (1) Argument from indistinguishability

Aquinas argues that there are not two or more gods because nothing would distinguish them.[17] At first, this seems false. Of course, two divine beings would probably not be distinguished by mass, colour, or spatial location since these are properties of contingent things whereas, precisely, divine beings are not contingent. However, why could one god not know more mathematics than another, or be more interested in creating fish than another? Polytheistic religions have many ways of distinguishing their gods.

Let us suppose, however, that God 1 differs from God 2 on account of properties $P_1, P_2, \ldots, P_n$. Since they differ on these properties, it is possible for a divine being to have or not have them. God 2 might have learnt more mathematics so that he would have been just as learned as God 1. God 1 might have had the same interest in fish as God 2. So if they are two gods, it is possible that they be the same god. However, this is absurd. Two distinct things cannot be the same thing.

---

[17] Aquinas, *Summa Contra Gentiles*, book I, ch. 42, sect. 3.

Against this argument, one can object that it may not be possible for the gods to share the same properties. Zeus and Cronus cannot share the property of 'being Zeus' and they cannot share the property of 'not being Zeus'. Furthermore, suppose Zeus necessarily exists only because Cronus necessarily wills that Zeus exist, and suppose, moreover, that it is necessarily true that Cronus exist regardless of what anyone wills. In such a case, let us say that Zeus has the property of 'being eternally begotten by an aseity'. Under the given suppositions, it is not possible that both these gods share this property, and it is not possible that they both share its negation. The above argument is thus not conclusive.

## (2) Argument from conflict

Since, by definition, divine beings have libertarian free will, it follows that if there are more than one of them then they may disagree. For example, one may decide to maintain Mars in existence but the other, his will being independent of that of the first, may decide to destroy Mars. If divine beings have equal power to create and destroy, the possibility of such a conflict implies the possibility that Mars both be maintained in existence and also, at the same time, destroyed. Since this is impossible, there can be at most one divine being.

To this it may be objected that, although a divine being has the power to create or destroy, the exercise of this power may none the less be limited by a second divine being. God 1 could create or destroy but only in so far as the stronger God 2 permitted. Nor is there anything untoward if the two divine beings are sometimes in conflict. Two virtuous political leaders will sometimes disagree but, just as often, they will find a way to resolve their difference. The two gods might take turns giving way to each other, or the stronger god might generously decide always to give way to the weaker god. In some way or other, the gods would all live together peaceably. Thus the above argument is not conclusive.

## (3) Argument from genuine love

In Chapter 5 we show that, necessarily, divine beings are good. Since divine beings are necessarily divine, it follows that divine beings are necessarily good. Hence if there are two (or more) of them then, necessarily, they love each other. It is necessarily true that Zeus loves Cronus and that Cronus loves Zeus. However, as we showed in Section III of the previous chapter, a love that is necessitated is inferior to a love that stems from an exercise of libertarian free will. Zeus is confronted by someone whom he must love with a love that is therefore not genuine. Cronus loves Zeus with the same inferior love. Indeed, we may imagine that Zeus creates a human being, Deucalion, in order to love him. Since Zeus does not have to love Deucalion—he did not have to create him—Zeus can love him with a true love. Moreover, Deucalion, we may suppose, freely chooses to love Zeus. In such a case there is a love between Zeus and Deucalion which is superior to the love between Zeus and his fellow god Cronus. However, this is absurd. Hence we may conclude that there is at most one divine being.

# 3

# Omnipotence

THE difficulty with the concept of omnipotence is not so much to prove that a divine being is omnipotent as to give a good definition of 'omnipotence'. Everyone knows the riddle about whether God can create a stone he cannot lift. Moreover, most would agree that, although it is a silly riddle, it points to a real problem: what exactly is meant by 'omnipotence'? In his article 'Omnipotence', Geach argues that this question cannot be answered: there is no good way of defining 'omnipotence' and so we had best call God 'almighty' and let it go at that.[1] Traditionally minded philosophers, such as Flint and Freddoso, have produced definitions of 'omnipotence' which avoid the difficulties raised by Geach (and others) but these definitions are rather long and clumsy—notably because they are tied to time. What is defined is not 'omnipotence' but 'omnipotence at time $t$', and the algebra of the time line tends to make these definitions less than elegant. For example, in 'Maximal Power' Flint and Freddoso claim that

$S$ is omnipotent at $t$ in $W$ if and only if for any state of affairs $p$ and world-type-for-$S$ $Ls$ such that $p$ is not a member of $Ls$, if there is a world $W^*$ such that
  (i) $Ls$ is true in both $W$ and $W^*$, and
  (ii) $W^*$ shares the same history with $W$ at $t$, and
  (iii) at $t$ in $W^*$ someone actualizes $p$,
then $S$ has the power at $t$ in $W$ to actualize $p$.[2]

In this chapter we give a definition of 'omnipotence' which is less technical than the above. Moreover, it does not presuppose that God is omnipotent only in time. Our definition will say something not only about God's powers but also about his freedom to exercise them. Finally, since (like Flint and Freddoso) I am a libertarian, I

[1] Peter Geach, 'Omnipotence', *Philosophy*, 48 (1973), 7–20.
[2] Thomas P. Flint and Alfred J. Freddoso, 'Maximal Power', in *The Existence and Nature of God* (Notre Dame: University of Notre Dame Press, 1983), 99. For another definition, see Edward Wierenga, 'Omnipotence Defined', *Philosophy and Phenomenological Research*, 43 (1983), 363–76.

shall not define 'omnipotence' in such a way that everything is determined by the will of an omnipotent being.

Our definition draws on a treatment of 'powers' given by Kenny. In the first section of this chapter, then, we offer a summary and elaboration of that treatment. In the second section we look at some of the problems involved in defining 'omnipotence', and in the third section we criticize Ross's anti-libertarian definition of that concept. In the fourth section we give our own definition and in the fifth section we show that it does allow that persons with libertarian free will co-exist with an omnipotent God. Finally, we argue that a divine being is necessarily omnipotent and we reflect on the relation between God's omnipotence, his free will, and his uniqueness.

# I

The words 'power', 'ability', and 'capacity' in ordinary language are not interchangeable. A very rich sot has a great deal of political power but little political ability. An Oxford don has a great capacity for speech but no speaking ability. A 12-year-old genius has the capacity to vote but not the power. For the purposes of this work, however, we shall take these three words in a more technical sense, one in which they *are* interchangeable. In particular, we shall not be discussing political or legal powers.

Roughly speaking, a person has the power to do something if and only if he does it, in the appropriate circumstances, because he wants to. For example, Professor Smith has the power to speak German just in case he does so, in the appropriate circumstances, because he wants to. One can also talk about natural powers. According to Harré and Madden in their carefully worked out account of natural powers:

'X has the power to A' means 'X will do A, in the appropriate conditions, *in virtue of its intrinsic nature*'.[3]

For example, 'copper has the power to conduct electricity' means 'copper will conduct electricity, if it is in its solid state, if there is

[3] R. Harré and E. H. Madden, *Causal Powers* (Oxford: Basil Blackwell, 1975), 86.

electricity to be conducted, etc., in virtue of the fact that the copper atom has a single electron outside the filled 4d shell'.[4] There is no sharp line between personal and natural powers. Going to sleep, weeping, scratching, and competing with the other fellow are examples of powers which are personal to the extent that they are exercised at will and natural to the extent that they are exercised in virtue of a person's intrinsic nature. Moreover, there are some powers which a person exercises simultaneously at will and in virtue of his intrinsic nature, for example, breathing or calling for help.

A power must be distinguished from its exercise. As Harré and Madden point out,

A power can be exercised over and over again or not exercised at all. So the possession of a power is different from the exercise of a power. A power is possessed through time.[5]

Suppose one has the power to speak German. Suppose also that one is visiting a dentist in Frankfurt. One wants to say some things in German, possibly some very nasty things, but with one's mouth full of dental dubieties, one can hardly groan. At least one still has the power to speak German. The power cannot be used or exercised in the particular circumstances but it is still there.

The distinction between a power and its exercise is made by Pelagius. Augustine quotes him as saying that, although God gives the ability to speak, it is he, Pelagius, who uses this ability.[6] Ceasing to use the ability is one thing but ceasing to have the ability is quite another. Augustine contemplates various ways in which Pelagius might cease to have the ability to speak. The idea of permanent bandages intrigues him. Temporary bandages would, of course, deprive Pelagius only of the opportunity to speak and not of the ability itself, but Augustine is thinking of 'closing and shutting the mouth with bandages, as to be quite incapable and opening it, and to put the opening of it out of our power'.[7]

Anselm distinguishes between a power and the conditions necessary to its exercise. One may have perfectly good vision, for example, but not see a mountain either because there is no

[4] R. Harré and E. H. Madden, *Causal Powers*, pp. 22–5.
[5] Ibid., p. 94.
[6] Augustine, *De Natura et Gratia*, XLV.
[7] Ibid.

mountain around or no light or there is something covering one's eyes.[8]

> We have no ability which, if taken by itself alone, would suffice to any actual deed; nevertheless, when those things are absent without which our abilities cannot do the least thing, we are still said to have these abilities in us without any distinction.[9]

Thus 'a man has the ability to see the sun even when the sun is absent, because he would be able to see it if it were present.'[10]

Note that the fact that there are certain conditions necessary to the exercise of a power does not imply that the power itself is conditional. An elderly woman might have the conditional power of 'getting around if the weather is good', but a young woman does not have the power of 'getting a tan if the weather is good'. What the young woman has is simply the power to get a tan, a power which is exercised only if the weather is good.[11]

Austin distinguishes abilities from the opportunities necessary to their exercise. He examines the idea that, given an opportunity to $x$ and an overriding desire to $x$, one has the ability to $x$ if and only if one does $x$.[12] Against this idea Austin notes that an ability, even in the best of circumstances, occasionally fails to be exercised. A good golf player may have the opportunity to hole a very short putt, an overriding desire to hole it, and the ability to hole it, but still (surprise!) not hole it.[13] Conversely, a poor player may, by very good luck, get a hole in one without exhibiting any skill or ability to get a hole in one.

The best work done on this subject is in Anthony Kenny's *Will, Freedom and Power*. Kenny remarks that a capacity must be distinguished from its exercise.

> Consider the capacity of whisky to intoxicate. The possession of this capacity is clearly distinct from its exercise: the whisky possesses the capacity while it is standing harmlessly in the bottle, but it only begins to exercise it after being imbibed.[14]

---

[8] Anselm, *Truth, Freedom, and Evil*, trans. and ed. Jasper Hopkins and Herbert Richardson (New York: Harper and Row, 1967), 128–9.

[9] Ibid., pp. 127–8.  [10] Ibid., p. 141.

[11] J. L. Austin, *Philosophical Papers*, 3rd edn. (Oxford: Oxford University Press, 1979), 225.

[12] Ibid., p. 226.  [13] Ibid., p. 218.

[14] Anthony Kenny, *Will, Freedom and Power* (Oxford: Basil Blackwell, 1975), 9–10.

Corresponding to the distinction between capacity and exercise is a distinction between the 'can' of ability and the 'can' of opportunity. To say 'she can speak Russian' may mean that she has the capacity to speak Russian (she was brought up by Russian parents) or it may mean that the circumstances are such that she has the opportunity to use this capacity (she is visiting Moscow) or it may mean both these things at once.[15]

In Section V below we use the distinction between powers and their exercise to show that God can create a person with libertarian free will by means of limiting not his power to control things but merely the opportunity for its exercise.

Kenny investigates the logic of powers. That one does something does not imply that one has the ability to do it. For example, one may spell 'seize' correctly (half the time) without having the ability to spell 'seize' correctly.[16] That one has the ability to do $x$-or-$y$ does not imply that one has either the ability to do $x$ or the ability to do $y$. For example, one may have the ability to get a head or tail on a single toss of a coin without having either the ability to get a head on a single toss or the ability to get a tail on a single toss.[17] That one has the ability to do $x$, and if he were doing $x$ then he would be doing $y$ does not imply that he has the ability to do $y$. For example, a cook has the ability to make a cake and, since there is in fact no flour, if he were making a cake, he would be making a cake without flour but this does not imply that he has the ability to make a cake without flour.[18]

Three other non-implications can be added to those which Kenny gives. First, that one lacks the ability to do $x$ does not imply that he has the ability not to do $x$. For example, a horse lacks the ability to solve third-order differential equations but this does not mean that it has the ability not to solve third-order differential equations. Indeed, 'the ability not to solve third-order differential equations' is properly understood as 'the ability to refrain from solving third-order differential equations' and this ability is possessed only by keen but self-disciplined mathematicians.

Second, that one has the ability to do $x$ and also the ability to do $y$ does not imply that he has the ability to do $x$-and-$y$. For example,

---

[15] Anthony Kenny, *Will, Freedom and Power*, pp. 131–2.
[16] Ibid., p. 136.          [17] Ibid., pp. 136–7.
[18] Ibid., p. 157. See also John Thorp, *Free Will* (London: Routledge and Kegan Paul, 1980), 28–30.

one may have the ability to order the butler to bring *crème de menthe* and also the ability to leave the liqueur to the butler's disretion but one would not have the ability to do both at once. Again, God has the power to make people who never sin and also the power to make people who decide on their own whether or not to sin but this does not mean that God can do both these things at once.

Third, that one no longer has the opportunity to exercise a power does not imply that one no longer has the power. For example, suppose I have run out of water in the middle of a desert and it is certain that I shall die of thirst. Although I no longer have the opportunity to exercise the power to drink, I still have that power. Again, suppose that some event has already occurred. Then God no longer has the opportunity to exercise the power to prevent it from happening. In spite of this, however, he still has the power itself to prevent the thing from happening, so that he can prevent similar things from happening (if they have not already happened).

It is useful to distinguish proper powers from relative powers. A proper power is one which is proper to the person possessing it in the sense that it does not cease to exist unless there is some change in its possessor. The power to play an errorless game of noughts and crosses (tick-tack-toe), and the power to spell the word 'cacography' are two examples of proper powers. A relative power is one which presupposes a relation between the possessor of the power and his environment such that the power may cease to exist if there is a change not in the possessor but merely in the environment. The power to beat anyone at Sleepy Wool Manor at noughts and crosses, and the power to spell 'cacography' better than Smith are two examples of relative powerrs. If I teach someone at Sleepy Wool Manor how to play an errorless game of noughts and crosses I thereby lose the power to beat anyone at Sleepy Wool Manor at noughts and crosses. However, this involves a change not in me but in my student. In particular, I do not relinquish the proper power to play an errorless game of noughts and crosses.[19]

Powers can be limited or curtailed in various ways. First, the actual power may be destroyed. If it is a proper power this will involve some change in its possessor but if it is a relative power it need only involve a change in the surroundings. If I commit suicide I shall no longer possess the power to play an errorless game of

[19] W. S. Anglin, 'Can God Create a Being He Cannot Control?', *Analysis*, 40 (1980), 222–3.

noughts and crosses (assuming the game is not played in the next world), and if I teach someone at Sleepy Wool manor how to play an errorless game of noughts and crosses I shall no longer possess the power to beat anyone at Sleepy Wool Manor at noughts and crosses.

Second, certain conditions necessary to the exercise of the power may not be met. If we run out of writing-materials at Sleepy Wool Manor then I shall not be exercising my ability to play an errorless game of noughts and crosses. Note that we may run out of writing-materials on purpose. Without ceasing to have the ability to play an errorless game of noughts and crosses, I can choose to put myself in a situation where I cannot exercise that power.

Third, one can curtail a power by exercising another power whose exercise is inconsistent with the exercise of the power in question. If I devote myself entirely to noughts and crosses then I shall not have time to do elaborate chemical experiments. Again, if God exercises his power to give created beings an autonomous role in deciding the future of the universe then he cannot at the same time exercise his power of ensuring that everything in the universe goes according to his perfect will. This third case may be seen as a version of the second.

In Section V we shall use the distinction between proper and relative powers to show that any limitation imposed on God by the existence of persons with free will does not jeopardise his omnipotence.

## II

Defining 'omnipotence' is not an easy matter, and it will be instructive to examine some of the difficulties before giving our definition. We shall begin by reviewing four theories of omnipotence which, as Geach has shown, involve inconsistencies.

The first of these four theories is that God is omnipotent because he can do anything whatsoever, whether it is possible or not. This is not a popular view. With the exception of a few extremists like Shestov (who believed that God could change the past to make it have been the case that there was never any evil), most philosophers agree that omnipotence need not be understood as implying the power to do things that are logically impossible.[20] Some limitations are in order. Thus Geach rejects the theory of omnipotence according to which God can do anything whatsoever in favour of the theory that God's omnipotence consists in the fact that

a proposition 'God can do so-and-so' is true when and only when 'so-and-so' represents a logically consistent description.[21]

However, this theory also is wrong. 'Making a mistake in simple arithmetic' or 'making a decision not made by God' are logically consistent descriptions and yet it is not possible that God have the power to do these things. Thus Geach turns to a third theory, that God's omnipotence consists in the fact that

A proposition 'God can do so-and-so' is true when and only when 'God does so-and-so' represents a logically possible proposition.[22]

This theory also must be rejected. For the sentence

God preserves Marilyn's virginity

represents a logically possible proposition, and yet, given the fact that Marilyn has already lost her virginity, it is not true that

God can preserve Marilyn's virginity

Finally, Geach tries a fourth theory of omnipotence which is like the third theory except that God's omnipotence does not require that he be able to change the past (for example, undo the past fact that Marilyn lost her virginity). This theory also fails because the sentence

God does what I am thinking of

represents a logically possible proposition, and yet, if what I am thinking about is squaring the circle using only ruler and compass, it is false that

God can do what I am thinking of.

As another example,

God destroys the world with a flood

---

[20] Lev Shestov, *Athens and Jerusalem*, trans. Bernard Martin (Athens: Ohio University Press, 1966), pp. 62, 68–9, 219, 411–12, and 434. See also René Descartes, 'God Can Do the Logically Impossible', in *The Power of God*, ed. Linwood Urban and Douglas N. Walton (New York: Oxford University Press, 1978), 37–40.     [21] Geach, 'Omnipotence', 13.     [22] Ibid.

is logically possible, and yet, given that God promised Noah that he would not destroy the world with a flood, and given that God cannot break a promise, it is not true that

> God can destroy the world with a flood.[23]

Geach concludes from his examination and rejection of these four theories that God is better said not to be 'omnipotent' but 'almighty'—'almighty' in the sense that he can create worlds, foresee the future, raise the dead, and so on.[24] As we shall see, however, it is quite possible to give a reasonable definition of 'omnipotence' which avoids the difficulties Geach raises. Flint and Feddoso have already given one such definition and, in Section IV below, we shall give another. Geach simply gave up too easily.


# III


Having been alerted to some of the traps surrounding the concept of omnipotence, let us consider Ross's definition of it. In his *Philosophical Theology* he claims that

*S* is omnipotent if and only if for every logically contingent state of affairs, *p*, whether *p* or −*p* is the case is logically equivalent to the effective choice, by *S*, that *p* or −*p* (respectively).[25]

For example, if God is omnipotent and it is true that

> Difficult Douglas is picking his nose

then it is God's effective choice that Difficult Douglas is picking his nose. In general, if there is an omnipotent being in Ross's sense, every contingent event which occurs is effectively chosen by him.[26] Hence, as Ross himself realises, the fact that God is in this sense 'omnipotent' implies that God cannot create a being he cannot control.[27] In particular, God cannot create a being with libertarian

---

[23] Genesis 9: 11; Numbers 23: 19; 1 Samuel 15: 29; Titus 1: 2.
[24] Peter Geach, 'An Irrelevance of Omnipotence', *Philosophy*, 48 (1973), 327–33.
[25] James F. Ross, *Philosophical Theology* (New York: Bobbs-Merrill, 1969), 211. Calvin would accept Ross's definition: *Institutio Christianae religionis*, iii. 23.
[26] See J. L. Mackie, 'Omnipotence', in *The Power of God*, pp. 84–6.
[27] Ross, *Philosophical Theology*, p. 216.

free will for, in so far as that being had libertarian free will, God would not have control over its choices. Its choices would not necessarily correspond to any effective choices made by God. According to Ross, an omnipotent being's choice is a 'sufficient and necessary cause of whatever finite and contingent events occur in the universe'.[28]

Ross's definition of 'omnipotence' is unsatisfactory because it clashes with our pre-analytic notion of that concept in three ways. First, it follows from his definition but not from our pre-analytic notion of 'omnipotence' that an omnipotent being lacks the power to leave things alone, to leave them to their own devices. Second, it follows from Ross's definition but not from our pre-analytic notion that an omnipotent being effectively chooses every evil thing that happens and is thus not wholly good. Third, it follows from Ross's definition but not from our pre-analytic notion that an omnipotent being who issues commands either lies or is always obeyed. Because it is packed with these repugnant doctrines, Ross's definition must be rejected. We shall examine these three points in turn.

In his article 'Ross on Omnipotence', Mann points out that on Ross's definition an omnipotent being lacks the power to refrain from effectively choosing $p$ and, at the same time, refrain from effectively choosing $-p$.[29] An omnipotent being is not able to forbear from making a choice between $p$ and its negation. In this sense, an omnipotent being is like a busybody who lacks the power to leave things alone. For example, if there is an omnipotent being, the fact that an electron jumps from one shell to another at exactly three o'clock rather than one minute later is not a random event but a consequence of the omnipotent being's specific choice that it jump exactly when it does jump. Hence, if Ross is right, an omnipotent being lacks the power to create a universe which contains random events.

Does the fact that an omnipotent being cannot forbear from willing whatever happens, or the fact that, in particular, he cannot create a universe containing random events (or persons with libertarian free will) mean that he is less powerful than an omnipotent being ought to be, given our intuitive notion of 'omnipotence'? The answer is yes, and for the reason given in

---

[28] Ibid., p. 247.
[29] William E. Mann, 'Ross on Omnipotence', *International Journal for Philosophy of Religion*, 8 (1977), 142–7.

Urban and Walton's article 'Freedom Within Omnipotence'.[30] They argue as follows:

Suppose there are two types of very powerful beings. *A* can create worlds over which he can exercise complete control. He can strictly determine every outcome. *B* can create all the worlds *A* can, but he can also create worlds partially governed by chance, and he can create worlds in which there are free beings over which he has no control as long as they are free. Which of these beings has the *greater* power? We think *B* has. For *B* can create many different kinds of worlds. The being who can only create worlds over which he has complete control does not have as many abilities as the one who can create worlds of different sorts.[31]

On our pre-analytic notion of omnipotence, the very powerful being *A* cannot be omnipotent if there is the possibility of a much more powerful being *B*. The conception of omnipotence which Ross gives does not do justice to our intuitive notion of an omnipotent being.

A second objection to Ross's definition of omnipotence is that it implies that, if there is an omnipotent being, he wills every evil thing that happens. Suppose Cain kills Abel. Then, according to Ross, this is logically equivalent to the effective choice, by the omnipotent being, that Cain kill Abel. Indeed, Cain can argue that he is only carrying out the effective choice of an omnipotent being, a being whose choice is a 'sufficient and necessary cause of whatever finite and contingent events occur in the universe'. Thus, on Ross's definition, an omnipotent God would be a direct cause of evil. Furthermore, if this is so, the only way to retain the notion that God is good is to deny that evil is really evil. One might say, for example, that because it serves some higher purpose, the evil in the world is not really evil. However, the view that evil is good is as heartless as it is ostrich-like. Moreover, according to our pre-analytic notion of omnipotence, there is nothing in that concept which implies that an omnipotent God is the author of every evil. On the contrary, it can be argued that if a being is omnipotent then, having the power to resist temptation and the ability to see the wisdom of doing so, he would have no choice but to do good.[32] If

---

[30] Linwood Urban and Douglas Walton, 'Freedom Within Omnipotence', in *The Power of God*, pp. 192–207.   [31] Ibid., pp. 205–6.

[32] Cf. Richard Swinburne, *The Coherence of Theism* (Oxford: Clarendon Press, 1977), 182.

anything is implicit in the concept of omnipotence, it is that an omnipotent being is *not* a direct cause of evil. For Ross an omnipotent being is like a totalitarian bureaucracy which prescribes in exact detail every single thing which is to be done—and is thus rightly blamed when things go wrong. However, according to a more usual conception, an omnipotent being is more like an absolute monarch who, out of respect for his subjects, allows them certain discretionary powers—and who is thus not necessarily at fault when things go wrong.

A third objection to Ross's definition of omnipotence is that it rules out the possibility of disobeying a truthful omnipotent being, a possibility which we think is *not* ruled out when we think of an omnipotent God. For example, suppose the omnipotent being tells Adam that he wills that Adam not eat a certain apple but Adam then eats the apple anyway. Since Adam eats the apple it follows, on Ross's definition, that the omnipotent being wills that Adam eat the apple. How can this be? Does the omnipotent being will that Adam eat the apple or not? If he does not will that Adam eat the apple (as one would suppose from the command) then how can it be that he is effectively choosing that Adam eat the apple? If he does will that Adam eat the apple (as one would suppose from the effective choice) then how can he be telling the truth when he tells Adam that he wills that Adam not eat the apple? On Ross's view, the omnipotent being lies to Adam, telling Adam that he wills that Adam not eat the apple when all the time he secretly wills that Adam do the opposite of what he is telling Adam to do. One thinks of C. S. Lewis's devil tempting the Venusian Eve. The devil tells her that God secretly wills that she disobey God's command. Lewis's point, of course, is that it is not God but the devil who is the liar. It is the devil, not God, who calls 'evil good, and good evil'.[33] Eve cannot claim that in her disobedience she would really be obeying some 'secret will' of God. Thus, once again, Ross has surreptitiously packed a highly controversial doctrine in his definition of 'omnipotence'. There is nothing in the pre-analytic notion of that concept to warrant the conclusion that an omnipotent being is disobeyed only in so far as he is a liar.

---

[33] C. S. Lewis, *Voyage to Venus* (London: Pan Books, 1953), 102–11. The scripture verse is Isaiah 5: 20.

## IV

If Ross's definition of 'omnipotence' is unacceptable, what shall we put in its place? In his elegant work *The God of the Philosophers*, Kenny suggests that God's omnipotence consists in 'the possession of all logically possible powers which it is logically possible for a being with the attributes of God to possess'.[34] Since no power would be such that it is logically possible for a being with the attributes of God to possess unless it were in itself logically possible, we can simplify this to say that God's omnipotence consists in the possession of all powers which it is logically possible for a being with the attributes of God to possess. This does not mean, however, that God always has the opportunity to exercise these powers. Kenny writes:

> It is logically possible to possess a power, I suggest, if the exercise of the power does not as such involve any logical impossibility. When I say that the exercise of the power does not *as such* involve any logical [im]possibility I mean that there is no logical incoherence in the description of what it is to exercise the power. For a power to be a logically possible power it is not necessary that every exercise of it should be coherently conceivable, but only that some exercise of it should be.[35]

For example, God

> has the power to do what I am thinking of. It is true that if I am thinking of something which it is impossible to do, then an omnipotent God cannot, on that occasion, exercise the power he has of doing what I am thinking about. But powers are not tied to particular occasions, and it is not necessary, for a power to be genuinely possessed, that it can be coherently exercised on all occasions and in all circumstances. Though God has the power to do what I am thinking of, he cannot exercise this power if I am thinking a nonsensical thought.[36]

Kenny's distinction between powers and their exercise enables him to disarm the examples which led Geach to renounce the notion of 'omnipotence'. For example, on Kenny's account God still has the *power* to preserve Marilyn's virginity—even though he no longer has the opportunity to exercise this power because Marilyn has now lost her virginity. Again, God retains the *power* to

---

[34] Anthony Kenny, *The God of the Philosophers* (Oxford: Clarendon Press, 1979), 98.          [35] Ibid., p. 96.          [36] Ibid., p. 97.

destroy all things of flesh in a flood—even though he cannot exercise his power now that he has promised not to.

Kenny has given a very nice solution to the problem raised by God's inability to change the past—and without introducing time or temporal slices of possible worlds into the definition of 'omnipotence'. One merely observes that although God can no longer exercise the power to prevent a certain past event he none the less still has the power in question.

Note that, as it stands, Kenny's definition of omnipotence applies only to God. It is true, of course, that only God can be omnipotent, but this is something which ought to be proved subsequent to a definition of the form '$x$ is omnipotent if and only if $Fx$'. We shall now give such a definition.

In defining '$x$ is omnipotent', we must be careful not to give a definition according to which some obviously nonomnipotent being comes out 'omnipotent'. We would not, for example, want to say that

$x$ is omnipotent
if and only if
$x$ possesses all the powers which it is logically possible for a being with the attributes essential to $x$ to possess.

For then 'the man who can only scratch his ear' will end up, on the definition, being 'omnipotent'.[37] As Mackie notes of definitions of this kind:

any thing would be omnipotent if it could do all that it was logically possible for that thing to do. That is, a thing's being omnipotent would mean only that practical possibility, for that thing, coincided with logical possibility and this might hold where both sorts of possibility were extremely limited.[38]

For example, a special pumpkin might possess all the powers which it is logically possible for a pumpkin to possess but still be unable to create a world or foresee the future or raise the dead. To be omnipotent, it is not enough to be able to do everything which you might possibly do: you have to be the *sort* of being who can do all

---

[37] Alvin Plantinga, *God and Other Minds* (Ithaca: Cornell University Press, 1967), 170.
[38] J. L. Mackie, 'Omnipotence', in *The Power of God*, p. 77–8. See also Ross, *Philosophical Theology*, pp. 206 and 209.

the things God is said to do. Thus, since no pumpkin can do the
things God does and still be a pumpkin, one of the requirements for
being omnipotent is being a nonpumpkin. In giving a proposition
equivalent to '$x$ is omnipotent' we have to place some restriction on
the sort of being $x$ can be. Now one of God's fundamental powers
is the power knowingly to create and destroy. If anything is going
to be omnipotent, presumably it will be able to create and destroy
any contingent thing it wants. Thus we might generalise Kenny's
definitions as follows.

> $x$ is omnipotent
> if and only if
> $x$ is a person who has the power knowingly to create or
> destroy any contingent entity and
> $x$ possesses all the powers which it is logically possible for a
> person with the attributes essential to $x$ to possess.

Is this definition satisfactory? No, for it suffers from three
defects.

1. The definition fails to exclude the possibility that $x$ might
essentially lack some power which another being, also able to
create and destroy contingent things, might not lack. To be
omnipotent, $x$ has to be such that there is no possible being who
possesses all the powers $x$ has and more besides. For example, $x$ is
not omnipotent if, although he can create or destroy worlds, he is
by nature incapable of doing algebraic topology, or by nature
incapable of loving thieves. Thus we need to replace the second
condition of our definition by a stronger condition such as

> it is not logically possible that there be some person who has
> all of $x$'s powers and more besides.

Is this condition strong enough, or is it, perhaps, too strong? One
might object to it that if a divine being is impeccable then, on the
emended definition, he will not be omnipotent, since there is the
possibility of a divine being who has unlimited powers to create or
destroy and also the power to sin.

To this objection I reply that it is not clear that there really is this
possibility. The fact that a being can knowingly create or destroy
contingent things may well entail that he knows too much to be
able to sin. Sin may require a certain ignorance. In any case,
however we define 'omnipotence', we shall be doing it badly if it

turns out, on our definition, that the Christian God is not omnipotent. To avoid any possible problems, then, I suggest that the second condition be:

> it is not logically possible that there be some person who has all of $x$'s powers and also some other power whose possession is compatible with $x$'s being necessarily omniscient and necessarily good.

2. The definition does not say anything about the exercise of $x$'s powers. If a being is omnipotent, he may himself do things which limit the exercise of his powers. For example, if he creates a stone, he thereby makes it impossible that he exercise his power never to create a stone. Or if he promises never to create a dragon and if he is, moreover, necessarily a promise-keeper, he thereby becomes unable to exercise his power to create a dragon. On the other hand, if he is omnipotent, it is not the case that some other independently acting being can limit the exercise of his powers. If a person has all sorts of powers but cannot exercise any of them without, say, the permission of someone whose existence and will are at all times beyond his control, then he is not omnipotent, at least not on my intuitive notion of 'omnipotence'. Hence we shall elaborate the definition by adding the condition that

> there is no limitation on the exercise of $x$'s powers that does not have its source in an exercise of $x$'s libertarian free will.

Note that this condition implies that no omnipotent being is such that, by nature, he must defer to any other omnipotent beings there may be in matters concerning, say, the creation.

3. The definition, as it stands, suffers from a failure to distinguish between proper and relative powers. Recall from Section I above that a proper power is one which is proper to the person possessing it in the sense that it does not cease to exist unless there is some change in its possessor. A relative power, however, is one which presupposes a relation between the possessor of the power and his environment such that the power may cease to exist if there is a change not in the possessor but merely in his environment. With our definition of 'omnipotence' as it now stands, an omnipotent being possesses all the powers, both proper and relative, which he might possibly possess. Thus an omnipotent being possesses the relative power to beat everyone at Sleepy Wool

Manor at noughts and crosses, and also the relative power to spell 'cacography' better than Smith. Moreover, if someone at Sleepy Wool Manor learns to play an errorless game of noughts and crosses or if Smith finally learns how to spell 'cacography' then the omnipotent being loses these relative powers and thus ceases to be omnipotent. In general, any change in the circumstances which implies that the omnipotent being, while himself remaining the same, loses a relative power also implies that he ceases to be omnipotent. To avoid this unpalatable conclusion we must emend the definition to refer only to nonrelative powers.

The final version of our definition is thus as follows.

$x$ is omnipotent if and only if

(i) $x$ is a person (with libertarian free will) who has the power knowingly to create or destroy any contingent thing; and

(ii) it is not logically possible that there be some person who has all of $x$'s nonrelative powers and also some other nonrelative power whose possession is compatible with $x$'s being necessarily omniscient and necessarily good; and

(iii) there is no limitation on the exercise of $x$'s powers that does not have its source in an exercise of $x$'s libertarian free will.

This definition avoids the traps pointed out by Geach. It avoids the untenable consequences of Ross's definition. It does not clash with our pre-analytic notion of omnipotence. And it preserves all that is good in Kenny's definition.


# V


Given the above definition of 'omnipotence', we now show that it is possible for there to exist an omnipotent being and a separate person with libertarian free will. We give three arguments.


## (1) Nonrelative powers only


Kenny thinks that, using his definition, it can be argued that God cannot create a being he cannot control. To quote Kenny in full:

The power to create a being that one cannot control and thereby give up one's omnipotence is not a power that could logically be possessed by a being who had the attributes of God including immutability.[39]

Clearly Kenny thinks that God would give up a power and hence (on Kenny's definition) his omnipotence if God created a being he could not control. But which power? There are three possibilities:

1. The power to create a universe such that everything in it is controlled by God
2. The power to control everything which God might possibly create
3. The power to control every currently existing thing.

God has the first power because he has the power to create a deterministic universe (and also the power to cause an indeterministic universe henceforth to be deterministic). However, God would retain this power even if he created a being he could not control. Thus, presumably, this is not the power Kenny has in mind. God has the second power if and only if he does not have the power to create a being he does not have the power to control. Whether or not God has this power is what is at issue and hence Kenny can hardly be taking it as a premiss that God has this power. Thus it seems it is the third power which is involved in Kenny's argument. Kenny assumes that there was some time at which there was no being which God did not have the power to control. Given this initial situation, the creating of such a being would entail the giving up of the third power.

If we suppose, on Kenny's behalf, that in creating a being with libertarian free will God is actually giving up the third power then it does follow on Kenny's definition of omnipotence that God ceases to be omnipotent. However, we saw above that Kenny's definition needed correction. We had to rewrite it so as to limit God's omnipotence to nonrelative powers. Now, is the power to control every currently existing thing a proper power, a relative power, or neither? The creation of a being which God does not have the power to control does not involve any change in God himself. He does not thereby become less strong. Thus it is not a proper power. On the other hand, this power does presuppose a relation between God and the contents of the present universe such that the power

[39] Kenny, *The God of the Philosophers*, p. 98.

may cease to exist if there is a change not in God but only in the universe. Thus it is a relative power. Hence given *our* definition of omnipotence (which implies that an omnipotent being need have only nonrelative powers), it follows that the loss of this power is compatible with God's remaining omnipotent. Therefore it is quite possible that an omnipotent God, without ceasing to be omnipotent, create a being he cannot control.[40]

## (2) Limitations of opportunities

In the previous section we assumed, on Kenny's behalf, that if God created a being with libertarian free will then God would thereby give up the power to control every currently existing thing. However, would God have to give up this power in order to create a being which he could not control, or would it suffice if God merely gave up the opportunity to exercise this power? If one takes the phrase 'God can create a being he cannot control' to mean 'God can create a being he lacks the power to control' then Kenny is right that God relinquishes a power if he creates such a being. However, one might take the phrase 'God can create a being he cannot control' to mean 'God can create a being which he lacks the power or the opportunity to control'. This latter statement is implied by the statement 'God can create a being which he has the power but not the opportunity to control'. If one understands the phrase 'God can create a being he cannot control' in the second way then Kenny is wrong to conclude that God relinquishes a power if he creates such a being.

Granted, however, that God has the power to control every currently existing thing, how might it come about that God not have the opportunity to exercise this power? One way would be for God to create a rational being and say to her, 'I promise to maintain you in existence forever and let you make choices independently of my will.' Since it is logically impossible that God should break a promise (we may assume), the promise precludes the exercise of God's power to control every currently existing thing. Thus, for example, the rational being might rob a bank in spite of the fact that God wills that she not rob a bank. When we saw her robbing

---

[40] Anglin, 'Can God Create a Being He Cannot Control?', pp. 220–3.

the bank, we might ask whether God could control her. There is clearly a sense in which the correct answer is *no*—not if God made the promise he did make.

## (3) Logical impossibility

In harmony with Kenny, J. L. Mackie writes:

there is a fundamental difficulty in the notion of an omnipotent God creating men with free will, for if men's wills are really free this must mean that even God cannot control them, that is, that God is no longer omnipotent.[41]

In answer to this argument, first note that an omnipotent being does have the power to make human beings will whatever he wants them to will. It is just that if he does this, they are not willing freely—in the libertarian sense. Libertarian free will is defined in such a way that you do not have it if God brings it about that it is somehow determined that you will what he wants you to will, and hence, in so far as you are exercising libertarian free will, it is logically impossible that God bring it about that it is somehow determined that you will what God wants you to will. It is in this sense, and only in this sense, that 'God cannot control them'. Since, however, even Mackie does not require that omnipotence extend to what is logically impossible, it is not necessary to follow him to the conclusion that 'God is no longer omnipotent'.[42] Because it is logically impossible that it be determined that someone will something with libertarian free will, it is without prejudice to God's omnipotence if there are persons exercising libertarian free will.

More subtly, Mackie goes on to suggest that an omnipotent being might ordinarily allow people to exercise libertarian free will but intervene when he saw that they would will wrongly if he did not intervene.[43] The cases in which they willed rightly would thus be perfectly typical exercises of libertarian free will but there would be no cases of willing wrongly. In this way an omnipotent God could create people with libertarian free will but, assuming God is also good, he could *not* create people with the sort of free will

[41] J. L. Mackie, 'Evil and Omnipotence', in *The Power of God*, p. 28.
[42] Mackie, 'Omnipotence' in ibid., p. 83.
[43] Mackie, 'Evil and Omnipotence', in ibid., p. 28.

which includes evil in its scope. It is not possible that there be both a good omnipotent being and a separate being with libertarian free will who might actually use his will do to evil.

Against this argument, first note that it is not clear that God knows what a human being would do if God did not intervene. Consider the two counterfactuals

> If I, God, were not to intervene then Marilyn would decide to seduce Professor Smith

and

> If I, God, were not to intervene then Marilyn would not decide to seduce Professor Smith.

There is nothing in counterfactual logic which implies that these two propositions are not both false. Moreover, if they are both false then no one can know either of them to be true—not even God. This is because, if they are both false, there is simply no fact about what Marilyn would do if God were not to intervene. There is simply nothing to be known. If both counterfactuals are false then it is not logically coherent to suppose that God could 'see' what would be willed if he were not to intervene, and then intervene to prevent it.

Note that since exercises of libertarian free will are indeterminate, there is no reason to think that if Marilyn is going to will that $p$ then something prior to that act of will indicates that she is going to will that $p$. There need be nothing to 'see' that would 'look' different if she was about to will that not-$p$. In exactly the same situation $S$, she might be going to will that $p$—or she might be going to will that not-$p$. In so far as her will is free in the libertarian sense, there is no infallible sign, prior to her choice, of what in fact she is going to will.

Note also that, even if we assume that God has foreknowledge of all future events, it still does not follow that he can 'see' what Marilyn is going to decide and prevent her from so deciding. For in that case she will not so decide and God's foreknowledge will tell him only that she will not so decide. It will not tell him what she would have decided had he not intervened.

Also against Mackie's argument, recall from the first chapter that an event is determined not only if God directly brings it about but also if it is the case that, were it not going to occur in an undetermined way, God *would* make it occur. Whether God directly causes it to occur or whether he simply ensures somehow that it occur, it is still determined. Hence if the situation is as Mackie suggests, it is determined that human beings decide rightly and only rightly and hence, by the definition of libertarian free will, they do not so decide with libertarian free will. It is as if a person had to go into one of two rooms but, perhaps unknown to him, one of them was locked. Even if he at once entered the unlocked room, we could not say that he had any 'liberty of indifference' in the matter. Of course, he would in some important sense be 'free' but there would not be the two-way possibility which is essential to the notion of libertarian free will. The 'possibility' which Mackie suggests is actually an impossibility and, as such, it is outside the scope of God's powers.[44]

I conclude that an omnipotent being can co-exist with some other being who has libertarian free will, and who might actually use that libertarian free will to do evil.

# VI

Suppose there is a being who has the power to create or destroy any contingent thing. Can we prove that he is omnipotent?

Normally we think about the exercise of a power as tied to a certain context. What is peculiar about God's power to create contingent things is that there need be no context at all for this act. Usually the exercise of a power is made possible or impossible by the circumstances. However, a being who can create or destroy contingent entities can also create or destroy circumstances. For example, to heal cancer, God does not have to separate the noxious cells from the healthy ones and then remove the noxious cells from the body. He can heal cancer simply by ceasing to maintain the cancerous cells in existence. They just disappear. Now because God has this power over the context or circumstances of his acts, it is hard to imagine any but a logical limitation to his powers. In short, there is nothing to prevent him from having the powers that an omnipotent being has.

[44] Clement Dore, 'Plantinga on the Free Will Defence', *Review of Metaphysics*, 24 (1971), 699–701.

Although the above suggests that a divine being is omnipotent, it does not actually prove that he has every power (of the type required by the definition of omnipotence). For there may be some powers which are not directly related to creating and destroying contingent things—for example, the power to do the mathematics of category theory—which none the less befit an omnipotent being. It is hard to think of a power that could not find expression in terms of the existence of contingent things—even a very abstract mathematical theory can usually be instantiated in terms of the laws of some possible contingent universe—but it none the less seems a possibility. Perhaps the divine being is simply less capable of rejoicing than he might be.

On the other hand, the claim that the divine being has some but not all the powers he might have is not a natural claim. What powers does God lack which none the less befit an omnipotent being? Why does he lack them? Unless we want to adopt a purely arbitrary position which raises unanswerable questions, we had best say that the divine being is omnipotent. Indeed, one of the roles which 'God' plays in intellectual life is that of ultimate answer. God is a terminus for our intellectual longings. If, however, there is some arbitrary and unknowable cut-off point beyond which God has no powers then we shall have reached not a terminus but a void—as when a traveller finds that the road simply stops in the middle of a forest.

There is another consideration as well. If simplicity and completeness are tokens of truth in scientific theories then so they can be taken in religion as well—for religion, precisely, is a kind of quest for some unified whole. Furthermore, if simplicity and completeness are criteria of truth then it is false that there is an arbitrary and unknowable cut-off· point for God's powers. The natural and simpler view is that the divine being is omnipotent.

Granted the above considerations, it follows that being divine entails being omnipotent. Suppose that this is indeed so. If, as we showed in the second chapter, a divine being is necessarily divine then it follows that a divine being is necessarily omnipotent. Indeed, we might have defined a divine being as a noncontingent, necessarily omnipotent being.

To conclude this chapter, let us reflect on the relationship among God's omnipotence, his free will, and his uniqueness. Suppose there are (at least) two omnipotent divine beings. Since both have libertarian free will, it is logically possible that the first decides to maintain Mars in existence and the second decides to replace Mars with a belt of asteroids. Since each is omnipotent, each can exercise his powers independently of the other and hence it is possible that Mars be maintained in existence and, at the same time, be replaced by a belt of asteroids. To say that the divine beings would have to work out a compromise on this is to say that they can hamper each other—and hence they are not really omnipotent (in the sense defined above). If they are really both omnipotent then it is possible that Mars both exist and, at the same time, not exist. The original assumption that there are (at least) two omnipotent divine beings has led to a contradiction. It must therefore be rejected. We may conclude that there is at most one omnipotent divine being.

# 4

# Omniscience

## I

THE fact that the divine being is omniscient—or at least very knowledgeable—follows from the fact that he knowingly created a very complex universe, or simply from the fact that he is omnipotent and thus has the power to give a correct answer to any question. Indeed, omniscience is often thought of in terms of propositions. Not only does God not believe any false proposition but, more important, if any proposition is true then God knows it is true.

There are (at least) two sorts of knowledge which it might seem that an omniscient being would possess. First, he would know for any situation what would happen if such and such were the case, and, second, he would know of any future event whether it would be the case. Both these assertions, however, are highly controversial.

Let us consider the first case. Does an omniscient being know whether $q$ would occur if $p$ were the case? If one of the counterfactuals

>  If $p$ were the case then $q$ would be true

and

>  If $p$ were the case then not-$q$ would be true

is true then, indeed, the omniscient being can tell you whether it is $q$ or not-$q$ that would be the case. However, there is nothing in counterfactual logic that would preclude the possibility that both propositions be false, and then, of course, an omniscient being cannot know either of them, and hence cannot tell you whether $q$ or not-$q$ would be the case. For example, it may be that both the following are false:

> If the car had cost 10 per cent more, Marilyn would (still) have bought it

and

> If the car had cost 10 per cent more, Marilyn would not have bought it.

If they are both false then you cannot learn anything by asking an omniscient being whether, if the car had cost 10 per cent more, Marilyn would have bought it. The omniscient being will not know, and simply because there is nothing to be known. There is no fact about what would have happened.

The second case concerns the omniscient being's knowledge of the future. (Even if the omniscient being is timeless—a possibility I try to keep open in this book—he can still have knowledge of the future in the sense that he can communicate his knowledge of a timelessly known event to a prophet for whom the event is in the future.) An omniscient being can tell you whether Smith will decide to marry Maid Marilyn only if one of the following is true:

> Smith will decide to marry Maid Marilyn

or

> Smith will not decide to marry Maid Marilyn.

However, if (thanks, say, to some difficulty about future contingent propositions in relation to two-valued logic) neither is true then an omniscient being will not be able to answer your question about whether this decision will be made. Again, this is not a fault of the omniscient being but rather a problem having to do with the indeterminacy of certain future events.

Christian tradition does not say much about whether God knows what *would* happen in every merely hypothetical case. Thus a traditional Christian can argue (as I shall) that God lacks this knowledge. On the other hand, Christian tradition is very strongly in favour of the thesis that God has complete, detailed knowledge of the future—for this, precisely, is the whole basis of prophecy. The Bible presupposes that God (and God alone) has unlimited foreknowledge.[1] The Nicene Creed affirms that God 'has spoken

---

[1] Ecclesiasticus 23: 19–20; 39: 19–20; Isaiah 41: 22–3; 48: 5; Daniel 13: 42; Matthew 26: 34; John 14: 29; Hebrews 4: 13.

through the prophets'. Aquinas (in line with many other Fathers and Doctors of the Church) held that God knows future contingent events.[2] The First Vatican Council states: 'For "all things are naked and open to His eyes", even those which by the free action of creatures are in the future.'[3] The question is not *whether*, on a Christian view, God has knowledge (timelessly or otherwise) of future events, but merely *how* he has such knowledge. Further-more, it is not just Christian tradition that interprets God's omniscience in such a way that it includes complete foreknowledge: many major religions hold the same view. For how else can true prophets make detailed predictions about future events—and how else can God exercise a providential control over the future? To deny that God has complete foreknowledge—for any reason whatsoever (e.g. one's version of libertarianism seems to conflict with it)—is to make a radical departure from a number of very important religious traditions, including the one whose cornerstone is the prophet Jesus.

In what follows, I first argue that an omniscient being does not always know what would happen in every given hypothetical situation. I then try to show how an omniscient being might none the less have complete knowledge of future events. In particular, I attempt to show that God can have foreknowledge of decisions made by human beings with libertarian free will. My treatment of this problem is similar to that found in Talbott's article 'On Divine Foreknowledge and Bringing About the Past'.[4] However, I take a more detailed and 'mechanical' approach, and I also answer some objections that have not yet been answered in the 'literature'. I close this chapter by suggesting a way in which God's foreknowledge (as I understand it) interacts with his providence.

## II

Let us say that a person has *middle knowledge* if for every pair of propositions of the form

---

[2] *Summa Theologiae*, 1a.57 art. 3.

[3] John F. Broderick, *Documents of Vatican Council I* (Collegeville, Minnesota: The Liturgical Press, 1971), 41.

[4] Thomas B. Talbott, 'On Divine Foreknowledge and Bringing About the Past', *Philosophy and Phenomenological Research*, 46 (1986), 455–69.

If *p* were the case then *q* would be the case

and

If *p* were the case then *q* would not be the case

that person knows (at least) one of them to be true. In particular, if *p* describes some circumstances in which a person with libertarian free will is faced with a decision, and *q* describes his making that decision in one way rather than any other, then a person with middle knowledge knows which one of $p \: \square\!\!\rightarrow q$ and $p \: \square\!\!\rightarrow \neg q$ is true, and hence knows what would be decided. For example, a 'middle knower' knows which of the following is true:

If Smith had gone to Brown's he would have ordered steak

and

If Smith had gone to Brown's he would not have ordered steak.

Counterfactuals, such as the above, whose consequent involves a choice made with libertarian free will are called 'counterfactuals of freedom'. Note that, thanks to the indeterminacy of exercises of libertarian free will, the consequent of such a counterfactual is not tied to the antecedent by means of a rigid causal or logical connection.

If there is a person with middle knowledge and if *p* and *q* are any propositions then at least one of the two counterfactuals $p \: \square\!\!\rightarrow q$ and $p \: \square\!\!\rightarrow \neg q$ is true. (They are both true only if *p* is impossible.) A person with middle knowledge knows of every set of circumstances what would happen in those circumstances, and thus there is something definite that would happen (one of *q* and $\neg q$). Conversely, if—as we shall argue—there are propositions *p* and *q* such that both $p \: \square\!\!\rightarrow q$ and $p \: \square\!\!\rightarrow \neg q$ are false then no one, not even God, has middle knowledge.

When someone says

If *p* were the case then *q* would be the case

he may mean one of several things. He may mean that

Facts like *p* (almost) always lead to facts like *q*.

Or he may mean that

> $p$ is true and, although it rarely leads to a fact like $q$, in this case it did.

As an example of the latter, suppose I claim that

> If Marilyn had rolled the die she would have got a three or higher.

I do not know that Marilyn did roll the die but you do know this and you also know she got an ace. So you reply:

> If Marilyn had rolled the die she would have got an ace.

No doubt there are other ways of using counterfactuals. For example, in hopes of convincing some gullible soul that I have occult knowledge, I might say

> Marilyn has not rolled the die but if she had rolled it—in a perfectly random way—she would have got a six.

None the less, when the antecedent is false, a counterfactual is typically used to express some causal connection between the antecedent and consequent. This causal connection may only be of a statistical nature but in a typical counterfactual utterance some claim is being made about the antecedent 'leading to' the consequent. For the typical counterfactual to be true, the event described by the antecedent must tend to bring about or make more probable the event described by the consequent. For example, assuming Marilyn has not tossed the coin, it seems that the counterfactuals

> If Marilyn had tossed the coin, she would have got heads

and

> If Marilyn had tossed the coin, she would have got tails

are both false because there is no deciding link from antecedent to consequent. The one outcome does not follow any more than the other.

For what follows, we define three types of true counterfactuals. A counterfactual is *trite* if it is true by virtue of the fact that its antecedent and consequent are both (at some time) true. A counterfactual is *tight* if its antecedent is false (but not impossible), and it is true by virtue of the fact that the event described by the antecedent would be a (near) sufficient cause of the event described by the consequent (in the understood circumstances). We might say that the truth of a tight counterfactual is grounded in the very high probability of the consequent given the antecedent (and background information). Finally, a counterfactual is *loose* if its antecedent is false (but not impossible) and it is true in spite of the fact that it is not tight. (We exclude counterfactuals of the form 'even if . . . still . . .'.) For example, if it is true, the following counterfactual is loose:

> If Marilyn had tossed the coin—in a perfectly indeterministic manner—she would have got tails.

Note that if God has middle knowledge then there are many loose counterfactuals.

We now have the following argument against middle knowledge. Let

> $A$ = God puts Woody Allen in the Garden of Eden.
> $B$ = Woody Allen rebels against God.

Then $A$ is false but not impossible and $A \square\!\!\rightarrow \neg B$ is the statement

> If God were to put Woody Allen in the Garden of Eden then Woody Allen would not rebel against God.

Assuming that Woody Allen has libertarian free will which extends to evil, this counterfactual is not tight. Nor is its mate $A \square\!\!\rightarrow B$. Now (1) there is no cause or reason on account of which Woody Allen would do better than Adam—and Adam rebelled in spite of all God had done for him; and (2) there is no cause or reason on account of which Woody Allen would do as badly as Adam—the lovely garden, etc. would give him an incentive to be grateful to God rather than rebellious. Thus there is nothing that would make $A \square\!\!\rightarrow \neg B$ true rather than $A \square\!\!\rightarrow B$. There seems, moreover, to be no way, even in principle, of verifying or falsifying either counterfactual. From the 'symmetry' of the example, it follows that there cannot be any overriding reasons that would support one counterfactual at the expense of the other, or undermine one counterfactual to the profit of the other. The two counterfactuals have a kind of metaphysical parity in relation to truth and, since they cannot both be true, it follows that they both must be false.

Since neither of the counterfactuals is true, we may conclude that there is no middle knowledge. In particular, an omniscient being does not know what would happen if, instead of Adam, God were to put Woody Allen in the Garden of Eden.

There are at least three objections to the above argument. First, one may object that the truth of one of the two counterfactuals (and the falsity of the other) is grounded in Woody Allen himself. The one counterfactual is true rather than the other simply on account of what Woody Allen himself would choose.

To this objection I reply that since, as we may suppose, Woody Allen never has and never will be in the situation in question, he cannot contribute to the actual truth, if such there be, of one of the counterfactuals. An actual state of affairs (e.g. a proposition's being true) cannot be caused by a purely hypothetical event.[5]

Second, one may object to my argument that God might just put Woody Allen in the Garden of Eden and not meet with any rebellion. In such a case, those who have maintained that $A \ \Box\!\!\rightarrow \neg B$ can say, 'we told you so. What we said was true all along. Indeed, this proves that $A \ \Box\!\!\rightarrow \neg B$ would still have been true, even if $A$ had never been true.'[6]

To this I reply that my opponent's counterfactual is trite rather than loose. We are not discussing trite counterfactuals and, moreover, there is no reason to hold that trite counterfactuals would still be true even if they were not trite. Trite counterfactuals are not typical counterfactuals—their antecedents are not false—and they cannot be used as a basis for inferring properties of other kinds of counterfactuals.

Third, it may be objected that there are counterfactuals of freedom such that even human beings know they are true. For example, Freddoso knows that

were I [Freddoso] offered a no-strings-attached grant to do research for five years and to do just as much teaching as I cared to do, I would freely accept it.[7]

Freddoso remarks that 'if even *we* can have some limited

---

[5] For more on bringing about the truth of counterfactuals of freedom, see William Hasker, 'A Refutation of Middle Knowledge', *Nous*, 20 (1986), 545–57.

[6] Alfred J. Freddoso gives this argument in the introduction to his translation of Part IV of Luis de Molina's *Concordia* (Ithaca: Cornell University Press, 1988), 73.

[7] Ibid., p. 79.

knowledge of conditional future contingents, it is hardly surprising that *God* can know them'.[8] In other words, because we humans have knowledge of counterfactuals of freedom such as the one above, *a fortiori*, God has knowledge of them and of many other such counterfactuals. There are thus many loose counterfactuals and nothing prevents an omnipotent, omniscient being from having middle knowledge.

Against Freddoso, it may be pointed out that some counterfactuals of freedom are tight. The causal connection in a tight counterfactual need not be so strong as to preclude an exercise of libertarian free will. Recall that the antecedent of a tight counterfactual can describe a *near* sufficient cause for the consequent. This, precisely, is the case in Freddoso's example. What Freddoso knows is true simply by virtue of the fact that academics who love research (and money?) at least as much as Freddoso does very rarely if ever turn down no-strings-attached grants. This is just an instantiation of some statistical law in Psychology. The fact that we know a tight counterfactual, moreover, has no implications for the possibility of loose counterfactuals. God does know what Freddoso would do if offered the grant in question but this does not mean that there is anything to know about what Freddoso would do if offered a mere two-year grant with a couple of strings attached.

Suppose Professor Smith says

> If I were to make a pass at Marilyn today, she would accept at once.

We realise that Smith would never make a pass at anyone, but we object to his statement on the grounds that Marilyn would be equally balanced between a desire to gratify her teacher, and a repugnance she would feel at the idea of doing so. Smith replies that this is merely to say that his counterfactual is not tight. He agrees that it is not tight but he points out that the counterfactual with the same antecedent and the opposite consequent is not tight either. He then assures us that the original counterfactual is loose. Smith admits that there is no 'ground' for the truth of the original counterfactual; he admits that he cannot say how he knows it to be true; he just knows it, he asserts. At this point we conclude that there is no more philosophy to be done, and we walk away. As we

---

[8] Ibid

go, we hear Smith protesting, 'but God would know!' We, however, realise that even God cannot make a non-fact into a fact merely by wishing to know something.

To conclude this section I sketch a second argument against middle knowledge. This second argument depends on a number of theological assumptions and it may not be as philosophically interesting as the main argument given above.

Suppose God has middle knowledge. Then, prior to his decision to create Gabriel, God knew that

> If I, God, were to create Gabriel then he would be a very happy person in heaven

—since that, in fact, is how it turned out. Since, however, some persons go to hell (e.g. Lucifer), the fact that God has middle knowledge implies that he created them *knowing* that if he created them they would go to hell. However, since God is good, he cannot create someone in the knowledge that, if created, they would go to hell. No, he could not do this in order to bring about a much greater good. For then he would be using the persons who would go to hell as a mere means to an end, and this would not be worthy of God.

If God has middle knowledge then Lucifer can rightly complain, 'God, you created me, knowing I would be miserable, and, whether you did this for some great good or not, you did not show proper respect for my person. Why did you not create only those whom you knew would be happy? Was it for some good so great that it can really justify your exploiting me, as a mere tool?'

In order to counter this charge, we must agree that God does not have middle knowledge, that, (metaphysically) prior to his creating Lucifer, God looked forward to a love relationship with him. (God's foreknowledge of Lucifer's fall was, as I shall explain below, dependent on that fall, and it was not possible that this knowledge— unlike middle knowledge—play a role in God's decision to create Lucifer.)

## III

In the previous chapter we argued that it is possible for there to exist both an omnipotent being and another being who exercises libertarian free will. In this section we shall show how there might exist both a being with foreknowledge and another being whose free decisions are foreknown by the first being. What we shall argue is that the foreknower's knowledge of future free decisions can be a kind of *a posteriori* knowledge acquired by means of the operation of temporally backwards causality. The future event causes the past foreknowledge of it. This is admittedly a paradoxical notion but it does not, as I shall argue, involve any logical impossibility. Indeed, my position has already been argued by philosophers such as Talbott and Dummett, and I shall mainly be repeating their arguments.[9] In the next section I shall answer some objections to backwards causality, including one proposed by Kenny and one proposed by myself.[10]

What is 'backwards causation'? When we look at a star five light-years away, we are observing what happened on that star five years ago. The photons that are now entering our telescope left the star five years ago. In this way the past is having an effect on us. We are experiencing its traces. By analogy, we may suppose that, as well as being affected by traces from the past, God (or his prophet, if God himself is not in Time) is affected by what we might call 'hansels' from the future. The future event will set off a causal chain of events whose effects in the present allow God to 'see' the future event. What he 'sees' now is the way it is because the future event will be the way it will be. Thus if the future were different from what it will be then what God is now 'seeing' would be different. Although the past is now 'gone' we still have the traces of it and, in an analogous way, although the future has not yet occurred, God already has hansels of it. The usual asymmetry of past and future is thus broken down in the special case of foreknowledge. Suppose, for example, that God's foreknowledge is due to backwards causation and that one Saturday the charming Maid Marilyn decides to consent to the wiles of Wily William. Then, in deciding to consent, Marilyn is deciding which bit of information God had

[9] See Michael Dummett and Anthony Flew, 'Can an Effect Precede Its Cause?', *Aristotelian Society Supplementary Volume*, 28 (1954), 27–62, and Michael Dummett, 'Bringing about the Past', *Philosophical Review*, 73 (1964), 338–59, and also Michael Dummett, 'Causal Loops', in *The Nature of Time*, ed. Raymond Flood and Michael Lockwood (Oxford: Basil Blackwell, 1986), 135–69. See also Michael Scriven, 'Randomness and the Causal Order', *Analysis*, 17 (1956), 5–9.

[10] See W. S. Anglin, 'Backwards Causation', *Analysis*, 41 (1981), 86–91, and Kenny, *The God of the Philosophers*, pp. 103–9.

about her on the previous Wednesday (assuming God is in Time). Whether she realises it or not, she is making the past event (of God's knowing she would consent) be what it was.

Before we involve ourselves in the nest of problems which the concept of backwards causation raises, let us examine the way in which it does solve the conflict between foreknowledge and free will. This conflict is well expressed in terms of an argument advanced by Aquinas:

the following is a conditional that is true: *If God knew that this is going to happen it will happen*—because knowledge is only of what is true. And its antecedent is absolutely necessary: first, because it is eternal, and also because it is expressed as having taken place. Therefore whatever is known by God is necessary.[11]

We can formalise this argument as follows. Let $p$ be some proposition describing a future contingent event. For example, let $p$ be 'Marilyn will consent on Saturday'. (We assume that her consent is an act of libertarian free will.) Let $Kp$ be the proposition 'God knew that $p$'. Then the argument runs:

$$\Box (Kp \Rightarrow p)$$
$$\Box Kp$$

$$\Box p$$

Needless to say, the inference pattern is valid and the first premiss is true. Thus if we wish to escape the conclusion that the contingent statement $p$ is 'necessary', we must challenge the second premiss.[12]

Why is it 'necessary' that God knew that Marilyn would consent in some sense of 'necessary' according to which we cannot say that an act of libertarian free will (e.g. her consent) is 'necessary'? Why is it that if something is 'eternal' or past then it is 'necessary' in some sense in which a contingent statement (e.g. a statement

---

[11] *Summa Theologiae*, 1a.14 art. 13.

[12] This argument is treated in a number of places. See Peter Geach, *Providence and Evil* (Cambridge: Cambridge University Press, 1977), 21; Anthony Kenny, 'Divine Foreknowledge and Human Freedom', in *Aquinas*, ed. Anthony Kenny (London: Macmillan, 1969), 255–70; Kenny, *The God of the Philosophers*, pp. 51–61; J. R. Lucas, *The Freedom of the Will*, pp. 71–7; A. N. Prior, *Past, Present and Future* (Oxford: Clarendon Press, 1967), 113–36; and Richad Sorabji, *Necessity, Cause and Blame* (London: Duckworth, 1980), 112–13.

describing an act of libertarian free will) is not? We shall examine eight senses of 'necessity' and show that the argument fails in every case to establish a contradiction between foreknowledge and free will. It is in connection with the last two interpretations of 'necessity' that we use the concept of backwards causation to undermine the argument.

## (1) Necessity = Pastness

If the necessity operator is interpreted 'it has already become the case that' then we can take the second premiss of the argument to be true. However, the conclusion of the argument is then simply 'it has already become the case that *p*'—e.g. 'it has already become the case that Marilyn will consent next Saturday'. But then some further argument is needed to show that this conclusion is incompatible with its being undetermined in some way that *p*. For although it seems obvious to some thinkers (e.g. J. R. Lucas) that there is an incompatibility, to other thinkers (e.g. Storrs McCall) the opposite seems obvious.[13] Indeed, one can understand

> It has already become the case that Marilyn will consent next Saturday

as meaning simply

> There was some time in the past, previous to the event of Marilyn's consenting on the particular Saturday

—and this latter statement has no implications with regard to the freedom of her consent. Moreover, one can argue that just as the fact that

> It will be the case next year that I won a game of pure chance on the day before my fifth birthday

does not imply that that past event was not contingent, so the fact that

---

[13] Storrs McCall, 'Objective Time Flow', *Philosophy of Science*, 43 (1976), 340–1.

It has already become the case that Marilyn will consent next Saturday

does not imply that that future event will not be contingent. Thus if necessity is taken to mean pastness, Aquinas's argument fails to establish any contradiction between the past foreknowledge and the future free decision.

## (2) Necessity = Timeless truth

If the necessity operator is interpreted 'it is timelessly true that' then similar remarks apply. For one can hold that

It is timelessly true that Marilyn consents on Saturday the—of June, AD 20—

without committing oneself to the view that her consent is not free in the libertarian sense. The fact that an act of will can be dated has no implications for its freedom—or, if it does, then this needs to be shown by some further argument.

## (3) Necessity = Broadly logical necessity

If the necessity operator is interpreted 'it is logically necessary that' or 'in all logically possible worlds it is true that' then the second premiss of the argument is false. For there are many possible worlds in which, say, Marilyn remains on the straight and narrow, with the upshot that God foreknows that she will remain on the straight and narrow, and God does not know (because it is not true) that she will consent to do evil. In general, as our argument itself shows, it is logically necessary that God know that $p$ only if it is logically necessary that $p$. However, $p$ is here a contingent proposition, one describing an undetermined event.

## (4) Necessity = Nomological necessity

If the necessity operator is interpreted 'it is nomologically necessary that' or 'it is determined by a previous state of the universe together with natural laws that' then the second premiss of Aquinas's argument is false. For on a libertarian view of free will, a proposition $p$ asserting the occurrence of a future free decision is not nomologically necessary and hence neither is God's knowledge of it. Given the same laws of nature and the same 'initial situation', it is possible both that Marilyn succumb and also that she not succumb. Hence it is nomologically possible that God knew she would succumb and also nomologically possible that he knew she would not succumb. Neither is nomologically determined.

## (5) Necessity = Deistic determinism

If the necessity operator is interpreted 'it is deistically determined that' or 'it is irrevocably commanded by God that' then, again, the second premiss is false. For it is deistically determined that God know that $p$ only if it is also deistically determined that $p$. But $p$ describes an act of libertarian free will and thus it cannot be determined in this way.

## (6) Necessity = Epistemic certainty

If the necessity operator is interpreted to mean 'we can have certain knowledge of the fact that' then there is no harm is accepting the truth of the second premiss ('we can have certain knowledge of the fact that God knows that $p$') and also the truth of the conclusion ('we can have certain knowledge of $p$'). For we need not suppose, unless we want to beg the question, that future events cannot be known as certainly as past events. I know for certain that my girlfriend will visit me tonight, and I know that she will do so freely. I am not, on the other hand, quite certain about some past events (e.g. who did I see in my dream last night?) and I have no way of finding out what occurred before the Big Bang.

Note that when we say that some future event is epistemically certain, we do not mean that we can know about it even if we are going to use that knowledge to ensure that the event will not occur. Rather we mean that it is a definite fact knowable by anyone who will not 'bilk' it. We discuss the problem of 'bilking' in the next section.

## (7)  Necessity = Causal independence

If the necessity operator is interpreted 'it is outside our present causal control that' then, thanks to the possibility of backwards causation, we need not take the second premiss to be true. For if backwards causality is a possibility then it is possible to affect the past. We cannot change the past, of course, but we can now make it have been what it was. For example, Marilyn can now make it the case that God previously knew she would consent to the wiles of Wily William.

## (8)  Necessity = Fixity or unalterability

If the necessity operator is interpreted 'it is now unalterable that' then we can understand this in two ways. First, we can take it to mean that we cannot now make a true statement about the past or future false. The second premiss would read 'we cannot now change the true fact that God knew that $p$'. Since we cannot change the past, this premiss is true. However, so is the conclusion of the argument—which is 'we cannot now change the fact that $p$'. For although we can change our *plans* for the future, we cannot change the future itself, as it truly will be, after all the altering of plans is done. If it is true that $p$ then we cannot somehow make it also true that not-$p$.[14]

Second, we can take the necessity operator to mean 'it is now unalterable that' in the sense that we cannot now make a true statement about the past or future true. If, however, we are allowing the possibility of backwards causation, the second premiss is false on this interpretation—just as it is false when necessity is interpreted to mean causal independence. For, given backwards causation, it is not true that we cannot now make it have been the case that God knew that $p$. In deciding whether or not to consent, Marilyn is now deciding which bit of knowledge God actually had about her on the previous Wednesday. She is now bringing it about that God previously had the particular knowledge he did.

[14] Kenny, 'Divine Foreknowledge and Human Freedom', p. 267 and *The God of the Philosophers*, p. 106.

It is worth noting that the so-called 'fixity' of past events—which is supposed to make them unamenable to backwards causation—is not a property intrinsic to those events. They do not harden with age. An astronomer who observes some event which occurred on a star ten light-years away does not observe any property of the event which could be called 'fixity'. Indeed, according to the special theory of relativity, the same event, with all the same intrinsic properties, can be a past event in one frame of reference and a future event in another frame of reference. 'Fixity' is not an intrinsic property of events but rather a relation between an event and an agent who has no control over the event. With respect to such an agent, the event is fixed. Usually the fact that an event has already occurred does mean that it lies outside the control of any (human) agent in the present and so we tend to think of past events as 'fixed'. However, this, precisely, is not the case where backwards causation is at work. We have now the power to decide what God previously knew about us.[15]

The argument we have been studying tries to establish a contradiction in the notion of foreknowledge of future contingent events. Were it successful, we should have to say that God (or his prophet) has complete foreknowledge only if there are no future acts of libertarian free will. The argument is an attempt to take some sort of necessity accruing to past events (e.g. God, or his prophet, knew that $p$) and shift it on to a future event (e.g. $p$) which does not, however, share, this necessity. What we have shown above, however, is that, given backwards causation, there is no sense in which past events are necessary but future contingent events are not. In so far as future free decisions are not necessary, the previous foreknowledge of them is not necessary either. Thus there is no reason to think there cannot be an omniscient being whose omniscience includes complete foreknowledge and another being who will, in the future, exercise libertarian free will. Indeed, if the notion of backwards causation is the only notion which can be used to answer the argument presented by Aquinas then it follows from the premiss that the divine being has foreknowledge of free decisions that there actually is backwards causation.

---

[15] Storrs McCall, 'Objective Time Flow', pp. 340–1 and pp. 351–3. Also Richard Sorabji, *Necessity, Cause and Blame*, pp. 114–15.

IV

We now consider six objections to the idea of backwards causality.


## (1) Definitional argument

An immediate objection to the notion of backwards causality is that the concept of causation implies, by definition, that it is the past event which causes the future one. However, that depends on one's definition of causality. As, for example, Ehring has shown in his article 'Causal Asymmetry', there is no need to build a temporal direction into the definition of cause.[16] One can say which of two causally linked events is the cause and which the effect without making reference to time. Thus it is really to beg the question if one insists that the very *meaning* of causation implies that the cause is not later than the effect.

(Roughly speaking, Ehring says the following. Suppose we have two events $e_1$ and $e_2$ of which we know that one is the cause of the other—they are 'causally connected'. Then $e_1$ is a cause of $e_2$ if and only if there is another event $e_3$ (the relevant *circumstances*) such that $e_3$ is causally connected to $e_2$ but not to $e_1$. For example, scratching a match is a cause, not an effect, of its lighting since the presence of oxygen is causally connected to the match lighting but not to its being scratched.)


## (2) Argument from entropy

Most laws of nature are time-reversible. For example, one can use Newton's laws to calculate not only where a planet will be in ten seconds but also where it was ten seconds ago. As far as these laws are concerned, there is nothing to preclude backwards causation. Moreover, not only backwards causation but even time travel into the past is compatible with the general theory of relativity. Gödel has proved that there are cosmological solutions of the gravitational equations and hence logically possible worlds such that

[16] Douglas Ehring, 'Causal Asymmetry', *Journal of Philosophy*, 79 (1982), 761–74.

by making a round trip on a rocket ship in a sufficiently wide curve, it is possible in these worlds to travel into any region of the past, present, and future, and back again, exactly as it is possible in other worlds to travel to distant parts of space.[17]

Indeed, Gödel allows that this universe itself might be one of those universes in which time travel into the past is possible.[18] Thus it is possible that, for example, God wait until the end of time and then travel back into the past and tell his younger self everything he has observed, including all the free decisions of persons with libertarian free will.

There is, however, one law of nature which does seem to imply that causality works in one temporal direction only. This is the Second Law of Thermodynamics, which is also called the Law of Entropy. It is according to this law that, as time goes on, energy becomes less 'available', arrangements of particles less ordered, heat distribution more uniform, and information less precise. For example, suppose we open a small vial of tear-gas in order to put an end to a noisy party in the Warden's Lodgings. The tear-gas is soon mixed with the air and 'the sprawlers' revelry is over'. Although it is possible, it is extremely improbable that the tear-gas remain in or return to the open vial: the process works in one direction only. Of course, increase in entropy is a consequence of many physical processes, including those which are initiated by agents exercising libertarian free will. Thus since (1) causes are characterised by a lower degree of entropy than their effects, and (2) entropy increases with time, it follows that there can be no backwards causation and no foreknowledge of physical processes which depends on backwards causation.

In answer to this argument, we first note that the Law of Entropy is statistical. Thus it is not only logically possible but quite in harmony with the Law of Entropy itself if a gas occasionally does not diffuse through a room or even if, having diffused through the room, it spontaneously returns to the vial whence it came. Thus even within the confines of the Law of Entropy there can operate some mechanism whereby God obtains from the future information which has the same degree of entropy as the events it reports.[19]

[17] Kurt Gödel, 'A Remark about the Relationship between Relativity and Idealistic Philosophy', in *Albert Einstein: Philosopher-Scientist*, ii, ed. Paul Arthur Schilpp (New York: Harper and Brothers, 1959), 560.

[18] Ibid., p. 561.

[19] Michael Scriven, 'Randomness and the Causal Order', pp. 5–9.

The second and more important point to be made, however, is that the Law of Entropy need not apply to information gathering which involves God. God is not a physical substance and thus there is no reason to think that the laws of thermodynamics apply to him. The Law of Entropy is intended to cover only purely physical processes. Thus it is irrelevant to the sort of backwards causation related to foreknowledge.

### (3) Kenny's argument

Another putative difficulty for backwards causation is presented by Kenny in *The God of the Philosophers*.[20] If there is backwards causation, how, asks Kenny, are we to distinguish between past and future? We cannot, of course, say that the past is the period of time in which causes occur. To this question Kenny himself gives an answer, namely, that the past is the period in which the vast *majority* of causes occur. If, thanks to backwards causation, there are a few cases of 'premembering' the future, or entropy decrease with time, these can be sufficiently rare that there is no serious question as to which period of time is the past and which the future. However, Kenny rejects this answer for the case which interests us:

if we imagine God as exercising reverse causation as frequently as would be necessary to provide an explanation of omniscient foreknowledge of free human actions then the distinction between past and future again becomes blurred.[21]

Although Kenny thinks that backwards causation might be a possibility, he does not think there could be as many instances of it as would be required to explain God's foreknowledge of free human actions (assuming, I suppose, that there are quite a few of these actions).

In answer to this argument, note that the case of God's foreknowledge need be the only case of backwards causation. Every other case of causation could be the regular forwards kind. Thus there is really no reason to worry that the distinction between past and future might become 'blurred'. Furthermore, God does not have to 'exercise reverse causation' at all frequently. Indeed, why

[20] Kenny, *The God of the Philosophers*, pp. 103–9.
[21] Ibid., p. 109.

would God have to exercise reverse causation more than once? Why could he not simply wait until the end of Time and then make it have been the case that he always knew what he will then know (at the end of Time) simply from having observed it? Of course, it may be that there is no 'end of Time'. In some possible worlds persons go on exercising libertarian free will forever. Yet even in those worlds it would suffice for God's having foreknowledge if once every $10^{1000}$ years he brought it about that he previously knew everything he had observed up until the end of that $10^{1000}$ year period. One case of backwards causation every $10^{1000}$ years would hardly suffice to blur the distinction between past and future.

Perhaps what bothers Kenny is not mere foreknowledge but God's interaction with human history to the extent that it is based on foreknowledge. Perhaps Kenny thinks that this interaction would involve enough backwards causation—or even time travel— to blur the distinction between past and future. For example, suppose that at three o'clock, when Difficult Douglas begins to write his final exam, God foresees that at six o'clock Douglas will pray that he wrote a good paper. (We are assuming, with Kenny, that God is in Time.) On the basis of this foreknowledge, God helps Douglas, at around four o'clock, to remember all those silly Greek verbs he never had much time for. However, at three o'clock God also foreknows the final shape of the paper, as it will be at six o'clock, thanks partly to God's help at four o'clock. One might think of God making two trips in a time machine. On the first trip he travels from three to six o'clock to hear the prayer and then returns to three o'clock when he decides that at four o'clock he will intervene to give Douglas a hand with those verbs. On the second trip he travels from three to six o'clock to find out what the finished paper is like and then returns, again, to three o'clock. Thus Kenny says, 'God should perhaps be pictured not as inhabiting a stationary tower, but as travelling from point to point of the field in a time machine.'[22] Moreover, if God does this often enough, there may be some blurring of past and future.

The answer to this, however, is that the imagery is wildly excessive. To say that God interacts with human history on the basis of his foreknowledge is not to say anything about time travel. There is no reason why at six o'clock—without any time travel—

[22] Ibid., p. 106.

God cannot simply make it have been the case that at three o'clock he had knowledge of everything he is aware of at six o'clock, including both the prayer and the completed paper. This would require only one exercise of reverse causation and no time travel. Hence, at three o'clock, God would know about the prayer—which he would then, at three o'clock, decide to answer at four o'clock—and also about the final shape of the paper, as it would be, thanks partly to God's intervention at four o'clock.

Yet how, it may be asked, can God decide whether or not to answer the prayer when he knows already, at three o'clock, that he will answer the prayer? How can it be that God decides—and decides freely—to help Douglas when God already knows he will decide to help Douglas? It seems that we have to have two Gods at three o'clock. There is a younger God who has time-travelled to six o'clock only once and learned only about the prayer. Now he is back at three o'clock deciding whether or not to answer the prayer. There is also at three o'clock an older version of the same God. This one has already made the decision to help Douglas at four o'clock and has made a second time-trip to six o'clock and learned about the final shape of the paper. With time travel it is, of course, possible to have several versions of oneself around at the same time, and some of these versions may well know the outcome of decisions which other, younger versions are still in the process of making.

Again the answer is that there are ways much less extravagant than time travel to explain how God might freely make a decision which he knows he will make. Indeed, one can point to examples in which even human beings foreknow which decisions they will freely make. Quinn gives an example in his article 'Divine Foreknowledge and Divine Freedom'.

Suppose Smith knows that, if White invites him to the evening concert tomorrow morning, he will then decide to go that evening, and that, if he decides to go, he will go. And now suppose that Smith learns that White will invite him to the concert tomorrow evening. Smith, knowing a bit of logic, infers that he will then decide to go to the concert and that he will go to the concert that evening. Thus, it would appear, Smith knows what he will decide to do before he makes his decision and he knows what he will do as a result of that decision before he makes it.[23]

[23] Philip L. Quinn, 'Divine Foreknowledge and Divine Freedom', *International Journal for Philosophy of Religion*, 9 (1978), 234. See also Jonathan Harrison, 'Dr Who and the Philosophers or Time-Travel for Beginners', *Aristotelian Society Supplementary Volume*, 45 (1971), 18.

The fact, then, that God foreknows which decision he will freely make does not imply that he is a time-travelling dromomaniac, still less that there is a blurring of past and future.

Again, the fact that God knows what he will decide does not necessarily mean that this knowledge is available to him in such a way that it can influence his decision. God *qua* decision-maker may have to put aside some of the information he has *qua* foreknower. In the case of human beings, at any rate, some sort of psychic compartmentalization is quite possible. For example, you may know perfectly well that you love Marilyn and have decided to marry her. However, in a dream, you are not aware of this knowledge and you are therefore deliberating about whether to say 'yes' to her proposal. The knowledge that you have already said 'yes' is not available to you in the dream. Similarly, it may be that somehow God's foreknowledge that he will help Douglas is 'not available' to God while he is deciding whether to help Douglas.

Finally, we should note in answer to Kenny that in some possible universes (e.g. ones in which time is cyclic) there may be no absolute past and future—just as in the actual universe there seems to be no absolute up and down. The fact that there was no absolute past or future but only different directions of time would not, moreover, imply there was no omniscient being with knowledge of all the free choices there would ever be.

## (4) Reverse fatalism argument

A fourth difficulty for foreknowledge based on backwards causality is the 'Reverse Fatalism Argument'. This argument has been refuted by Dummett.[24] Put in terms of foreknowledge, it might run as follows.

> At six o'clock it is either true or false that God knew at three o'clock what would happen at six o'clock.
>
> If it is false then no amount of backwards causality is going to change the given past fact.

---

[24] Dummett, 'Bringing about the Past', pp. 338–59. See also Roderick Chisholm and Richard Taylor, 'Making Things to Have Happened', *Analysis*, 20 (1960), 70–6.

If it is true, however, then there is no need for God to exercise reverse causality in order to make it true. Why should he bother bringing about what has already happened anyway?

Thus, either way, backwards causality is ineffectual.

This argument is paralleled by Douglas's argument:

At three o'clock it is either true or false that at six o'clock it will be true that I got down to my work at three o'clock.

If it is false then no amount of ordinary causality is going to change the given future fact.

If it is true, however, then there is no need for me to exercise ordinary causality in order to make it true. Why should I bother bringing about what will in the end happen anyway?

Thus, either way, ordinary causality is ineffectual.

In both cases, of course, the point is that the non-present event does not occur *regardless* of what happens in the present. Just as the future event is not given regardless of what happens now but only *because* of what happens now, so the past foreknowledge is not given regardless of whether God now exercises reverse causality (to make himself have known the future) but only *because* he now exercises reverse causality. The past was what it was and the future will be what it will be only because of what happens in the present.

It is queer to think of someone acting to bring about what has already happened—especially if he knows or is in a position to know that it has already happened—but this is only because we do not ordinarily have control over the past. If someone told us that it was only thanks to something he did in 1980 that he passed an exam in 1970, we would rightly regard him with suspicion. However, if God made a similar claim, we could not dismiss it out of hand. It is, at any rate, not logically impossible even in the case of a human being.

The following example may make it clearer how someone might bring about a past event, even one which he knows has happened. Professor Smith is reading a very exciting account of the conversion of King Clovis. He knows perfectly well that Clovis converted to Christianity but, while he is reading, he enters into the anxieties of Queen Clotilda and begins to pray along with her: 'Lord Jesus, please bring Clovis to the true faith!' Now it is at least logically possible that, at the time at which Clotilda was praying, God, foreknowing that Smith would add his prayers to hers, decided to give Clovis the additional grace in response to which Clovis actually did come to the true faith. It is also possible that God did this *only* because, as he foreknew, Smith would add his prayers to those of the Queen. Thus Clovis would not have been converted were it not for Smith's future prayers.

According to the Reverse Fatalism Argument, the fact that something has already happened means that it cannot now be caused to have happened. However, as Dummett has pointed out, this is analogous to saying that the fact that something will in the end happen means that it cannot now be caused to happen. Thus, in whichever way the latter implication fails, the former fails also.

## (5) Bilking Argument

If backwards causation is possible, then, says the Bilking Argument, one could either prevent a necessary cause from happening after its effect had already occurred, or make a sufficient cause happen after its effect had already not occurred. Hence one could have an effect without its cause, or a cause without its effect. For example, if God already believes you will sit down, you can belie his belief by not sitting down, thus 'bilking' the alleged connection between present cause (sitting) and past effect (foreknowledge of sitting).[25]

One reason this argument is not conclusive is that it may be that the future cause is less than, say, ten years in the future but more than ten light-years away from anything which might bring it about or prevent it. For example, suppose that, thanks to backwards causation, Isaiah foreknows that in some uninhabited solar system fifteen light-years away some event C will occur in five years. This suggests that the backwards causation somehow involves speeds greater than the speed of light (e.g. it might depend on 'tachyons'). Isaiah, however, cannot travel faster than the speed of light and hence there is no nomological possibility of his bilking the

---

[25] This difficulty has been raised by many philosophers. See Chisholm and Taylor, 'Making Things to Have Happened', pp. 76–7; Dummett and Flew, 'Can an Effect Precede Its Cause?', p. 57; Kenny, *The God of the Philosophers*, pp. 56–7; J. L. Mackie, *The Cement of the Universe* (Oxford: Clarendon Press, 1974), 178; N. Pike, *God and Timelessness* (New York: Schocken Books, 1970), 58.

backwards causal connection by preventing $C$ from occurring. He simply cannot get there in time.

What is really wrong with the Bilking Argument, however, is that it presupposes that the past was whatever it was regardless of what occurs in the present or future and this, precisely, is what is at issue. For the question we are discussing is whether it is at least logically possible that a past event be subject to a present event and therefore not fixed or given in any sense in which a future event is not.

Let $C$ be a cause (e.g. I sit) and $E$ its effect (e.g. God believes at some time that I sit). Suppose that $C$ is necessary and sufficient for $E$. In the case in which $C$ occurs before $E$, if $C$ does not happen then $E$ will not happen but if $C$ does happen then $E$ will happen. Whether or not $E$ occurs is fully explained by saying that $C$ did or did not occur. Similarly in the case in which $C$ occurs after $E$, if $C$ does not happen then $E$ did not happen but if $C$ does happen then $E$ did happen. Whether or not $E$ occurs is fully explained by saying that $C$ will or will not occur. Thus if you prevent a past-directed cause $C$ from happening, you bring it about that the past effect $E$ did not occur. The reason it did not occur is simply that its cause will not occur. If you make a past-directed cause $C$ happen you bring it about that the past effect $E$ did occur. The reason it did occur is simply that its cause will occur. Thus, whatever you do, you cannot leave $E$ without $C$ or bring about $C$ without $E$ having occurred. (We are assuming that $C$ is necessary and sufficient for $E$.) Suppose, for example, that $E$ has already occurred. Suppose also that it is entirely up to you whether to bring about $C$ or not. The fact that $E$ has occurred does not imply that you will *have* to bring about $C$ but it does imply that, as a matter of contingent fact, you will bring about $C$. This is strictly analogous to the case of future-directed causes. Suppose that $E$ will in the end occur and that it is entirely up to you whether to bring about $C$ or not. The fact that $E$ will occur does not imply that you *had* to bring about its previous cause $C$ but it does imply that, as a matter of contingent fact, you did bring about $C$. The only necessity involved is that of the connection between $C$ and $E$. There is no necessity in $C$ itself (unless we have a special case where it is necessary that $E$ occur). Thus, returning to the case in which $E$ precedes $C$, if it is entirely up to you whether to bring about $C$ or not and you intend to wait until $E$ occurs and then prevent $C$ from happening, then you will be waiting forever. Neither $E$ nor $C$ can occur in that case.

Note that we must not be misled by the fact that, in English, we use the sentence 'if $p$ happens then $q$ will have to happen' to mean 'necessarily, not-$p$ or $q$'. For example,

> If Karen goes to the party, she will have to take the bus

means *not*

> If Karen goes to the party, it will be a necessary truth that she takes the bus

but rather

> Necessarily, if Karen goes to the party, she will take the bus.

In logical symbolism, the difference is between $\Box \ (p \Rightarrow q)$ and $\Box \ (p \Rightarrow \Box \ q)$. Thus if I say

> If I sit down now then it will have to have been the case that God knew I would sit down

the 'have to' applies to the connection between the two events and not separately to the consequent. We cannot conclude from the 'have to' that any necessity accrues to the past event itself.

Note also that the above discussion moves on a metaphysical rather than an epistemological or psychological level. No doubt it would be interesting to enquire how a person's beliefs about $E$'s occurring relate to his causing $E$ to occur. Can someone work for a goal he believes he is destined to achieve? Can he work for a goal he feels sure he has already achieved? Can someone bring about a past event in the belief that that is what they are doing? However, we must not let these questions confuse our thinking about the purely metaphysical possibility of backwards causation. For these questions have to do with the psychology of agents and are only indirectly related to the question of the logical possibility of temporally backwards causality.

Let us take a concrete example. The Bilking Argument might be put in the following way.[26] Normally, a time bomb explodes a few microseconds after the timer goes off. If there is backwards causation, however, one can build a time bomb which explodes a few microseconds *before* the timer goes off. Let us define a *tachyon*

---

[26] See William Lane Craig, 'Tachyons, Time Travel, and Divine Omniscience', *Journal of Philosophy*, 85 (1988), 135–50.

*bomb* as a time bomb which explodes before its timer goes off and which, when it explodes, destroys its timer in the process. For example, suppose that the timer goes off at time $t$ and the explosion occurs at time $t - e$. In that case, the timer is destroyed at $t - e$ and no longer exists at time $t$. The effect (the explosion) is thus left without its cause (the timer going off). If backwards causality is possible then a tachyon bomb is possible. However, as we have just shown, a tachyon bomb is not possible.

To this I reply that, of course, it cannot be the case that first, at time $t - e$, there is an explosion, and then, second, at time $t$, the bomb that caused the explosion is sitting in the middle of the debris, its timer just going off. However, this does not mean that backwards causation is impossible: it just means that backwards causation with bilking is impossible. Logic itself provides an adequate explanation as to why the tachyon bomb will just not go off.

Note also that the Tachyon Bomb Argument presupposes that if there is backwards causation then some engineer can use it to link a future physical cause to a preceding physical effect. However, this may not be so. The argument itself may give us some reason to think that there is no backwards causation unless it works via some non-physical event (e.g. an event in the mind of God).

Finally, there is no danger that God himself will contribute to the Tachyon Bomb Project by agreeing to push a certain button when he gets the right signal from the future. God knows that backwards causality works only if it is not bilked. In particular, if it is necessary that God knows all future events then logic itself ensures that God will not succeed in any bilking projects which would undermine this knowledge—and God has enough sense not to try to do the logically impossible.

As another concrete example, let us consider these ideas in terms of a version of the Newcomb Paradox.[27] Placed before you is a title-deed to a beautiful mansion somewhere in the world, and a large sealed envelope. You have the choice of taking just the sealed envelope, or else taking both the sealed envelope and the title-deed. This latter option is called 'being greedy'. Thanks to

---

[27] Robert Nozick, 'Newcomb's Problem and Two Principles of Choice', in *Essays in Honor of Carl G. Hempel*, ed. Nicholas Rescher (Dordrecht-Holland: D. Reidel Publishing, 1969), 114–17 and 134–42. I treated this problem in 'Backwards Causation'. Dummett has since taken up a similar treatment of it in 'Causal Loops'.

backwards causation, God has already observed what you will do and has done the following:

> If you will choose just the sealed envelope, he has put in it a title-deed to a beautiful mansion somewhere in heaven;
>
> if you will choose both the sealed envelope and the title-deed to the beautiful mansion somewhere in the world, he has left the sealed envelope empty.

You know that God has done this and you want the heavenly mansion much more than the earthly mansion (although you do want the earthly mansion too). What should you do?

It might seem that you ought to be greedy since God has already either put the title-deed to the heavenly mansion in the sealed envelope, or he has not. If he has, then you get both mansions, and, if he has not, you get the earthly mansion along with a free envelope. Either way you are better off being greedy.

However, if we are taking the hypothesis of backwards causation seriously, then the past event of God's putting or not putting the title-deed in the envelope, although it cannot, of course, change, is not fixed and unalterable in any way in which present or future events are not fixed and unalterable: it was whatever it was depending on your future choice. You will decide what God did do. You cannot change the past by your choice but you do affect it. A past event which really depends on a present choice is no more or less fixed and unalterable than a future event which depends on a present choice. Thus you cannot take the contents of the envelope as given regardless of your present choice. They are what they are, yes, but what they are depends on your decision. You cannot take the contents of the envelope for granted.

A second argument for being greedy is that an 'intelligent, well-informed and perfect well-wisher' who knew whether the sealed envelope was empty or not would advise you to be greedy.[28] Since what an intelligent, well-informed, and perfect well-wisher would advise you to do would be in your best interests, you should indeed be greedy.

Against this argument, note that if the envelope is full, the well-wisher, being intelligent and well-informed, knows that it is full only because you will reject any advice to be greedy. Thus he does

[28] Don Locke, 'How to Make a Newcomb Choice', *Analysis*, 38 (1978), 19.

*not* advise you to be greedy because intelligent persons do not waste their breath giving advice they know will be rejected. Moreover, if the envelope is empty, the well-wisher knows that it is empty only because you will foolishly choose to be greedy. Thus he does *not* advise you to be greedy because well-wishers do not contribute to the folly of those whom they wish well.

The point is that a well-wisher's knowing the contents of the envelope presupposes God's having made his past decision and that, in turn, presupposes your going to make the particular decision you will in fact make. The well-wisher is thus confronted with a *fait accompli*. It is not temporally but causally 'too late' for him to advise you. He is at the end of a causal chain which begins with your future decision.

At this stage it may be objected that if you *yourself* know whether the envelope was empty or not, it would surely make sense to take both the envelope and the title-deed to the earthly mansion, and surely knowledge cannot affect the contents of an envelope. Thus even if you did not know whether the envelope was empty, you should still be greedy.

In answer to this objection, note that a pair of events, one the cause (your actual choice) and the other the effect (God's foreknowledge of your actual choice) is sometimes contingent for its occurrence on a certain condition being met. For example, the pair of events consisting of my scratching a match and the match lighting does not occur unless there is oxygen. In the same way, the pair of events consisting of my planning a surprise for you and my succeeding in carrying out this plan is contingent for its occurrence on your ignorance of the future. Again, Professor Smith growls at Marilyn if and only if he is angry at his wife, and this only because he does not realise he is being unfair to Marilyn. Thus there is no harm done to the possibility of backwards causation if it is admitted that, in certain cases, the pair of events, one the cause and the other its previous effect, does not occur if someone has too much information. It may well be that God's foreknowledge of your choice is contingent upon the fact that he has not told you about it. The envelope does have to be sealed. In this sense, knowledge *can* affect the contents of an envelope.[29]

We conclude, finally, that it is not possible to 'bilk' God's

[29] For a delightfully written treatment of this point, see Jerry L. Walls, 'A Fable of Foreknowledge and Freedom', *Philosophy*, 62 (1987), 67–75.

foreknowledge either in the case of the Newcomb choice or in any other case.

## (6) Circular causality

A sixth argument against the possibility of backwards causation beings by noting that causes are supposed to explain their effects. However, if there is backwards causation then there is circular causation and hence circular explanation. However, circular explanation does not explain anything. For example, consider the following case reported by C. G. Jung. A student

> went to Spain, and there, in one of the streets, he recognized the city of his dreams. He found the square and the cathedral, which exactly corresponded to the dream-image. He wanted to go straight to the cathedral, but then remembered that in the dream he had turned right, at the corner, into another street. He was curious to find out whether his dream would be corroborated further. Hardly had he turned the corner when he saw in reality the carriage with the two cream-coloured horses

—just as they had been in the dream.[30] Let us suppose that this is a true story and that the future event was actually the cause of the previous dream. Then (1) the student's turning right at the corner in reality was caused by his remembering that he did so in the dream (together with his curiosity, etc.); (2) his remembering that he did so in the dream was caused by his doing so in the dream; and (3) his doing so in the dream was caused by his doing so in reality (assuming, as we are, that the dream was brought about by backwards causation). The possibility of backwards causation thus gives rise to the possibility of circular causation or circular explanation. However, circular explanation is no explanation at all.

In answer to this objection, first note that when we ask for an explanation of some event *E*, we are usually satisfied if we are told about another event *C* which is its cause. We do not usually need to go on and ask for an explanation of *C* and, if we did, we would not necessarily learn anything more about *E*. For example, if I ask you why you think Marilyn cares for you and you tell me that Marilyn

<hr>

[30] C. G. Jung, 'Synchronicity: An Acausal Connecting Principle', in *The Collected Works of C. G. Jung*, vol. 8, trans. R. F. C. Hull, ed. Sir Herbert Read *et al.* (London: Routledge and Kegan Paul, 1969), 522.

sent flowers, I do not need to go on and ask why Marilyn sent flowers. If I do, then I may learn only that it was your birthday—which does not tell me more about why you think Marilyn cares for you. Occasionally, however, one is not satisfied merely to know which event gives rise to the event in question, but one needs to know also what gives rise to the cause event. A good student is not satisfied with Kepler's Laws until he has studied Newton, and he is not satisfied with Newton's Laws until he has derived them from Einstein's Laws. If one continues to enquire in this fashion, asking about each cause in turn, one can run into either an infinite chain of causes or else a circle. For many purposes, however, it is sufficient just to give one cause without giving the cause of the cause. For such purposes there is nothing vicious about circular causality. For example, I can explain why Marilyn came to the party by saying that William came to the party—and this explanation is acceptable even if it is also true that William came to the party because Marilyn came to the party. Or I can explain why Professor Smith is putting a lot of energy into his classes by saying that he has some very enthusiastic students—and this explanation is acceptable even if it is also true that the enthusiasm of the students can be explained by Smith's putting a lot of energy into his classes. It is like the case of a cardboard box whose four flaps are imbricated in such a way that each prevents the one to its right from opening. Flap 1 stays in place because flap 2 stays in place, flap 2 stays in place because flap 3 stays in place, flap 3 stays in place because flap 4 stays in place, and flap 4 stays in place because flap 1 stays in place. All four flaps stay in place because of the way they are attached to the box, together with the geometry of their imbrication. In the case of Jung's dream example, each link in the event-dream-memory-event circle is explained by the previous link. The whole circle must, of course, be explained by something else. Perhaps it was brought about by God.[31]

The six objections to backwards causation which we have considered have allowed us to clarify a position which still remains intact: it is logically possible that there be instances of temporally backwards causation and, in particular, it is logically possible that God (or his prophet) foreknow libertarian decisions. There is a way

---

[31] Anglin, 'Backwards Causation', pp. 89–91. David Wiggins gives another example of nonvicious circular causality in *Sameness and Substance* (Oxford: Basil Blackwell, 1980), 159. See also sect. V in Dummett's 'Causal Loops'.

for an omniscient being to know about the future, even when the future is not determined.

## V

To close this chapter, let us assume that God has complete foreknowledge due to backwards causation, and let us suggest a way in which it might interact with his care of the world. After all, one reason that Christians hold that God has foreknowledge is that, without it, he could not exercise a very sure providence over creation.

God obviously cannot use his foreknowledge to bilk foreknown evils but there are none the less ways in which he can use it to govern the world. For example, suppose that God foresees that in two hours Mr James Philanthropist will decide to go out and give $200,000 to the first person he meets. This is a decision made with libertarian free will. Of course, God also knows who will receive the money but, in responding to this decision, God sets aside his knowledge of the recipient. (We ourselves know many things of which we are not immediately conscious so, presumably, this is possible for God.) Now there is a needy Christian poet in the city. If God were to do nothing at all, the $200,000 would go to one of the already rich persons walking in the street near the home of James Philanthropist. However, God inspires the poet to go out to the rich man's house and stand right in front of his door. As planned, James Philanthropist makes his decision, leaves his home, finds the poet standing right in front of him, and gives him the $200,000. God has used his foreknowledge to make the world better.

Note that (1) God knew the poet would get the money and (2) the poet does not get the money because God knew he would but because God foreknew something else, something which did not entail that the poet get the money. God has used his foreknowledge of one part of the future to exercise his providence in another part of the future.

# 5

# God's Goodness

WE begin this chapter by arguing that the divine being is morally good. We also argue that it is necessary that he be morally good. We then try to answer some questions about God's moral goodness. If it is necessary that he be morally good, can he deserve praise for being morally good? How can he be morally good if he freely chooses to create a universe in which a person with free will may do evil? To reply to the latter question, we shall invoke the Principle of Double Effect.

## I

What do we mean when we say that someone is morally good? Roughly speaking, we mean that he avoids evil (that is, he fulfils the minimum requirements of moral duty) and, moreover, he sometimes performs works of supererogation (that is, he does good deeds beyond the call of duty). Obviously, this is not the only way to characterise moral goodness but, equally obviously, we cannot here enter into a long discussion of various ethical theories. In order to fix our ideas, it will be useful to have some definition of moral goodness, but our particular choice for the definition is, admittedly, arbitrary. Also arbitrary is our presupposition that morality is objective, that statements of the form 'it ought to be the case that $p$' are true or false.[1]

Our definition of moral goodness is as follows.

> A person $x$ is morally good
> if and only if
> $x$ never freely chooses to do what he believes is evil
> and
> $x$ sometimes freely chooses to perform what he believes is a
>     supererogatory act.

[1] For a defence of this view, the reader may wish to consult chapter 11 of Richard Swinburne, *The Coherence of Theism* (Oxford: Clarendon Press, 1977).

It is assumed that $x$'s choices are free in the libertarian sense and thus, on account of the second condition, no one is morally good unless he have libertarian free will. Note that $x$ can be morally good even if it is determined that he never freely choose to do what he believes is evil. Indeed, on many libertarian accounts, it is possible to fulfil the minimum requirements of moral duty, and to do this in a morally significant manner, even though it is determined that one should do this. For it is possible that it is determined that one should do this only because one has freely chosen (in the libertarian sense) to put oneself in a situation where it will be so determined. For example, although the saints in heaven cannot sin, they none the less deserve credit for not sinning since the reason they cannot sin is that they freely chose to let God's grace fix them in goodness.

There are a number of reasons to think that God is morally good in the above sense. One reason is that there are human beings who become morally good. Since the creator is not inferior to the creature, it follows from this that God is morally good. Another reason is that God gives us many blessings we are not entitled to. He has put us in a beautiful universe, he has answered many of our prayers, and he has died for us, to free us from evil. For a Christian, it is proof of God's own love for us, that Christ died for us while we were still sinners.[2]

What we wish to show in this section is not merely that God is morally good but that, necessarily, he is morally good. To this end we shall assume that he is necessarily divine, necessarily omnipotent, and necessarily omniscient. This assumption is defended in previous chapters. In Sections V and VI of Chapter 2, we showed that an individual is a divine being if and only if it is necessary that he be a divine being. In Section VI of Chapter 3, we argued that it is necessary that God be omnipotent. At the beginning of Chapter 4 we noted that being omnipotent entails being omniscient—and from this it follows that if it is necessary that God be omnipotent then it is necessary that he be omniscient.

The arguments we are going to give may be sketched as follows.

Necessarily, God is divine, omnipotent, and omniscient.

Being divine, omnipotent, and omniscient entails being morally good.

Thus, necessarily, God is morally good.

[2] Romans 5: 8. See also John 10: 11 and 1 John 3: 16.

We might express this in logical symbols as follows. Let 'g' denote whoever it is who is the divine being. (If 'Yahweh' is a proper name of the divine being, let $g$ = Yahweh.) Let

$Dx$ = $x$ is a divine being
$Px$ = $x$ is omnipotent
$Sx$ = $x$ is omniscient
$Mx$ = $x$ is morally good. .

Our argument has the following form:

$\square$ $(Dg \& Pg \& Sg)$
$\underline{\square \ \forall \ x \ (Dx \& Px \& Sx \Rightarrow Mx)}$
$\square \ Mg$

What we need to establish is the truth of the second premiss.

If God is not morally good then either he fails in his moral duty (he sins) or he fails to undertake any work of supererogation. Now no one fails in his moral duty unless he lacks a complete awareness of the nature or the consequences of his acts. Thus no one who is omniscient can fail in his moral duty. Furthermore, failing to do your duty involves preferring yourself to the highest good, which is the divine being. Since the divine being cannot prefer himself to the divine being, it follows that he cannot fail in his duty. Again, no one sins unless he acts against what he values, and no one acts against what he values unless he is partially ignorant or confused. Hence no omniscient being sins.[3] From these arguments we may conclude that being divine, omnipotent and omniscient entails being sinless. Since, necessarily, God is divine, omnipotent, and omniscient, it follows that he is impeccable. Thus if God is not morally good it has to be because he never undertakes any work of supererogation.

Is there a possible world in which God never chooses to perform a supererogatory act? On a Christian view, there are possible worlds in which God never creates anything and in which he therefore shows no superabundant love or care for his creation. However, even in these possible worlds he may none the less promote positive values, such as happiness, simply by instantiating those values more fully in himself. Since there is no largest infinite cardinal number, there is no upper limit to the amount of, say, happiness which God can enjoy. Furthermore, since God is

---

[3] See Swinburne, *The Coherence of Theism*, p. 202.

omniscient, he realises that a state of, say, greater happiness is more valuable, and he realises that his omnipotence will enable him to enter into such a state without any prohibitive costs. Realising this, God chooses one of these higher states and enters into it. Being omniscient and omnipotent entails choosing a state of, say, happiness for oneself or for one's creation which is not merely morally acceptable but supererogatorily good. We may conclude that it is necessary that God choose to do at least one work of supererogation. Hence, given what we established above, it is necessary that God be morally good.

Let us end this section by asking six questions.

(1) If it is necessary that God is morally good, does he deserve praise for being morally good?

There are many works of supererogation which God might choose to perform. If he picks one that is particularly generous, or involves a special sacrifice on his part, then he can be praised for having chosen that one rather than some less exalted one. For example, God can be praised for coming as a human being to save us from evil rather than leaving us with what we deserved.[4]

(2) Doesn't God's omnipotence include the power to do evil?

No, because, as we have just shown, this is not a power which it is logically possible for a divine being to possess.

(3) How can God have libertarian free will if it does not extend to evil?

As we argued in Chapter 1, libertarian free will implies the possibility of doing evil only in the case of limited beings such as ourselves. The fact that God can choose among many good things does not imply that he can choose evil. God can choose between giving a human being justice or mercy—but he cannot choose to do an injustice to a human being.

(4) How can God be morally good when he maintains a murderer's bullet in existence, rather than destroying it in mid-flight?

If in every case God negated the normal consequences of an evil decision (e.g. the murderer's decision to pull the trigger) then he would turn the world into a fairy tale, and undermine the dignity of

---

[4] See Edward R. Wierenga, *The Nature of God*, forthcoming, chapter 8.

free agents. If we are not to be treated as mere children, God must respect our decisions and the normal consequences of them. We must be able to stand by what we choose to do. In the next chapter we shall say more about why God allows evils which are not themselves wicked decisions (e.g. atomic bombs, cancerous cells in otherwise healthy children).

(5) If God is necessarily morally good, can he be tempted to sin?

Consider the following two examples. First, Brown goes to Smith and says, 'why don't you murder the Chairman of the Philosophy Department? You're too clever to be caught. You'll get his job and his beautiful young wife as well.' Smith is shocked by this idea and makes a point of mentioning it to the dean.

Second, Brown makes the same proposal but, in this example, Smith is rather inclined to act on it. It is not without some glee that he fantasises about it. Fortunately, Smith had a strict Anglican upbringing and it is actually psychologically impossible that he murder anyone. Smith makes an effort to think about other things, and gradually ceases to consider Brown's proposal.

In the first case I think one might argue about whether Brown tempted Smith to commit murder, or merely tried to tempt Smith to commit murder. In the second case, however, I think it is clear that Brown did tempt Smith, and that Smith was tempted. According to the seventh edition of *The Concise Oxford Dictionary*, to 'tempt' is to entice or incite, and Smith was certainly enticed or incited to murder the Chairman. There is nothing illogical in saying that Smith was tempted to commit murder although, of course, he could not possibly have done such a thing.

If it is necessarily true that God is never even inclined to do what he believes is wrong then it may follow that he cannot really be tempted. However, the mere fact that he is necessarily morally good (in our sense) does not imply that he cannot be tempted. If the Incarnation is possible then it is possible that God experience desires just as we do, and it is possible that he feel attracted by, say, an adulteress. An adulteress would probably not waste her time with him if she thought he was impeccable, but if she thought he was just another man, she might well display her charms and he might well be enticed or incited to fall in with her plans.

Even if a person resolves to think about only what is good, he may still experience brief day-dreams or attractions which entice him to do evil. Whether he wills it or not, his psyche may throw up ideas or desires which he ought to reject if he wishes to avoid sin. The mere fact of having such ideas or desires is not, however, sinful. On the contrary, it is just the normal functioning of the human psyche as it considers different possibilities. Sin is committed only if the person chooses to dwell on these ideas or desires, or if he chooses to implement them.

We conclude that there is nothing in the logic of temptation which suggests that being tempted is being sinful. It is quite possible that an impeccable person be tempted.

(6)   Would a morally good God create a universe which, thanks to persons with free will, might contain moral evil?

In the last section of this chapter we argue that God was under no moral obligation to refrain from creating a universe containing persons with libertarian free will extending to evil.


# II


Pike claims that God is not morally good if he creates a universe containing the mere possibility of evil.[5] In Section IV of this chapter I am going to reply to Pike using the Principle of Double Effect. In this section, however, I want to mention the 'standard' reply, namely, the appeal to some sort of utilitarianism. For one common response made by theists to worries about the compatibility of evil and a morally good God is that the evil is outweighed by good. God's creating a universe that might contain evil is justified if it contains more good than evil and, moreover, this good is not possible without at least the risk of some evil.

I do not want to challenge this sort of reply. However, the reason I prefer the reply I give in Section IV is that the utilitarian theist is faced with some tricky questions I hope to avoid.

(1)   What about the fact that, since there is no largest cardinal number—no maximum—God cannot really maximise utility?
(2)   Is there a danger that God will create persons in order to

---

[5] Nelson Pike, 'Plantinga on Free Will and Evil', *Religious Studies*, 15 (1979), 456.

augment utility rather than creating utility for the benefit of persons?

(3) Can God be said to do supererogatory deeds?

It would be worthwhile to investigate the extent to which a theist can consistently make use of various forms of utilitarianism. Needless to say, such an investigation would occupy a book of its own. In this book, we shall present a nonutilitarian answer to Pike.


## III


If we do not take a utilitarian perspective, how shall we show that it is morally permissible for God to create someone with libertarian free will in the knowledge that that person might (or would) do evil? One way is to use the Principle of Double Effect. For the Principle of Double Effect lays down certain conditions under which, as many people agree, it is morally permissible to do something even though it may well result in evil. In what follows we first state the Principle and give some examples of its application, showing how, in many cases, it matches our moral intuitions. We next defend it against some alleged counterexamples. Finally, we use the Principle of Double Effect to prove that it is morally permissible, in certain cases, for God to create a person with libertarian free will who will choose to do evil.

The Principle of Double Effect presupposes a theory of action. According to this theory, we can think about a particular person (an 'agent') performing a particular 'act' $A$ as a 'means' to bring about an intended goal or 'end'. Moreover, we can distinguish this end from the various other consequences of the act. These are categorized as 'side' or 'subsequent' consequences of the act. More precisely,

> $S$ is a side consequence (or effect) of bringing about an end $E$
>    using means $A$
> if and only if
> (1) $S$ is a consequence of $A$ and
> (2) $E$ is not a consequence of $S$ and
> (3) $S$ is not a consequence of $E$.

Moreover,

> *S* is a subsequent consequence (or effect) of bringing about an
>      end *E* using means *A*
> if and only if
> (1)  *E* is not a consequence of *S* and
> (2)  *S* is a consequence of *E*.

Being exhausted might be a side effect of becoming rich by working
hard, and being arrogant might be a subsequent effect of becoming
rich by means of working hard.[6] Note that the person's 'working
hard' should not be described as his 'making himself exhausted'—
as if he intended to become tired as well as rich.

Also important in describing or understanding his act are the
agent's motives and beliefs. Here we shall simplify the theory of
action by assuming that the motives are always good and the beliefs
are always correct. We also assume that the agent is acting freely.
At least in the case of God, all these assumptions are appropriate.

Unfortunately, this is not the place to elaborate on or defend the
theory of action we have just sketched. In particular, we cannot
enter into the debate over whether the side effects should be
considered as somehow part of the act. We shall merely assume
that there are cases in which the side effects are distinct from the
act.

The Principle of Double Effect applies in cases where the means
*A* and the end *E* are both good (or, at least, neutral) but where the
side or subsequent consequences *S* are bad. What it says, roughly
speaking, is that the act is morally permissible if *E* cannot be
brought about without bringing about *S*, and if the goodness of *E*
outweighs the badness of *S*.

For example, suppose Jennifer likes Sam and Bob equally, and
either of them would be thrilled to be asked out by her. However, if
Jennifer asks Sam out, his ex-girlfriend, Alice, will feel a pang of
jealousy, whereas if Jennifer asks Bob out, nothing bad will happen.
Assuming that Jennifer does not wish any harm on Alice, we can
describe a pang of jealousy as a side effect of Jennifer's asking Sam
out (in order to have a good time with Sam). If Jennifer is a good
classical utilitarian, she will feel obligated to invite Bob rather than
Sam but, on the Principle of Double Effect, it is morally permissible

---

[6] Kenny, *Will, Freedom and Power*, pp. 57–8.

for her to ask Sam out if the goodness of their evening together outweighs the badness of Alice's pang of jealousy. Here

$A$ = asking Sam out
$E$ = enjoying an evening with Sam
$S$ = Alice's feeling jealous.

Our precise version of the Principle of Double Effect is adapted from one given by Mangan in his article 'An Historical Analysis of the Principle of Double Effect'.[7]

> The Principle of Double Effect is the principle that it is morally permissible for a person $P$ to bring about a good end $E$ using means $A$ and thereby producing bad side or subsequent effects $S$
> *if*
> (1) $A$ is morally permissible and
> (2) it is not in any practical sense possible for $P$ to achieve $E$ without either using a morally impermissible means, or else producing side or subsequent effects at least as bad as $S$ and
> (3) the good of $E$ outweighs the bad of $S$ and
> (4) $P$ does not want $S$, producing it only because of (2) and (3).

We presuppose that $P$ is fully aware of what he is doing and, in particular, that he foresees the production of the side or subsequent effects $S$.

As Connell emphasises in his article in the *New Catholic Encyclopedia*, the Principle of Double Effect has wide applicability:

the aviator who tests planes in order to improve aeronautic equipment, the doctor who treats patients affected with contagious diseases, the policeman who attempts to capture an armed criminal—all these are lawfully using the principle of the double effect, the bad effect being the hazards they are incurring to their own life or health, the good effect being the benefits they are conferring on society.[8]

Dunstan notes that the Principle of Double Effect justifies the action of a ship's captain who, in order to save many lives, orders

[7] Joseph T. Mangan, 'An Historical Analysis of the Principle of Double Effect', *Theological Studies*, 10 (1949), 43.

[8] F. J. Connell, 'Double Effect, Principle of', in *New Catholic Encyclopedia*, iv, ed. William J. McDonald (New York: McGraw-Hill, 1967), 1021.

the closing of some watertight doors in the knowledge that a few members of the crew will be trapped behind them and drown.

The action is necessary to save the ship and as many as possible of her company. If some of the crew are trapped behind the closed doors, the captain is not culpable in law or morals for their death—though he would have delayed so long as possible to enable them to escape. Their death would be a secondary and unintended effect of a necessary act.[9]

As another example, it follows from the Principle of Double Effect that

it is all right to raise the level of education in our country, though statistics allow us to predict that a rise in the suicide rate will follow.[10]

The unintended subsequent effect of some additional suicides is outweighed by the intended end of raising the level of education.

We should also give a couple of examples where the Principle of Double Effect does *not* justify an action. Suppose that the only way I can save Marilyn's life is by means of smashing Jennifer's skull. (I leave it to the reader to invent a situation in which this would be true. Perhaps the case of craniotomy would do.[11]) Here the action itself is wrong—it is a case of grievous assault—and hence condition (1) of the Principle is not met. As another example, suppose I have sexual intercourse with Marilyn (who is now married to Professor Smith). The end is sexual adventure and romantic emotions. The side effect is the undermining of Marilyn's marriage. The Principle of Double Effect does not justify our liaison because the means to the end may properly be described as 'committing adultery' and this is in itself morally bad. Furthermore, the joy and excitement of sex are not proportionate to the good of marriage. Conditions (1) and (3) of the Principle are not met.

Are there any cases in which the Principle of Double Effect would lead one astray? Foot thinks there are. Suppose that

---

[9] G. R. Dunstan, 'Double Effect', in *Dictionary of Medical Ethics*, ed. A. S. Duncan *et al.* (London: Darton, Longman & Todd, 1981), 145. A similar example is given in Michael J. Costa's excellent article, 'The Trolley Problem Revisited', *Southern Journal of Philosophy*, 24 (1986), 437–49.

[10] Philippa Foot, *Virtues and Vices and Other Essays in Moral Philosophy* (Oxford: Basil Blackwell, 1978), 19.

[11] For discussions of craniotomy, see James G. Hanink, 'Some Light on Double Effect', *Analysis*, 35 (1975), 147–51, and Robert Hoffman, 'Intention, Double Effect and Single Result', *Philosophy and Phenomenological Research*, 44 (1984), 389–94.

there are five patients in a hospital whose lives could be saved by the manufacture of a certain gas, but that this inevitably releases lethal fumes into the room of another patient whom for some reason we are unable to move. His death, being of no use to us, is clearly a side effect, and not directly intended.[12]

Foot thinks first that it would be wrong to go ahead and manufacture the gas, and second that, according to the Principle of Double Effect, it would not be wrong to do this. On the basis of this example, she rejects the Principle of Double Effect.

The first difficulty with Foot's counterexample is that it is hard to take seriously. How can it be possible that the manufacture of the gas *inevitably* releases lethal fumes into the room of another patient? For *what* reason are we unable to move him? Why can we not at least give him a gas mask?

The second difficulty with Foot's counterexample is that it is not obvious that it is wrong for the doctors to manufacture the gas, assuming it is the only way they can save the five patients. In Dunstan's example, the captain is *not* wrong to shut the watertight doors in order to save five persons even if, in so doing, he causes one person to drown. Nor is the captain wrong if the one person who thus drowns is an excellent swimmer who would have survived had the captain not closed the watertight doors. Foot's counterexample is not decisive.

A second possible counterexample to the Principle of Double Effect is this.[13] A doctor has a choice between (1) removing the diseased uterus of a pregnant woman in order to save her life, and (2) killing the foetus of the same pregnant woman in order to save both her life and her uterus. In both cases the foetus dies. In the first case, however, its death might be seen as a side effect of the removal of the uterus whereas in the second case its death is the means of saving both the woman and her uterus. Let

$A$  = removing the uterus
$A'$ = killing the foetus
$E$  = saving the mother
$S$  = destroying the uterus and depriving the foetus of its life support system

---

[12] Foot, *Virtues and Vices and Other Essays in Moral Philosophy*, p. 29.
[13] This example is taken from Paul J. Micallef, 'A Critique of Bernard Haring's Application of the Double Effect Principle', *Laval Theologique et Philosophique*, 38 (1982), 259–63.

If *A* is morally permissible but *A'* is not then conditions (1) and (2) of the Principle of Double Effect are met. We may also suppose that (3) and (4) are met. Hence on the Principle of Double Effect it is morally permissible for the doctor to remove the uterus. Common sense, however, would lead one to say that the doctor is morally obligated to take the second alternative, saving not only the woman's life but her uterus as well.

In defence of the Principle of Double Effect, I reply that common sense does not have much to say about uncommon moral dilemmas. If depriving someone of the means necessary to their living is as bad as killing them then the two alternatives are significantly different only as far as the uterus is concerned and the second alternative is to be preferred. This does not mean, however, that the first alternative is not also morally permissible. One wants to save the uterus, of course, but, on the other hand, one does not want to be the direct cause of the death of a foetus. This is a hard choice and one would have to be very confident of one's moral intuitions to declare one of the alternatives morally wrong.

A third possible counterexample to the Principle of Double Effect is the following.

A sixty-year-old male, with no living relatives or family, underwent a routine physical examination in preparation for a brief but much anticipated trip to Australia. During the examination, the physician discovered that the man suffered from a terminal case of cancer.[14]

The 60-year-old male asked if there was anything wrong with him.

The physician believed that the patient would not suffer from the cancer at all while in Australia and answered the question by saying, 'The examination shows that you have never been in better physical condition.' The physician had good evidence to indicate that no treatment would be effective against the cancer.[15]

Was the doctor's deception morally permissible? According to the Principle of Double Effect, it seems that it was. For (1) there is nothing intrinsically wrong about saying what one believes is false (e.g. one is allowed to do this on April Fool's Day); (2) the doctor wanted only the good effect that the man enjoy his holiday and not the bad side effect that the man be ignorant of his true condition;

[14] Tom L. Beauchamp and James F. Childress, *Principles of Biomedical Ethics* (Oxford: Oxford University Press, 1979), 259–60.
[15] Ibid.

and (3) the happy holiday was of greater value than the knowledge of the cancer. None the less, it may seem to some people that what the doctor did was wrong. It may seem that he owed it to his patient to tell him the truth. If that is so, the Principle of Double Effect leads one astray.

There are four ways to answer this objection to the Principle of Double Effect. First, one can maintain that the doctor did not, in fact, do anything wrong. Second, one can say that, although there is nothing intrinsically wrong about, say, a practical joker proclaiming something he believes is false, there is something intrinsically wrong about a doctor telling his patient something about his patient's health which he believes is false. It may be that the doctor's statement should be classified as a case of condescending paternalism, or as a breach of contract. If so, the first condition of the Principle of Double Effect is not met. Third, one can say that the man's ignorance of his true condition was not a side effect but a part of the means to his enjoying his holiday. If that is so, the Principle of Double Effect does not apply. Fourth, one can dispute the claim that the happy holiday was of greater value than the knowledge of the cancer. When a person is going to die, it is of the utmost importance that they know this, in order that they can prepare themselves spiritually.

We conclude that there is no reason to think that the Principle of Double Effect will lead one astray. On the contrary, it is a widely applicable ethical principle which often yields conclusions compatible with our moral intuitions. It respects (but does not insist on) the notion that the ends do not justify the means, and it throws light on many awkward cases. It is thus not unreasonable to adopt this Principle in trying to understand God's goodness in creating persons whom he knew would do evil.

## IV

In the case of most interest to us, the person *P* is God. The good end *E* is a universe containing finite persons who reason, create, take ultimate responsibility, choose their values, co-operate freely with God, love unconditionally, and keep promises—as we defined all these things in the first chapter. As we showed, such persons must have libertarian free will which extends to evil (i.e. may possibly be used at some time to do evil). This is a necessary condition of their being able to reason create, etc. The means A is creating a universe containing finite persons with libertarian free will (extending to evil), and helping (not forcing) them to use that free will to do only what is good. The bad side or subsequent effect S is the risk or reality of that free will being used to some extent to do evil. The universe may well contain moral evil, along with any suffering resulting from it.

Some thinkers disagree with this analysis. For example, Hick holds that moral evil is part of God's original plan.[16] It is not a side or subsequent effect but an intended means to the end. On all accounts, God brings good out of moral evil but, on Hick's account, God intends to have moral evil and thereby bring about good. Moral evil is part of the means God chooses to bring about E. (Roughly speaking, the idea is that God wants us to sin because if we sin we are in the best possible position to learn about justice, forgiveness, and the like, and our learning about these things would improve us.)

Against Hick's view, we can make the following seven points: (1) when a person does moral evil he sets himself against God and his conscience and is therefore not making any progress towards any 'greater good' in which he will live in harmony with God and his conscience; (2) although, without moral evil, there would be less long-suffering and forgiveness, there would also be more trust, prudence, peace, chastity, learning, generosity, and love; (3) Adam would have reached his full potential much sooner if, like the angel Gabriel, he had resisted the temptation to sin; (4) it is logically impossible for an essentially good God to intend that someone be morally evil; (5) it is logically impossible for an essentially truthful God to intend moral evil at the same time as he condemns it through his prophets; (6) it is logically impossible that God plan that a person be morally evil because it is logically impossible to plan an exercise of libertarian free will; and (7) God is not a heartless father who, when he sees his little daughter playing near the fire, hopes she will burn herself, because 'that would teach her a lesson'. I suggest, then, that we dismiss Hick's view that moral evil was part of God's original plan.

[16] John Hick, *Evil and the God of Love* (Glasgow: William Collins Sons, 1979), 316–27.

The first of the four conditions in the Principle of Double Effect is

(1)  *A* is morally permissible.

If God had middle knowledge then he might be able to choose a group of possible persons with libertarian free will extending to evil who, if they were created, would not do evil, and then create them. On the other hand, as Plantinga has pointed out, it may be that, no matter which group of persons with libertarian free will extending to evil God created, some of them would do evil.[17] In any case, as we argued in Chapter 4, God does not have middle knowledge. Furthermore, his knowledge of future events, being due to backwards causation, is logically subsequent to those events. Thus, in deciding to create a group of persons with libertarian free will extending to evil, God is, in effect, ignorant of the results of his decision. Prior to his deciding to create Mary, he does not know whether Mary would in fact do evil. If he chooses to create Mary, God is, in a sense, taking a risk.

One might take the view that it is always wrong to take any risk involving the possibility of moral evil. This would be an extreme view. It would, for example, imply that one ought not to have children if there is any chance that they will do something morally wrong. A more moderate view would be that it is sometimes morally permissible to risk the possibility of moral evil if (1) the risk is small, and (2) there is a way of repairing most of the damage if the worst comes to pass. In creating persons with libertarian free will extending to evil, God is not running a substantial risk that they will do evil. For he helps them in many ways to avoid evil. Indeed, ours is perhaps the only planet where persons have chosen to rebel against God. Furthermore, God has ways of repairing most of the damage of moral evil. He can call people to repentance, he can forgive them, and he can give them more blessings than they had before they sinned. Thus there is nothing intrinsically wrong if God creates persons with libertarian free will extending to evil. *A* is not in itself morally bad.

The second condition is

(2)  it is not in any practical sense possible for *P* to achieve *E* without either using a morally impermissible means, or else producing side or subsequent effects at least as bad as *S*.

---

[17] Alvin Plantinga, *The Nature of Necessity* (Oxford: Clarendon Press, 1974), ch. IX.

We argued in Chapter 1 that no finite person can reason, create, etc., unless he has libertarian free will which he might actually use to choose evil. We argued in Chapter 4 that God lacks the 'middle knowledge' that would allow him to create only those persons (if any) who would never misuse their libertarian free will. Thus there is no way for God to achieve $E$ except by running a risk of some moral evil. He has to 'take a chance' and, unfortunately, some persons do choose to do evil, and they influence other persons to do evil as well. God puts Adam in a very pleasant environment, one in which it is unlikely that Adam sin, but Adam chooses to do evil none the less. He influences his progeny to do evil, and they make the world a rather unpleasant place to live in, a place where it is often more likely than not that one will sin. None the less, if God did not run the risk of this happening, there would be no finite persons having the power to reason and to create, etc.

One might ask why God did not plan to annihilate any person who chose evil as soon as they had done so. Moral evil is habit forming. Morally evil persons entice others to do moral evil. Hence God might have lessened the magnitude of the possible disaster if he had designed persons with libertarian free will in such a way that they would self-destruct on sinning. God did not need to produce the side effect $S$ which is the actual amount of moral evil in the universe. He could have achieved $E$ with a less evil side effect $S'$, namely, the risk of moral evil but moral evil curbed by the instant annihilation of the evil-doer.

To this I answer that God's end is not to produce reason, creativity, unconditional love, and the like in the abstract but to create particular persons who reason, create, love unconditionally, and so on. Nor is it enough if some person or other does these things: God's aim is that each and every person he has created does these things. To put it precisely, God's aim $E$ is to create a universe containing finite persons such that (1) each is immortal (death notwithstanding); (2) each has the power to reason, to create, to take ultimate responsibility, to choose his own values, to co-operate freely, to love, to love unconditionally, and to make promises; and (3) if any of these person chooses to do evil, he is given every possible opportunity to repent. I conclude that, for the end $E$ which God hopes to achieve, condition (2) of the Principle of Double Effect is met.

The third condition is

(3) the good of $E$ outweighs the bad of $S$.

This condition is not satisfied unless it is reasonable for God to suppose that this universe containing persons who can reason, create, etc., will contain more good than evil. We may assume that God knows how to weigh out even infinite quantities of good and evil in such a way as to arrive at some comparable mathematical expectation for each of the different courses of action open to him. Moreover, it seems that God knows that, given his omnipotence, he can bring it about that there is more good than evil, even if many persons with libertarian free will choose to do evil. For God can bring most of them to repentance, or he can create new persons who will be likely not to do evil. Thus it is reasonable to suppose that the third condition is met.

The fourth condition is

(4) $P$ does not want $S$, producing it only because of (2) and (3).

God's original plan is not that good come out of evil but that greater good come out of good. He does not want even the risk of moral evil. He accepts this risk only because it is necessary to his achieving the good end $E$. As the prophets make very clear, God in no way wants people to sin.

Since all four conditions of the Principle of Double Effect are satisfied, it follows that it is morally permissible for God to create a universe containing a person with libertarian free will even though God knows that that person may (or will) do evil.

# 6

# The Problem of Evil

In this chapter we show that the existence of evil is compatible with the existence of God. We do this by means of a 'free will defence'. In Section I we recall some things said about evil by Plato, Augustine and Anselm. In Section II we consider the view that evil is privation. In the third section we give our Free Will Defence. The fourth section addresses the question of why God allows not only moral evil but also its consequences. In Section V we discuss the problem of 'natural evil'. We treat the question of hell in the chapter on immortality.

## I

We are very prone to blame not ourselves but others for evils in the world. If we think that there is a God we are tempted to put the blame on him. However, as the prophets reminded the ancient Israelites, it is not God's fault that things are bad but our own.[1] If only we all stopped doing evil we would have little cause to complain. Not only would we cease to suffer at the hands of other people but, according to Jeremiah at any rate, we would even cease to suffer various natural disasters. In the Old Testament, calamities such as famine and earthquake were understood to be a result of sin. Contemporary ecologists might be interested in Jeremiah's lament:

How long will the land be in mourning, and the grass wither all over the countryside? The animals and birds are dying as a result of the wickedness of the inhabitants.[2]

In response to what the prophets said, some people wondered why it was that God did not simply stop man sinning. If he was

---

[1] Proverbs 19: 3. See also Job 18: 8 and 19: 6.
[2] Jeremiah 12: 4. See also Jeremiah 5: 24–5 and Amos 8: 4–8.

Lord of all creation, how could anyone sin unless God himself were ultimately responsible? Ben Sira had an answer to this question.

Do not say, 'The Lord was responsible for my sinning,'
  for he does not do what he hates.
Do not say, 'It was he who led me astray,'
  for he has no use for a sinner.
The Lord hates all that is foul,
  and no one who fears him will love it either.
He himself made human beings in the beginning,
  and then left them free to make their own decisions.
If you choose, you will keep the commandments
  and so be faithful to his will.
He has set fire and water before you;
  put out your hand to whichever you prefer.
A human being has life and death before him;
  whichever he prefers will be given him.[3]

Ben Sira's answer is one of the earliest attempts to shift the blame for moral evil from God to man by means of an appeal to man's free will. Such an attempt is a Free Will Defence.

Free will plays a role in the Tale of Er, as it is reported in Book X of Plato's *Republic*. According to this myth, the souls who are about to go down to earth to be born are gathered together to choose what their future lives will be. Since at most one person can live one particular life, it is decided by lot who shall have first choice, who second, and so on. Er tells us that

the drawer of the first lot at once sprang to seize the greatest tyranny, and that in his folly and greed he chose it without sufficient examination, and failed to observe that it involved the fate of eating his own children, and other horrors, and that when he inspected it at leisure he beat his breast and bewailed his choice, not abiding by the forewarning of the prophet. For he did not blame himself for his woes, but fortune and the gods and anything except himself.[4]

The soul of Odysseus, however, draws the last lot of all

and, from memory of its former toils having flung away ambition, went about for a long time in quest of the life of an ordinary citizen who minded his own business, and with difficulty found it lying in some corner disregarded by the others, and upon seeing it said that it would have done the same had it drawn the first lot, and chose it gladly.[5]

---

[3] Ecclesiasticus 15: 11–17.          [4] *Republic* 619b–c.
[5] Ibid. 620c–d.

After the souls choose their lives in the order of their lots, they pass 'beneath the throne of Necessity'.[6] Their choice having been made, it is irreversible. Yet because it is they who choose their fate and not God who imposed it upon them, 'the blame is his who chooses. God is blameless.'[7] Let the tyrant complain to the gods about his bitter fate: still it is a fate of the tyrant's own choosing.

Plato's myth touches on a number of important issues. For example, choice is distinguished from both chance and necessity.[8] It is crucial to the Free Will Defence that there be choices which are neither 'mere random events' nor 'necessary outworkings of past states'. For if our choices are 'mere random events', no less than if they are 'necessary outworkings of past states', they cannot be the locus of responsibility for evil which they must be if the Free Will Defence is correct.

A second point implicit in the myth is that 'an ought need not imply a can'. If someone does evil of necessity, it does not follow that he is blameless since it may be his fault that it is necessary that he do evil. Suppose Smith knows that when he has drunk too much he cannot resist the urge to go for a drive. He then drinks too much vodka, goes for a drive, and kills someone in the resulting road accident. It will not do if he claims to be innocent on the grounds that when he has drunk too much he cannot resist the urge to go for a drive.

A third point suggested by the myth is that if present evils can be explained in terms of past decisions, the past decisions themselves need explaining. Why does the drawer of the first lot choose a life in which he eats his children? It would involve us in a vicious regress to suppose that at some previous time he had chosen a meta-life in which he would choose a life in which he would eat his children. Thus Plato needs to give some other reasons: 'in his folly and greed he chose it without sufficient examination.'[9] However, why was this soul greedy and foolish? To shift the responsibility for evils to some event in the past does not in itself help to explain them. Nor does it throw any light on the question of God's responsibility for them. Perhaps the unhappy tyrant is right to blame 'fortune and the gods and anything except himself' for, although it is he who chooses the unhappy life, it may be they who are responsible for the folly and greed without which he would have made a better choice.

  ⁶ Ibid. 621a.       ⁷ Ibid. 617e.
  ⁸ Ibid. 617e.       ⁹ Ibid. 619b–d.

In his later life at least, Augustine held a view similar to that presented in the Tale of Er.[10] Long ago, before we were born, we were in the Garden of Eden 'in Adam'. There, 'in Adam', we had the power to refrain from sinning and also the power to sin. Nothing in the circumstances nor in the will of God determined what Adam would do. Unfortunately, he sinned. Had he chosen to obey God he would have merited the boon of losing the power to sin but, since he chose to disobey God, he lost the power of being able to resist sin. Thus it is that we are all bound by sin, having all 'sinned in Adam'.[11] Jesus delivers some of us from the necessity of sinning but he does so by means of an irresistible grace. Those who are chosen are made to respond. Thus, since the time of Adam, we have not had any real choice between good and evil. Like the souls in the Tale of Er, we are now under the power of necessity.

Unlike Plato, however, Augustine attempts to give an account of exactly how things went wrong in the first place. He wants to know how it was that we, like Plato's tyrant, chose the wrong sort of life right from the start. Many of the arguments are found in Augustine's *De Libero Arbitrio*. As Augustine says in the *Retractions*:

We undertook this discussion because of those who deny that evil is due to free choice of will and who maintain that God, if this is so, deserves blame as the Creator of every kind of thing.[12]

*De Libero Arbitrio* opens with Evodius's question, 'is not God the cause of evil?'[13] Augustine gives the typical Free Will Defence in reply. There are two kinds of evil, moral evil and nonmoral evil (e.g. suffering). The second is a result of the first and the first results from the misuse of free will. Thus the blame for evil lies not with God but with those who misuse their free will.[14]

In the course of the dialogue, Evodius raises four questions each of which must be given a satisfactory answer if the Free Will Defence is to be maintained. The first question is how someone like

[10] *Actu Seu Disputatio Contra Fortunatum Manichaeum*, Disputation of the Second Day, 22–37; *De Civitate Dei*, XIV. 12–15; *De Correptione et Gratia*, X–XIV; *De Libero Arbitirio*, 3.18.51–3.21.59.

[11] This was the incorrect translation of Romans 5: 12 used by Augustine.

[12] Augustine, *The Problem of Free Choice*, trans. Dom Mark Pontifex, Ancient Christian Writers, No. 22, ed. Johannes Quasten and Joseph C. Plumpe (New York: Newman Press, 1955), 221.

[13] Ibid., p. 35.                                        [14] Ibid., pp. 35–6.

Adam (who was free) could possibly choose to do evil. Evodius says:

We believe that man was so perfectly formed by God and established in a life of happiness, that only of his own will did he come down thence to the troubles of mortal life. Yet while I hold this firmly by faith, I have never grasped it with my understanding.[15]

Hick makes the same point less reverently:

The notion that man was at first spiritually and morally good, orientated in love towards his Maker, and free to express his flawless nature without even the hindrance of contrary temptations, and yet that he preferred to be evil and miserable, cannot be saved from the charge of self-contradiction and absurdity.[16]

'Self-contradiction and absurdity' is a little too strong, for a person is not really free (in the libertarian sense) to love God unless he is free to consider and endorse the possibility of refusing to love God—not in order 'to be evil and miserable', of course, but in order to put his own narrowly conceived happiness above what he believes is right. For Adam did not know that his choice would make him 'evil and miserable' but he did know that it was morally wrong. None the less, there is some truth in Hick's remark. The difficulty can be put in the form of a dilemma. Either God made Adam in such a way that he was very unlikely to misuse his free will, or God did not. If the latter, then God is partially responsible for evil but if the former, how is it that Adam did misuse his free will? Augustine answers this question by saying that Adam was neither so wise that, like the saints in heaven, he really had no opportunity to sin, nor was he so foolish that God ought to be blamed for his evil choice.

Those who put the problem as follows think they are forming it very cleverly. If the first man was created wise, how was he seduced? If he was created foolish, why is not God the cause of vice, since folly is the greatest vice? As if human nature might not receive some condition midway between folly and wisdom, which could be called neither folly nor wisdom![17]

A sinless person in a wholly good world will have strong reasons

---

[15] Ibid., p. 58.
[16] Hick, *Evil and the God of Love*, p. 75.
[17] Augustine, *The Problem of Free Choice*, pp. 212–13.

for loving God (e.g. God's love for him). However, if the love is to be genuine, such a person must be free with respect to the decision to love God. At least once during his existence, the sinless person must have the opportunity of using his free will to choose not to love God (in order, say, to keep his love for himself). Since to refuse to love God is to do something evil—to break, in fact, 'the greatest commandment of the law'—that person must have the possibility of doing evil. Moreover, if this possibility is to exist, the sinless person cannot be omniscient, for no one would refuse to love God who knew the full consequences of doing so. And if the person is not omniscient, it might seem to him that he would be happier, at least in one respect, if he kept his love for himself rather than loving God. Thus it is conceivable that he not love God.

Consider this example. Professor Smith has repented of his carnal lust for Maid Marilyn and has become a fine Christian gentleman. One day, just as he is in the middle of the final chapter of his book on connubial harmony, his wife comes in bringing him some tea and sandwiches. Normally, of course, he would put aside his work and spend some time with her. Today, however, even though he believes it is wrong to do so, he gives the woman a furious look and growls, 'I'm right in the midst of my work!' He has rejected her love in favour of his own narrowly conceived happiness. Now no matter how much we build up Smith's character—short of making him so good that he is either a divine being or a being without libertarian free will—this little story, although the less likely to occur the more we do build up Smith's character, is at least intelligible.

Evodius's second question is this: 'explain to me, if you can, why God has given man free choice of will. For if man had not received this gift, he would not be capable of sin.'[18] Augustine replies that there would be no merit in our doing good deeds unless we did them of our own free will (rather than acting them out in accordance with some prearranged divine plan).[19] Since the capacity to earn merit is a good thing, God acted well in giving man free will. Note that in replying to this question, Augustine does not say that free will *per se* is a good but only that it is necessary to the good of earning merit.[20] As we showed in Chapter 1, some of the very greatest goods, including love and rationality, presuppose free will and the risk of sin.

---

[18] Augustine, *The Problem of Free Choice*, p. 74.
[19] Ibid., pp. 75–6, 131–2.          [20] Ibid., pp. 134–5.

The third question Evodius raises is whether God is not responsible for Adam's sin since God created Adam in the knowledge that, if he created him, Adam would sin.[21] Augustine replies by saying that (1) foreknowledge does not impose any kind of necessity, and (2) sinners are better than irrational creatures, so that God should not be blamed but praised for creating them.[22] In connection with this latter statement, Augustine invokes the 'Principle of Plenitude' that it is good for God to create as many different kinds of things as possible. Thus

there may be something in nature which your reason cannot conceive, but it is impossible that a thing should not exist which you conceive truly. You cannot conceive anything better in creation, which has escaped the Creator's thought.[23]

Augustine comes dangerously close to saying that the Principle of Plentitude implies not only that it is good that God create beings capable of sinning but even that it is good that God create sinners. Are sins (together with their punishment) necessary to the perfection of the universe?

The answer is as follows. The sins of themselves or the unhappiness itself are not necessary for the perfection of the whole; but the souls are necessary as souls.[24]

However, the question then arises as to why God did not create just those persons (like Mary and Gabriel) whom he foreknew would not sin, and not also those persons (like Adam and Lucifer) whom he foreknew would sin. If, as Augustine interprets it, the Principle of Plenitude is satisfied merely by creating every possible kind of being rather than every possible being of every possible kind, would it not have been better had God created only those human beings and angels whom he foreknew would not sin? Why was Adam in the Garden of Eden rather than Mary? Hick notes that it would be hard

to clear God from ultimate responsibility for the existence of sin, in view of the fact that He chose to create a being whom He foresaw would, if He created him, freely sin.[25]

However, as Hick also points out, it is not really a question of foreknowledge that is at issue. God is not 'foreseeing' what *will*

[21] Ibid., pp. 142–3, 149–50.
[22] Ibid., pp. 150–78.          [23] Ibid., p. 153.
[24] Ibid., p. 167.          [25] Hick, *Evil and the God of Love*, p. 75.

happen but what *would* happen. As in our chapter on omniscience, we could deny that, prior to his decision to create Adam, God knew what Adam would do if created, without denying the doctrine that God has foreknowledge. Moreover, if we do deny that God knew what would happen, we can exonerate him from any blame for creating beings whom he knew would sin (since he would not have had that knowledge). (Recall that if God's foreknowledge is causally posterior to the event then it cannot help God prevent that event.)

The fourth question raised by Evodius is whether the explanation for a morally evil choice really terminates with the person who makes it. Why should the 'buck stop there' and not with some event, causally prior to the choice, which would therefore draw some share in the responsibility for the choice? Human beings are very inquisitive. We do not feel entirely satisfied with the statement that someone chose $X$ for reason $R$ rather than choosing $Y$ for reason $S$ unless we are also told that (1) $R$ was the overriding reason, or (2) the person had reason $T$ for choosing to choose $X$ for reason $R$, or (3) given the state of the world or God's will at some time, the person *had* to choose $X$ for reason $R$. Were it possible to satisfy our curiosity in this respect, we might still want an explanation of the explanation we were given. Is there a reason $U$ on account of which the person had reason $T$ for choosing $X$ for reason $R$? Continuing in this fashion, we would either (1) go into an infinite regress, or (2) go in a circle, or (3) arrive at some ultimate explanans, such as God. In the case of many phenomena, a theist, at any rate, is happy enough if a sequence of explanation terminates with God. However, in the case of moral evil this will not do, since moral evil is something which God does not will and which is not in harmony with his nature. Hence one either goes into an infinite regress or in a circle—or else one picks some stopping place other than God, such as the free choice of the evil-doer, taking that as the ultimate explanans. Augustine adopts this latter option.

Evodius says

I should like you to tell me what is the cause of that movement by which this will turns away from the unchangeable good which is common to all, and turns towards private goods, whether belonging to others or below it, indeed to all changeable goods.[26]

[26] Augustine, *The Problem of Free Choice*, p. 138.

Augustine replies that there is no natural necessity involved, such as the necessity by which a stone falls to the ground, but that the will itself simply chooses to do evil. Evodius is not satisfied with this answer and he raises the question again a little later in the dialogue. This time Augustine retorts

> Since the will is the cause of sin, and you are looking for a cause of the will, if I can find this, will you not look for a cause of the cause I have found? What will satisfy these questions, what will put an end to our hesitation and discussion? You ought not to look further than the root.[27]

Although it is true that some sins are the result of previous sins (e.g. Adam's sin), the ultimate terminus of an explanation of sin is some exercise of libertarian free will which cannot itself be fully explained.[28] Sins 'are to be attributed to nothing but to their own wills, and we must not look for any further cause of sins'.[29]

Anselm gives the same Free Will Defence as Augustine.[30] However, he probes more deeply the matter of how exactly a very good person in very good circumstances can choose to do evil. His *De Casu Diaboli* is a meditation on the fall of Satan, Satan having been created as a good angel. Anselm agrees with Augustine that, ultimately, the only reason Satan chose himself over God was simply that that was what he did. However, Anselm tries to give a partial explanation for Satan's choice.

The *De Casu Diaboli* is a dialogue between a student and his teacher. The student wants to know why Satan did not will to receive God's gift of perseverance in the truth. Was it because Satan did not *will to will* to receive this gift? As student and teacher agree, such an answer would only lead to an infinite regress.[31] In any case, it was not that Satan did not will to receive the gift of perseverance *per se* but that he willed something which he knew was incompatible with receiving this gift, namely, he willed to obey no higher will.[32] Satan was given both a desire to be happy and a desire to do right.[33]

---

[27] Ibid., p. 190.

[28] See J. R. Lucas, *The Freedom of the Will*, pp. 42–3.

[29] Augustine, *The Problem of Free Choice*, p. 205. See also *De Civitate Dei*, xii. 7.

[30] Anselm, *Truth, Freedom, and Evil*, trans. and ed. Jasper Hopkins and Herbert Richardson (New York: Harper and Row, 1967), 182. See also *Cur Deus Homo*, xxiv.      [31] Ibid., p. 152.

[32] Ibid., pp. 154–7.      [33] Ibid., pp. 172, 175–6.

He knew that he could continue both to be happy and to do right if only he obeyed God. However, he also knew that he could become more like God in one respect and therefore happier in one respect if he ceased to do right by ceasing to obey a higher will.[34] What he did *not* know was whether he would be *on the whole* happier if he chose the second option rather than the first. Thus he had a real choice between (1) continuing to obey God in order to be happy and do right, and (2) rebelling against God in order to be in one respect happier than he would have been otherwise. The reason that God withheld from Satan the knowledge of the full consequences of rebellion was that if Satan

had known this, then even while willing and possessing happiness, he wouldn't have been able freely to will that thing which would make him wretched. And in such a case, he wouldn't have been just when he didn't will what he shouldn't, because he couldn't have willed it.[35]

In other words, if Satan was to have the opportunity to do something morally commendable, he had to be ignorant of the disasters which would follow if he did not do what was morally commendable. There had to be what Hick calls some 'epistemic distance' between Satan and God.[36] Had Satan been given knowledge of the consequences of rebellion, he would have avoided it not in a way that was commendable but because his knowledge made it necessary that he not rebel. 'It is not honourable,' says the teacher, 'to refrain from sinning simply because of hatred of punishment.'[37]

The student accepts this account of the fall of Satan but still wants to know *why* Satan chose to value happiness more than rectitude. After all, God gave Satan a desire to do right as well as a desire to be happy, and no doubt God arranged things so that it would be easier for Satan to choose to value rectitude more than additional happiness. On the student's behalf, we might also add that Satan must have realised that God is more worthy of love than Satan so that Satan had at least a *prima facie* reason for loving God more than himself, and hence obeying God rather than seeking his own greater happiness. Why, then, did Satan choose to put his additional happiness above rectitude? The teacher replies

[34] Anselm, *Truth, Freedom and Evil*, p. 188.       [35] Ibid., p. 189.
[36] Hick, *Evil and the God of Love*, p. 317.
[37] Anselm, *Truth, Freedom, and Evil*, p. 190.

Only *because he willed*. For there was no other cause by which his will was in any way driven or drawn; but his will was both its own efficient cause and its own effect.[38]

Nothing causes the will to rebel except itself. It, and it alone, puts itself into a state of rebellion. It is Satan himself who causes himself to rebel. This is the same answer that Evodius received, that 'we must not look for any further cause'.

On a determinist view of the universe, each event is the unique effect of previous states. Given the previous events (and the nature of the things in the universe, as expressed in scientific laws), only one sequence of succeeding events is possible. If it is possible that Satan choose rectitude then it is not possible that he choose additional happiness, and vice versa. However, what the Free Will Defence argues, precisely, is that evils are *not* always implicit in previous events nor in the nature of things in the universe. They can be traced back only as far as some free choice. It is there that 'the buck stops'. Indeed, there is ultimately always a mystery about any contingent fact (e.g. an act of libertarian free will) as to why it is so and not otherwise. For, in one sense, the only utterly complete explanations are logical deductions from logically necessary premises, and the conclusions of such deductions are not contingent but themselves logically necessary.[39]

## II

In our article 'Evil is Privation', Stewart Goetz and I claim that

little progress can be made in any philosophical discussion unless the participants know what they are talking about. Thus it *is* crucial in considering the question of God and evil to have a correct analysis of the concept of 'evil'. Only in the light of such an analysis can we go on to a profitable investigation of the question of God and evil, including an investigation of the question which we take to be just as crucial, namely, does God directly bring evil into being or merely allow it to occur.[40]

[38] Ibid., p. 195.
[39] Aquinas offered a Free Will Defence similar to Augustine's. See *Summa Contra Gentiles*, book III, chs. 10, 108–10, and 159–63, and *Summa Theologiae* 1a.19, 48–9, 62–3, 83, 1a3ae.79, 109, 112.
[40] Bill Anglin and Stewart Goetz, 'Evil is Privation', *International Journal for Philosophy of Religion*, 13 (1982), 11.

Before giving my version of the Free Will Defence, I shall thus try to say just what I mean by 'evil'.

The following five considerations suggest that evil is some sort of 'privation'—and thus God does not 'directly bring evil into being'.[41]


## (1) Pain

The sensation of pain is not in every respect an evil. First, we should note that pain is not the same as suffering.[42] Not only are there people who suffer without feeling pain but there are also people who feel pain without suffering. One does not have to be a masochist to take pleasure in the loudness of painfully loud music, or in the ache of the muscles in toe-touching. Second, pain is part of a warning system without which our bodies would easily be destroyed. Suppose you put your hand in a fire. If you feel severe pain, you withdraw your hand immediately and little harm is done. However, if you do not feel pain then you are in serious trouble. Worse than the fact that your hand is burning is the fact that your nervous system is not working. Perhaps you have become a leper! Third, pain can be useful as a form of punishment or behaviour modification. Perhaps it is only with the help of some mild amount of pain that certain smokers can give up smoking. Fourth, pain is a compound of a system whereby we acquire scientific or moral knowledge. For example, suppose Smith hits someone on the head. The victim is able to get up and go about his business but the next day he dies. If the victim does not feel any pain it will be harder to establish whether or not there was a causal connection between the blow and the death.[43]

If pain is not an evil in every respect, in which respects is it evil? Let us consider a toothache. Toothache is good in the sense that it gets you to the dentist. You feel pain but you save your teeth. It is also good in the sense that it gives you a reason to brush your teeth. However, suppose you are someone who always brushes their teeth. It is four in the morning and you have a raging toothache.

---

[41]  Much of the material in this section comes from 'Evil is Privation'.

[42]  Hick, *Evil and the God of Love*, pp. 331–3.

[43]  Richard Swinburne, *The Existence of God* (Oxford: Clarendon Press, 1979), 202–14.

You have to wait another five hours before the dentist will see you. There is no pain-killer and all the pharmacies are closed for the night. Whether the pain stops or not, you will certainly see the dentist the next morning. The pain, however, rages on. It is not serving any useful purpose. There seems to be no good in it. However, what, precisely, is the evil in it? The evil, it seems, is that it is completely disrupting your normal state of mind. You cannot sleep, read, or even think. The pain has taken over to the point where you can no longer function as a human being. The evil, it seems, is a privation of normal consciousness. Your tooth is deprived of its normal protection against decay, and you are deprived of the possibility of thinking pleasant thoughts, having a conversation, or sitting still.

## (2) Sin

It is one thing to let someone in India die (because you never donate money to charity) and quite another to fly to India to kill someone. In both cases someone dies but in the latter case there is something extra in the way of 'moral evil' or 'sin'.

Suppose that Smith puts poison in Mr Douglas's coffee in the hope that, once Mr Douglas is dead, Mrs Marilyn Douglas will be more open to romantic ideas. Part of what makes this murder is that it was pre-meditated in the awareness that it was not justifiable. Smith intends to kill Douglas and Smith is sane enough to realise that this is wrong. There is a discrepancy between what Smith is doing and what he thinks he ought to be doing.

A person has a certain vision of what the world ought to be like. He has an opinion about how it could be improved, and he knows of several things he could do to make it worse. A person also has a certain notion of rights and duties which fit in with this vision of how things ought to be. In the 'ideal world', promises are kept and life is respected. This capacity to 'see' a better world, and to recognise rights and duties, is called *conscience*.

Moral evil occurs, precisely, when persons do not follow their conscience, when they act against what they believe is right. Smith 'sees' that he ought not to kill Douglas but he does it anyway. Later, he may admit, 'I knew I should not have done it.' There is a lack of alignment between Smith's decision to kill Douglas and Smith's view of the right order of things. The hope of having Mrs Douglas for himself put him in a position where he was tempted, and what he was tempted to do was to ignore his conscience or perception of duty in favour of a well-concealed murder.

Deliberately killing someone in India is worse than letting someone in India starve because, in the former case, there is a greater nonfulfilment of one's perceived duty to respect and preserve life. There is a greater discrepancy between the person's choice and the dictates of his conscience. Murderers often have less peace of mind than those of us who consistently refuse to give money to Oxfam.

The above considerations suggest that we define 'moral evil' (or 'sin') as follows.

> $X$ is a moral evil
> if and only if
> $X$ is a choice made with libertarian free will
> and
> there is a lack of agreement between $X$ and the conscience of
>     the person choosing $X$.

If this is a sound definition then the evil in moral evil does consist in a kind of privation, namely the lack of agreement.

## (3) Destruction

Not every kind of destruction is evil. When a cow eats grass, the grass is destroyed but this is hardly a cause for moral indignation. This converse, however, is true: every kind of evil involves destruction. For example, death presupposes destruction, and hatred hopes for it. But destruction, precisely, involves privation. Again, we have a reason for associating evil and privation.

## (4) Loss

A typical evil often involves the loss of some transitory good or the failure to acquire some object of desire. Whatever accompanies typical examples of something is often characteristic of it. Thus privation may be seen as a characteristic of evil. For example, why are old people less good-looking than adolescents? It is because they have lost the smoothness of their skin. What was once nicely sculpted is now full of holes and hollows. Again, evil seems to be a kind of privation.

## (5) Disharmony

We remarked above that the bad thing about moral evil seems to be the psychic disharmony: the evil-doer is at odds with his own conscience. One can see disharmony in other kinds of evil as well (e.g. in ugly paintings). Since the essence of goodness, one might say, is order and harmony, and since evil is the opposite of good, it follows that the essence of evil is disorder and disharmony. Thus evil is essentially the privation of something.[44]

Having considered five reasons for associating evil with privation, we now present the traditional privationist theory. According to this theory, 'evil' would not show up on an inventory of the contents of the universe. It is not any actual entity but rather an absence of what ought to be present in actions or situations. Something is an evil in so far as it is defective or deficient.

Aquinas was a champion of the theory that evil is privation. He writes

evil is in a substance because something which it was originally to have, and which it ought to have, is lacking in it. Thus, if a man has no wings, that is not an evil for him, because he was not born to have them; even if a man does not have blond hair, that is not an evil, for, though he may have such hair, it is not something that is necessarily due him. But it is an evil if he has no hands, for these he is born to, and should, have—if he is to be perfect. Yet this defect is not an evil for a bird.[45]

Note that if a child is born with three hands, this is an evil because the child lacks the natural human form. There is some genetic defect.

[44] Augustine, *St. Augustin: The Writings against the Manichaeans and against the Donatists*, trans. Richard Stothert *et al.*, vol. iv of *A Select Library of the Nicene and Post-Nicene Fathers of the Christian Church*, 1st ser., ed. Philip Schaff (1887; rpt. Grand Rapids: Eerdmans, 1979), 145–50.

[45] *Summa Contra Gentiles*, book III, part I, ch. 6. For an excellent presentation of Augustine's views on the subject, see William Maker, 'Augustine on Evil: The Dilemma of the Philosophers', *International Journal for Philosophy of Religion*, 15 (1984), 149–60.

Aquinas held that moral evil involves the abandoning of a higher good (e.g. God) for some inferior good. When this happens, the will is no longer in the proper order with respect to God. The evil of moral evil is this lack of right order and the moral evil is worse as the deviation from the right order is greater.

Hence, a sin occurs in our will when, failing to observe this order, we desire what is only relatively good for us, in opposition to what is absolutely good.[46]

A number of things follow from the privationist view of evil and a number do not. One consequence is that a thing cannot be an evil in virtue of its possessing some property essential to its being what it is. The fact that a gun is capable of killing a human being does not imply that a gun is an evil. Similarly, the fact that a person is capable of not loving God does not entail that the person is evil. Moreover, there is no such thing as evil in the sense that there is a noxious miasma which goes by that name. Nor is there any devil whose essence is evil. For if evil is privation then each evil presupposes some good which is being destroyed by the evil but which none the less to some extent remains. Evil is like holes in a coat. The more holes, the worse it is—but there is no such thing as a hole in itself. If the coat is completely eaten up by moths then the result is not a pure, unadulterated hole. The coat is simply gone and nothing is left. Thus it is a consequence of the privationist theory of evil that there is no purely evil noncontingent being in the universe (e.g. a Manichean counter-god).

On the privationist view, nothing is evil unless it is in other respects good. Every defect presupposes something it is a defect of. The converse, however, need not be true. A healthy, normal frog is an unqualified good but a sick frog is not an unqualified evil. In so far as the frog still functions properly, it is a good. Looked at in this way, the universe itself is fundamentally good or at least neutral.

A nonconsequence of the privation theory is that there is no such thing as evil—in the sense that everything is jolly if only you look at it the right way. Privationists are making a claim not about the

---

[46] *Summa Contra Gentiles*, book III, part II, ch. 108. M. B. Ahern has a slightly different view of the privation in moral evil: see 'The Nature of Evil', *Sophia*, 5 (1966), 40–2.

truthfulness of sad newspaper headlines but about the *nature* of evil.[47]

A second nonconsequence is that every privation is an evil. One plant may deprive another of sunlight. A cloud may deprive them both of sunlight. However, there is nothing to say that plants are somehow entitled, in every case, to adequate sunlight. There is no lack of anything that *ought* to be there and hence no evil.

A final nonconsequence is that any sort of finitude or contingency implies evil. God might have created a universe consisting only of a meadow of flowers lit by an ever-shining summer sun. The fact that these flowers died and were replaced by new flowers would not make this universe an evil one. For the 'privation' would not be privation of anything that *ought* to obtain.[48]

Given the five considerations at the beginning of this section, we have good grounds for accepting the privationist theory as I have just presented it. In what follows, then, we shall assume that all evils are cases of inappropriate privation. Not much of what we say, however, will depend on this assumption. As a conceptual analysis of evil, the privation theory is useful to a theist who wishes to answer the question 'why does God create evil?'—when the questioner believes that evil is a substance which God injected into the universe. However, to answer the more sophisticated question 'why does God allow evil?' the privation theory is not particularly helpful. For if evil is like a hole, 'why does God not fill it up with good?' If evil is a lack or loss, 'why does God not make it up?' If evil is like a watch running slow, 'why does God not set it right?' An analysis of evil does contribute to theodicy—it provides an understanding of what the discussion is about—but it does not give complete answers to many key questions.

## III

In this section we explain why God allows moral evil. To fix our thoughts, let us imagine the following possibility. A philosophy student submits a first-rate thesis at a well-known university. The examiner makes her wait for six months for the oral defence.

[47] G. Stanley Kane, 'Evil and Privation', *International Journal for Philosophy of Religion*, 11 (1980), 44.          [48] Ibid., p. 46.

During the defence, the examiner asks misleading questions and, at one point, even shouts at the student. A week later the student learns that the examiner has failed her because, although the topic was approved by the Department, 'the thesis ought to have been written on another topic'. A formal appeal is launched, but the examiner and his cronies see that it goes nowhere.

We shall assume that the thesis really was first-rate—good enough that it might have been published as a book. We shall also assume that the examiner was clever enough to realise this. Before we ask why God allowed this injustice, let us ask why the examiner committed it. Was the examiner taking revenge for the fact that the student had complained about having to wait six months for the oral? Was the examiner befuddled by his investigations into the occult? If the examiner's behaviour can be explained in such a way that the injustice was *determined* then—from a libertarian point of view—there is less of a question of moral evil—unless the examiner can be blamed for the determining factors. Let us suppose, however, that God had given the examiner sufficient grace that he might have passed the candidate—or at least given the candidate the hope that the thesis would be accepted with some feasible amount of revision. Why, then, did the examiner do neither? As Augustine explains to Evodius, this is not a question to which one can expect a complete answer. For if, in order that the examiner have the opportunity to reason, create, love, and so forth, God gives him libertarian free will extending to evil then it is not impossible that the examiner misuse that free will—simply because he chooses to do so. We might model the inner state of the examiner as follows: 'either I can pass this thesis because, although the student irritates me, it is as good as many other passed theses, or I can fail this thesis because, although it is a satisfactory thesis, the student should suffer on account of her arrogant attitude.' The examiner has a reason for passing the thesis and a reason for failing it. He knows that, *qua* examiner, it is his duty not to act on the second reason, not even if he feels it more strongly than the first reason. None the less, the choice is 'up to him'. He decides to fail the thesis.

How is it possible that a good God allow the examiner to choose the alternative forbidden by his role as examiner, and probably also forbidden by his conscience? The answer is simply that such evils are a possibility given libertarian free will extending to evil. God's omnipotence does not extend to the impossible and it is impossible that God both give the examiner libertarian free will (which must, as we showed in the first chapter, extend to evil if the examiner is to have a chance at the high destiny God intends for him) and also prevent him from ever misusing it. The freedom of free will presupposes an indeterminacy which is not logically compatible with God arranging things otherwise.

What, however, if God had changed the circumstances so that the examiner would have been at least more inclined to be fair? This question assumes that God had not already done so. However, perhaps God had considered a number of alternatives: 'although I, God, do not middleknow what the examiner would do in these various hypothetical circumstances, it is none the less probable that in circumstances C he would behave himself.' The actual circumstances were, in fact, circumstances C but the examiner, although *very* inclined to do his duty, resisted this inclination and failed the student anyway. The examiner, we may suppose, had the help of some assistant examiner who was quite willing to pass the thesis. The student, we may suppose, answered all the questions very politely, even after the examiner had shouted at her. The circumstances *were* favourable to an honest appraisal of the thesis and yet the examiner unjustly failed it.

The following argument expresses my view as to how it is possible that God allow such evils to occur. Let

$p$ = God exists, is omnipotent, omnisicent, and morally good.

$q$ = God creates a world containing persons who can reason, create, be ultimately responsible for their decisions, choose their values, co-operate, love unconditionally, and keep promises.

$r$ = God creates a world containing persons with libertarian free will extending to evil (i.e. which might actually be used to do evil).

$s$ = Prior to his decision to create a group of persons with libertarian free will extending to evil, God does not, in effect, know how much evil (if any) they *would* do *if* he created them.

$t$ = There are some persons who make some morally evil choices.

Given what we have said in the previous chapters (where the reader will find an explanation of the meaning of the terms used in the above statements), there is good reason to doubt that the first four statements entail the negation of the fifth statement, that is, we may doubt that

$$\Box \ (p \ \& \ q \ \& \ r \ \& \ s \Rightarrow \neg t).$$

Thus we may take it as a premiss that

$$\neg \ \Box \ (p \ \& \ q \ \& \ r \ \& \ s \Rightarrow \neg t).$$

From this premiss it follows that the five statements are compossible, that is,

$$\Diamond \ (p \ \& \ q \ \& \ r \ \& \ s \ \& \ t)$$

and hence

$$\Diamond \ (p \ \& \ t).$$

In other words, it is possible both that there be an omnipotent, omniscient, morally good God and also some persons who make some morally evil choices.

A second argument for the compatibility of God and moral evil is the following. We use the notation $a \rightarrowtail b$ for

If $a$ were the case then it might be the case that $b$

and we take it, with Lewis, that this is equivalent to $\neg \ (a \ \Box\rightarrow \neg \ b)$, that is,

It is not the case that if $a$ were the case then it would not be the case that $b$.[49]

In other words, to use Goodman's term, $b$ is 'cotenable' with $a$.[50] Then we have the following:

$$\Diamond \ (p \ \& \ q \ \& \ r \ \& \ s)$$
$$\underline{p \ \& \ q \ \& \ r \ \& \ s \rightarrowtail t}$$
$$\Diamond \ (p \ \& \ q \ \& \ r \ \& \ s \ \& \ t)$$

---

[49] David Lewis, *Counterfactuals* (Oxford: Basil Blackwell, 1973), 2.

[50] Nelson Goodman, *Fact, Fiction and Forecast* (London: Athlone Press, 1954), 23. (On p. 22 Goodman gives a different definition of 'cotenability'. The two definitions are not equivalent. This is because cotenability is not a symmetric relation.)

The libertarian theist, as I characterise him, holds not merely that $p$ & $q$ & $r$ & $s$ is possible but also that $q$ entails $r$ and that $p$ & $q$ & $s$ is true. He thus has, in a sense, an *explanation* as to why moral evil exists as well as a proof of the logical compatibility of the statements $p$ and $t$.

If the above explains why there is *some* moral evil, it does not really explain why there is as much moral evil as there actually is. How is it that there is so much? In the next section, we shall show why God allows the consequences of moral evil. Now one of the consequences of moral evil is more moral evil. Evil-doers, by their bad example and their enticements, influence other people. Children brought up by parents who lie and steal will find it hard not to lie and steal themselves. If a married woman tries to seduce a young man, he will find it hard not to commit adultery. Furthermore, sin is habit-forming. Once you have cheated on your income tax or your spouse, you find you have a strong desire to do so again. Greed, lust, sloth, envy, and so forth can be pscyhologically addictive. Even without recourse to a theory of original sin or a discussion of the temptations provided by the devil, we can easily explain why there is so much moral evil in the world.

## IV

Granted that there is a reason why God allows moral evil, why does he allow its conequences?[51] It is one thing to will the death of your neighbour and quite another to shoot him. Now why could God not achieve the advantages of free will together with the advantages of social harmony by, say destroying the bullet in mid-flight?

Suppose God intervened every time an evil decision was about to have an evil consequence. The following things would happen.

(1) People would rarely repent of their evil decisions since these decisions would cause no visible harm.
(2) The ground would normally be hard enough to walk on but when, on account of his own recklessness, a person fell, the ground would become soft to protect him from bruises.

[51] Robert McKim, 'Worlds Without Evils', *International Journal for Philosophy of Religion*, 15 (1984), 161–70.

(3) If, by accident, I fired a gun at someone's heart, they would be killed, but if I did it with the intention of harming them, they would not be hurt at all. (For the additional possibility of God's intervening to prevent evil which is neither moral evil nor a consequence of moral evil, see the next section.)

(4) If a scientist did an experiment in order to discover the truth of some matter, he would get the results he would normally get in the actual world. However, if a scientist did the same experiment in order to show he was superior to a hated rival, he would not necessarily get those results.

(5) When the evil examiner went to write 'fail' in his report, he would find himself writing 'pass' instead.

(6) A student who decided to be lazy and not study would none the less do well on tests.

(7) If you intended to tell your husband that you wanted to leave him because you found Douglas more attractive, your lips would curl up in a delightful smile and you would exclaim, 'darling, I am so happy with you!'

(8) The hypocrisy of the above exclamation would not bother you. Since guilt is a painful consequence of moral evil, God would eliminate it too.

The above examples suggest that if God annulled all the bad consequences of evil decisions then things such as the following would occur.

(1) We would have trouble learning what was evil.

(2) We would have trouble learning the laws of nature and, as a result, the level of technology would be low.

(3) Intending to hurt someone would be an effective way to avoid hurting them inadvertently.

(4) God would be the cause of a great deal of lying.

(5) God would make people make a public show of loving God, even if they chose to hate him.

(6) People who hated other people because of their skin-colour would never feel guilt, remorse, or shame for this hatred.

(7) The world would lack some of the beauty it now has on account of its order and regularity.

(8) Instead of respecting their decisions, God would often undermine the choices made by human beings.

Point (8) is important. When a child makes a promise, his parents can annul that promise. However, if an adult makes a promise, it would be an affront to him if anyone tried to say that he was not bound to the consequences. Part of the dignity of being a normal adult is that you are responsible for your decisions. It may be that marriage to Marilyn *is* a bad idea (since you are already married to Marie), but if God makes it impossible for you to say 'I do' then he is exercising a suffocating and tyrannical paternalism which shows no respect for your power of judgement. There are many ways in which God could annihilate the consequences of moral evil. For example, he could simply adopt a policy of annihilating any person the moment that person made a morally evil choice, and instantly replacing that person with someone very much like him who had, however, never done evil. However, God's initial purpose in creating us was to love us and to win us to love for him and each other. The goal is partnership and friendship. In harmony with this goal, God respects our decisions, and gives us a way of coming to regret and repent of bad decisions. He treats human beings not like irrational children but like potential friends. He acts with tolerance and understanding, not with high-handed authoritarianism. Respecting our dignity and autonomy, he permits us to implement our decisions, even when they are evil.

In Chapter 1 we defended the view that human beings are more than mere actors with predetermined lines. On the contrary, human beings were created to be friends and associates of God. According to the second letter of Peter

the greatest and priceless promises have been lavished on us, that through them you should share the divine nature.[52]

The Bible describes those who choose to accept God's grace as his bride.

> Like a young man marrying a virgin,
> your rebuilder will wed you,
> and as the bridegroom rejoices in his bride,
> so will your God rejoice in you.[53]

On a high and exalted view of human beings, it is only appropriate that God allow us to make the world as we decide to make it.

---

[52] 2 Peter 1: 4.
[53] Isaiah 62: 5. See also 2 Corinthians 11: 2 and Revelation 21: 2.

Without destroying the dignity which he himself gives us, God could not negate all the bad consequences of evil decisions.

## V

The reader will not expect me to give a completely satisfying answer to a question that has bothered theists for over two thousand years, namely, 'why does God allow those evils which do not seem to be due to free will?' I do think the question has an answer but the best I can do is to offer a few clues.

First, let us give some examples of the sort of evil we have in mind.

(1) A person with terminal cancer feels pain which serves no apparent purpose.

(2) A person looks so ugly that no one wants to marry him.

(3) A person dies in an unforeseeable earthquake.

(4) A child drowns through nobody's fault.

(5) A young mother has terminal cancer.

(6) Some people born blind are mysteriously healed but most are not.

(7) A university professor, through no fault of her own, becomes incurably mad.

(8) It rains the whole summer.

(9) A person with a learning disability never learns to read.

(10) Animals tear other animals to pieces.

(11) There is a famine and thousands of people starve.

(12) A child is severely mentally retarded.

Theists have taken at least five different positions in an attempt to understand such facts.

## (1) Natural evils are not so bad

Human beings tend to react to 'natural evils' with fear and resentment. However, looked at in the proper 'philosophical' way, they are really not so bad. Indeed, the only real evil here is people's refusal to praise God for the realities of a contingent universe.

We should distinguish between pain, incapacity, and death, on the one hand, and suffering on the other.[54] For example, the Christian martyrs felt pain but, rather than suffering, they rejoiced in it. What is bad is not that, having bodies, we need pain to help keep them intact but rather the attitude of someone who rejects or resents this pain and thereby suffers. When a fox eats a chicken, we may assume that the chicken feels pain, but we need not think that it suffers. Suffering is a psychological state of rebellious persons. Again, since an eye is a contingent arrangement of matter, it is not surprising if a few people are born blind. This is obviously unfortunate but it does not prevent those people from living happy and useful lives. If they brood on the fact that they are unlucky then, of course, they will suffer, but there is no need for them to do so. Indeed, blind persons can be more cheerful than persons with perfect sight who choose to regard each little difficulty as a reason to get upset. Death, too, is not an evil but part of the natural cycle of life. From a theistic point of view, moreover, it can be the beginning of a much better existence. The evil connected with death is not so much the cessation of life as the selfish clinging to a useless grief.

Against the above, one may object that in certain cases suffering itself is an inevitable result of 'natural evil'. Suppose that, due to a chemical imbalance, a university professor becomes mad. Suppose also that part of her insanity consists in a constant feeling of dread. She is not in a position where she can take a positive attitude towards her condition. The disease itself determines that she be fearful and depressed. Examples such as these show that some natural evils are very bad indeed.

I do not want to belittle a real evil but, on the other hand, I do not want to be deceived by my emotions into thinking that something is worse than it really is. Of course, it is tragic that the university professor is locked in a state of fear and anguish on account of her mental illness. If we discovered that this illness had been deliberately inflicted on her by a jealous colleague, we would punish that colleague to the full limit of the law. If we discovered that some doctor had a cure for this illness but was deliberately withholding it, we would rightly judge him to be a sadistic scoundrel. In all this, however, we must realise that our human

[54] Romans 8: 18.

perspective is limited. In juridical or moral matters we must, of course, make judgements on the basis of the best knowledge available to us. However, this does not imply that there is no larger view, no more accurate view of things. We rightly condemn the sadistic doctor because, like ourselves, he should be acting on the presupposition that the woman's suffering is, on the whole, a bad thing. The data do not allow him to conclude otherwise. We cannot, however, condemn God for permitting the same evil because he may well know many things about the case which we do not. For example, God may know that it is only by means of witnessing this particular suffering that the professor's brother will be likely to come to his senses and choose to give up his sinful way of life. Indeed, God may know that, before she became ill, his sister told God that she would gladly do or undergo anything at all if only it could help save her brother's soul. Moreover, God may know that the suffering of the woman will somehow strengthen her spirit so that, in the next life, she will be capable of a far greater rejoicing in the divine beauty. Given only what we know, it is probable that the suffering of this woman is, on the whole, bad, and so we ought to end it if possible. Given the complete truth of the matter, however, it may follow that the suffering is a necessary part of some far greater good. From God's perspective, the illness may not be so bad after all. As Paul writes to the Romans, 'all that we suffer in the present time is nothing in comparison with the glory which is destined to be disclosed for us'.[55]

Against the above, one may object that God ought to give us a better understanding of suffering. If a child drowns, God ought to tell us if the child really did go straight to heaven. We should also be told (if it is true) that, if the child had lived, the bad example of his parents would have probably led the child to commit ghastly crimes.

To this I answer that God has already told us a great deal about why he permits evil. Many of the ideas in this chapter come from the Bible. Furthermore, it is not clear that we would benefit by being told more. We might lose some spiritual advantage if there was nothing left for faith. More likely, we simply would not understand the complete explanation. The fact that there is a complete explanation does not imply that we humans should be the

[55] Hick, *Evil and the God of Love*, pp. 331–3.

first to know about it, and it does not imply that we would comprehend the explanation. The fact that a high school student cannot understand advanced Number Theory does not mean that advanced Number Theory is not a precise and illuminating subject.

## (2)  All evils are moral evils

Augustine lived in an age which believed in demons (i.e. fallen angels) just as fervently as we believe in banks. Their activity was as widespread and pernicious as credit cards. Thus, in his age, it was perfectly reasonable to suggest that *every* disaster was a moral evil, or a consequence of a moral evil. If a person had cancer, it was because the devil had attacked his health (possibly using some biological means to do so). If a person died in an earthquake, it was because the demons had caused the foundations of the rock to shift. A person born blind had been blinded by something the devil had done. Demons could control the weather too, and it was their fault if there was a famine.

What are these demons? The demons are angels who exercised their libertarian free will to rebel against God. The devil is their leader, and he has decided to destroy all that is good on earth. The result is the widespread ruin we mistakenly call 'natural evil'. Even today, some Christians would argue that this is the correct picture. There really are demons, and if you wish to contact them (in spite of the great psychological and spiritual dangers) you need only play with a ouija board or attend a seance. Demons do indeed possess people (especially in non-Christian societies) and the proof is that (i) the possessed persons do things which surpass human powers (e.g. speak in languages they have never learned, or lift very heavy objects), and (ii) the possessed persons can be 'cured' not by psychiatry but only by exorcism. The best protection against demons is to become a Christian and 'plead the Blood of Jesus' (i.e. say a prayer in which you place yourself under the care of the sacrificed redeemer and his Holy Spirit). The best way to exorcise demons is to have some serious, humble Christians order them to leave 'in the Name of Jesus'.

Now it may seem that even if we accept this exciting picture of the world, we still do not have an adequate answer to the problem of 'natural evil'. For in a contingent world things fall apart quite naturally. Devil or no, a tile will occasionally break off a roof and kill someone walking below. Devil or no, a child will occasionally drown—though no one is at fault. When the disciples asked Jesus, 'who sinned, this man or his parents, that he should have been born blind?' the answer is

Neither he nor his parents sinned, he was born blind so that the works of God might be revealed in him.

Jesus then cures him, not by means of exorcism, not with any reference to the devil, but in a more 'natural' way:

he spat on the ground, made a paste with the spittle, put this over the eyes of the blind man, and said to him, 'Go and wash in the Pool of Siloam.'[56]

It seems, then, that some 'natural evils' are not tied to demonic activity. Given the vagaries of the weather, it will occasionally not rain for a long time. Given the vast genetic possibilities, a person will occasionally be too ugly to attract any suitors. This is just part of a contingent world. It does not want any demonic activity to explain it. Indeed, God could prevent such things only with an excessive 'super-natural' intervention.

I agree that, devil or no, in the 'natural' course of things, an animal will occasionally fall off a cliff, hurt itself, die, and leave its offspring starving. This can happen to a human being too. However, it should be made clear whether we are talking about 'nature' as God originally intended it before the rebellion of Satan, or 'nature' as it is now, after his rebellion. If you live in air, you may find it difficult to imagine living under water. Since we live in a fallen world, we may find it difficult to imagine what it would have been like without sin. None the less, I do not think we have to reject the idea that if those angels had not sinned then the 'natural' course of things would have included safeguards against pain or starvation, safeguards which are now lacking. It is not impossible that, in God's original plan, there was some 'natural' way in which animals avoided falling off cliffs, some 'natural' mechanism whereby humans avoided damage to their bodies without any really strong or unnecessary pain. When certain of the angels rebelled, the fabric of this original state of nature came undone and the result is the large number of 'natural' evils found in the world today. From our

[56] John 9: 1–7.

point of view now, the prevention of such evils would involve constant supernatural intervention but perhaps, in the original plan, God had in some subtle way built safeguards into the 'natural' course of things. These safeguards would have been destroyed by the rebellious angels. This explanation of natural evil is not, of course, going to win many converts among those who hold that everything should be explained in terms of an unchanging set of laws of nature. However, it may be a viable explanation for certain people who, unsatisfied with a materialistic or mechanistic view of the universe, prefer a more person-centred understanding of it.

## (3) Man's sin causes natural evils

The view is closely related to the previous one, only here the culprit is not Satan but 'Adam'. Human beings are seen as a collective unity. They form the nub or centre of creation (at least on this planet), and the proper relation between them and God is what holds the earth's ecosystem together. When human beings collect-ively reject God, this centre gives way, and the whole of nature falls apart, past, present, and future. Rocks and animals are affected no less than the human intellect.

In Judeo-Christian thought this idea is associated with the third chapter of Genesis. Before Adam sinned there was no pain or death. As John of Damascus puts it, 'there was neither rain nor tempest on earth'. However,

at the transgression the thorn sprang out of the earth in accordance with the Lord's express declaration and was conjoined with the pleasures of the rose, that it might lead us to remember the transgression on account of which the earth was condemned to bring forth for us thorns and prickles.[57]

Before Adam and Eve disobeyed God, they lived in perfect harmony in the Garden of Eden. After they sinned, they were thrown out, and God told Eve

I shall give you intense pain in childbearing, you will give birth to your children in pain. Your yearning will be for your husband, and he will dominate you.[58]

[57] John of Damascus, *Exposition of the Orthodox Faith*, ii. 10. See also Genesis 3: 18.	[58] Genesis 3: 16.

How is it that we all sin 'in Adam'?[59] How does a collective sin work? We can give some answer to these questions even without referring to a mystical unity of human beings. For people often sin—or fail to do good—by just not standing up against the sins of others. People often just 'go along with the crowd'. Like Gandhi, I could take a stand against war and racism. Like Socrates, I could question the competence of my leaders. Like Amos, I could divorce myself from our money-lusting economy. And if I do not take such a stand, how can I not share in a collective guilt?

The relationship between the 'fall of Adam' and natural evil can be seen in the following way. To the question 'why is there cancer?' one might reply, 'because we spend enormous amounts of energy and intelligence in the development and distribution of weapons. If all that time and talent had gone into medical research, we would long ago have found a cure for cancer.' To the question 'why are people killed in earthquakes?' one can answer, 'because we have not had enough sense to build our cities away from major earthquake zones'. To the question 'why is there famine and starvation?' a partial reply is, 'because we do not have a global system for sharing with each other, and because we are not always prudent in the number of children we beget'. To the question 'why is that girl too ugly to find a husband?' the answer might be, 'because we do not make the effort to free ourselves from aesthetic stereotypes, because we do not choose to look any deeper than the surface of a person's skin'. In short, there are many 'natural evils' which would not exist if only we human beings collectively chose to do good rather than evil. Someone who spends his life working for a cigarette company need not wonder why there is cancer.

It may be objected that the above is too simplistic. Even if we always acted wisely and well, there would still be a great number of natural evils. For example, it is naïve to think that if no one had ever sinned then no one would ever have died. The fact that animals tear other animals to pieces cannot be blamed on some 'original sin'. It may be that in heaven the 'lion will eat hay like the ox' but such a rosy picture is not true of this world.[60] Real lions have always had sharp teeth.

To this objection I answer that we are naïve only in that we do not know the deep connections which may exist between nature

[59] Romans 5: 12.
[60] Isaiah 11: 7.

and human sin. We cannot say that if no one had ever sinned then people would still have died, because the possibility evoked by the 'if' clause is too remote from our experience. If we do not have some special revelation (as in, say, the Bible), we cannot possibly tell what the world would be like if no one had ever sinned. It is true that in all our experience, animal bodies age and die. However, no one has yet explained the ageing process. No one knows if it can be halted or not. We do not know if a human being could survive indefinitely via a long series of operations in which small parts of his brain were replaced by plastic transplants. We are certainly nowhere near developing a technology for attempting such a thing. Nor do we know whether ageing and death were part of God's original plan. We are in one sense 'naïve' if we suppose that if no one had ever sinned then no one would ever die. However, we are equally naïve if we think we know this is false. Basically, we have no way of telling—unless God chooses to reveal it to us. The only really simplistic view in this area is the view that, without relying on a special revelation, we know the real fact of the matter.

## (4) Value of the natural order

Consider a universe consisting merely of angels with libertarian free will. Since angels are immaterial substances, there is no matter in this universe, and no laws of nature as we know them. This universe contains love, rationality, and many other good things but it lacks a certain completeness. There is no concrete expression of beauty. In particular, there are no sunrises, no laughing eyes, and no human beings. From this we may conclude that it is a good thing that the actual world contains matter, and that this matter is governed by patterns and regularities. Indeed, it is the order of the physical universe that, even if it is in a 'fallen' state, makes it both beautiful and useful for human beings. We can admire the laws of nature and we can exploit them to produce beneficial technology. It is only because light always obeys the same equation for refraction that we can chart the positions of the stars or build telescopes to look at them more closely. The regularity and durability of the physical universe give us a basis for our life, learning, and aesthetic pleasure. A whole new dimension of happiness is added thereby to the delights of the good angels.

Given the value of the natural order, we can answer the problem of natural evil in the words of Pope:

> Think we, like some weak prince, the Eternal Cause,
> Prone for his favourites to reverse his laws?
> Shall burning Etna, if a sage requires,
> Forget to thunder, and recall her fires?
> On air or sea new motions be imprest,
> O blameless Bethel, to relieve thy breast?
> When the loose mountain trembles from on high,
> Shall gravitation cease, if you go by?
> Or some old temple, nodding to its fall,
> For Chartres' head reserve the hanging wall?[61]

If God intervened to prevent every disaster, the natural order of the physical world would be disrupted. That would make the world less beautiful, and it would make the world less easy for us to manage.

Against this explanation of why God allows natural evils, it may be pointed out that God could intervene *occasionally*, performing a miracle, without thereby jeopardising the structure of the world. The world already holds together very nicely in spite of a great deal of randomness (e.g. at the subatomic level) and surely a little more irregularity would not hurt. Indeed, it would increase the regularity and beauty of the world if, for example, no one was ever born blind, or if everyone always looked physically attractive. Human beings are constantly trying to improve upon the 'natural order' (e.g. through technology) because, precisely, it is not as good as it might be. It has value but God could give it greater value by eliminating some natural evils.

To answer this objection, that God should intervene to prevent natural evils, I suggest that he already does intervene. If he intervened any more often, he would seriously undermine the causal order, destroying the beauty of the patterns of nature. Life would become a disjointed fairy-tale. It is like walking across a lawn. If it happens a few times, no harm is done. However, there is a certain threshold after which the more the lawn is walked on, the worse it becomes. A few exceptions cause no harm but there is a definite limit to the number of exceptions the lawn can bear.

---

[61] The quotation is from the *Essay on Man*. Martin Gardner gives it on p. 266 of his excellent book *The Whys of a Philosophical Scrivener* (New York: Quill, 1983). CHS. 15 and 16 of this book are devoted to the problem of evil.

## (5) Utilitarian answer

The utilitarian answer to the problem of natural evil is simply that natural evil is a means to a very good end. God allows the various diseases and disasters because it is only through them that we can develop in such a way as to enjoy everlasting happiness. Perhaps if we had not rebelled against God then these natural evils would not have been necessary. Given the actual state of affairs, however, they are an essential component in a process whereby God brings about a great utility for the universe. If a young mother dies of cancer, it is only because, in the long run, this will be of great benefit to mankind.[62]

To this it may be objected that the utilitarian cannot usually say why a *particular* natural evil could not be dispensed with. Why is it necessary for the greatest total happiness that *my* child drown? Would it really diminish the quantity of utility so much if we had more regular rainfall and thus less famine? Moreover, if natural evils are essential to the greater long-run happiness, why should we combat them? If a utilitarian theist claims that it was right that this young mother die of cancer then is he not dangerously close to saying that her doctor was wrong to try to prevent it? If natural evils are just a means to a better end then it seems that they are not so evil. Yet they are very evil indeed.

It may well be that in some cases it is better that a young mother not die of cancer. In such a case, God might use a doctor to heal her. In another case, however, the spiritual benefits of dying might outweigh the physical liabilities, and the doctor would find that the cancer was incurable.

Since we are not omniscient, it is not surprising if we cannot say, in each particular case, why *this* suffering contributes to a far greater good. However, we do have some idea as to why, in general, natural evils may lead to greater good. First, natural evils often incite people to repentance. For every one person who chooses to respond to the evil by rejecting God, there are a hundred who choose to respond by leading better lives. Second, we need not think that life ends in death. As we shall argue in the next chapter,

---

[62] For a sophisticated utilitarian theodicy, see Keith Chrzan, 'Linear Programming and Utilitarian Theodicy', *International Journal for Philosophy of Religion*, 20 (1986), 147–57.

human beings are immortal. Hence a sudden death due to some natural catastrophe may be a quick route to a much happier life in heaven. Indeed, from this point of view, if someone survives a natural catastrophe, he should react by saying, 'how unlucky I was that I did not go to heaven!' Of course, there may also be the possibility of hell. We shall discuss hell in the next chapter. Suffice it to say here that no one goes to hell unless he exercises his libertarian free will to reject God, and then freely chooses not to repent. Given the magnitude of God's love and power, we may be sure, moreover, that at most a few people actually go to hell. Although God cannot force us to love him, he has a great deal of patience, persuasion, and compassion.

## V

Suppose there are two Jews. One has rejected belief in God because his father died in a concentration camp. The other clings to belief in God because it was this belief for which *his* father died in the same concentration camp. The first Jew feels that evil is the overriding fact about human existence. The second Jew believes that the faith his father died for will triumph over all the Hitlers the world will ever produce. These two Jews decide to discuss the existence of God. Is it likely that their emotions will allow them to find a common truth about the matter? Will their reason transcend their histories and personalities in such a way as to allow them to agree? I believe it is possible—but only at the cost of a heroic effort. The problem of evil, more than any other, is an intellectual difficulty because it is first an emotional difficulty.

7

# Immortality

THE question of immortality is obviously bound up with the nature of human beings. It makes a difference whether (1) a human being is just a body, or (2) he is just a soul, or (3) he is a union of body and soul. Since this is not a book about mind-body dualism and the nature of human beings, I cannot go into detail as to why I prefer position (2). I shall make a few points in its favour, yes, but I certainly do not think that this chapter contains the definitive treatment on the nature of humans. For an excellent presentation of a dualist position, the reader may wish to consult Swinburne's *The Evolution of the Soul*.[1]

Let me begin this chapter by setting out a few 'points of reference'.

(*a*) Position (1) might well be incompatible with libertarianism. In order to have 'agent causality' as opposed to determinism or randomness, the libertarian is probably better off opting for (2) or (3).

(*b*) None of the three positions implies immortality or its negation. Even if we are merely bodies, it is still possible that God reassemble or repair us as often as necessary to keep us in existence for ever. Even if we are souls, it is still possible that we cease to exist at death. God might simply cease to maintain the soul in existence as soon as there ceased to be a body through which it could function.

(*c*) Although I prefer position (2), I certainly do not think the body unimportant. A person without a body is, to my mind, like a bird without wings. It is still a bird, I would maintain, but clearly a bird in a sad and incomplete state.

We have noted that the question of immortality is tied to the question of human personal identity. The question of human person identity, moreover, is tied to the question of how and when a human person begins to exist. If Smith begins to exist before he is

[1] Richard Swinburne, *The Evolution of the Soul* (Oxford: Clarendon Press, 1986).

conceived then he may well exist after he dies. However, if he begins to exist only when his reason develops (at, say, age 7) then he may well cease to exist when he becomes senile. One's view of the terminus of life is related to one's view of its beginning. Thus in the first section of this chapter, I ask 'when did Smith begin to exist?'. In the second section, I present my theory of what it is to be a human person, and, in the third section, I relate my view to that of Parfit. It is in the fourth section of this chapter that I argue that, only thanks to a free decision of God, we are immortal.

The fifth section of this chapter looks at the topology of immortality. I show, for example, that it is logically possible that a person be immortal and yet always live in the twentieth century. In the sixth section, I discuss the question of heaven and hell. I suggest that by sending persons to hell, God is merely respecting the choices they made when they were able to exercise libertarian free will. In the final section, I say what Smith is going to do in heaven (assuming he gets there), and I stress that it will be Smith himself (and not some other person evolved from Smith) who will be doing it.

## I

Smith, let us say, is born in Montreal on 11 May, about one thousand nine hundred years after Jesus allegedly rose from the dead. Smith's birth is a minor change in position relative to his mother. It involves nothing more important than a change in his feeding habits. More significant is the moment at which Smith began to exist.

Was there such a moment? Or was there merely some 'limiting' moment, a moment at which Smith did not exist but after which he did exist? Or has Smith always existed? Perhaps Smith is 'part of Adam' and, perhaps, Adam was created at the first moment of time so that, perhaps, there was no moment before which Smith did not exist.

Is Smith a material object, like a complicated jigsaw puzzle? If so, it is still not impossible that he existed at the beginning of time. For the very same atoms which, in their particular configuration, are Smith may have been together in that same configuration at the beginning of time. Imagine God labelling a certain collection of atoms, one by one, and bringing them together from time to time in just the same way—as a child might make and remake the same jigsaw puzzle. Then, just as we could say that the jigsaw completed now is the same as the jigsaw completed earlier, so we could say that the person living now is the same as the person living at the beginning of time.

Is Smith a memory? Must Smith be able to remember what it was like being X in order to be now the person X once was? Even if this were so, it would not make it impossible for Smith to have existed long before his birth. For, if Smith did exist then, it is not impossible that he remember it now, at least in part. Plato thought that we all remember something of our previous lives. And if Smith does not remember anything of his previous life, and it may yet come back to him. Memories sometimes do come back, perhaps even from time immemorial.

Is Smith one or more streams of consciousness? Even when Smith is in a dreamless sleep, certain unconscious activity occurs. For example, he notices when Marilyn stops snoring. He immediately wakes up and checks to see if she is all right. Even if Smith is a stream of consciousness, he may have existed for billions of years. The fact that he does not remember what he was conscious of does not prove that he did not have those images or feel those impressions. Perhaps he has had the same vivid dream night after night since the world first spun round its axis.

Is Smith a being whose identity is what it is because someone could know what it is? Is the person Smith was and continues to be tied up with the possibility of someone recognising him to be that person? Could the possibility of knowing a truth determine that truth in such a way that Smith existed in a previous life only if there is a way of finding out? Even if this were so, it may be that Smith did exist previously, for it may be that God recognises him to be the same person as Adam.

Is Smith an immaterial soul? He may need a body as badly as a bird needs wings, but none the less, he may be a soul. And perhaps someone long ago with just Smith's kind of intelligence and psychological orientation was the same soul which is and always has been Smith.

More soberly, let us suppose that Smith did not exist before the conception of his zygote. Did he come into being along with his zygote? Or was it, perhaps, when he first emitted brain waves? Did

Smith come into being when he first achieved consciousness of himself as an individual? Or was it when he was reborn in Baptism? Even if we suppose that Smith did not exist prior to conception, we are still not going to have an easy time deciding when he did begin to exist. Astrologers place great importance on the moment of birth. In this they are wrong—just as on account of the precession of the equinoxes, they are wrong about the actual positions of the sun, moon, and planets. The merely geographical transition from mother's womb to mother's arms is of little importance. However, if the moment of birth does not matter, with what moment shall we replace it?

Suppose that Smith did not come into existence at the moment of conception but at the time when he first acquired the property $P$. For example, $P$ might be the property of being aware of himself. The problem with this idea is that we can imagine there being some sort of extraordinary circumstances in which an ordinary adult ceases for a while to have property $P$. For example, he might lapse into a temporary coma. Because of this possibility, we are inclined to say that a person can none the less exist, as the same person, even if he lacks property $P$. In standard arguments about abortion, the pro-abortionist advances some property $P$ which, he says, a foetus must have before you can equate it in the relevant ways with a normal adult. The standard reply is to produce a counter-example in which a normal human being lacks $P$ for a while.

Even if we suppose that Smith did begin to exist at the moment of conception, there are still other problems. Could he have begun to exist at some other moment? According to some philosophers, no. If, for example, a phone call had interrupted his parents on that fruitful eleventh of August, then, in all probability, a different spermatozoon would have fertilised the ovum and, according to these philosophers, a different person would therefore have been conceived. Noting that an ovum dies within a month, Parfit makes the following claim

If a particular person had not been conceived within a month of the time when he was in fact conceived, he would in fact never have existed.[2]

[2] Derek Parfit, *Reasons and Persons* (Oxford: Oxford University Press, 1986), 352.

However, Parfit would have to admit that this is wrong. Given the fact that we freeze spermatozoa and ova, something very much like the following has probably happened a few times. A scientist has a single frozen spermatozoon and a single frozen ovum. He intends to put them together as a summer research project but, as things turn out, he fails to get around to it until the following winter. Since Parfit holds that who a person is is tied to the specific zygote from which that person grows, Parfit would have to admit that, in this case, the person could have been conceived six months before the time he was in fact conceived. Of course, the real issue is not that Parfit has overlooked a wonder of modern technology. The real issue is his blithely presupposed materialism. Suppose I say, 'if I had had different parents, Carol would have loved me'. Perhaps I am merely complaining that Carol detests me on account of my social class. Perhaps I am entertaining the idea that the particular spermatozoon and ovum which joined to form me might have been produced, atom by numerically identical atom, by a man and woman different from my parents (e.g. their identical twins) who might therefore have been my parents. Perhaps, however, I am simply operating under the concept that my identity cannot possibly be tied up in a particular microscopic bit of matter. We shall say more about this in Sections II and III below.

In *The Dialogue*, Catherine of Siena thanks God for his having created her. She is not just thanking him for having created some persons one of whom happened to be her. Rather she is thanking him for having created the unique person who she is—and not someone else he might have created instead. Addressing God, she says, 'you loved me before I existed' and 'whatever being I have and every other gift of mine I have from you'.[3] It is as if God were a master builder studying a collection of blueprints—one for a church, one for a supermarket, another for a museum. Each building has its merits and God examines each one carefully. Finally, he decides to build the little convent. 'Catherine House' is constructed. Nor does it matter whether God uses red bricks purchased from Company X or yellow bricks purchased from Company Y. The same little convent is brought into being.

On this view, God could have created me even if my parents had never met. 'Beginning with zygote Z' is not an adjective which has

[3] Catherine of Siena, *The Dialogue*, trans. Suzanne Noffke (New York: Paulist Press, 1980), 273–4 and 364.

to apply to me if I am to exist. But if the zygote does not matter, what does matter? If what is matter is immaterial then it is something immaterial that matters! This immaterial thing is the 'blueprint' or pattern for the soul. According to Catherine, when God creates a person he deliberately instantiates not merely a common noun concept—like 'human being'—but also a proper noun concept—like 'Catherine'.

If Catherine is right then, prior to the existence of J. R. Smith, there is a concept or type or essence of J. R. Smith which God can consciously choose to instantiate. One may object to this view that it seems to entail the possibility of God instantiating this essence more than once. Perhaps Smith and Catherine are both instantiations of J. R. Smith-hood. Unknown to either, it is necessarily true that $X$ is Catherine of Siena if and only if $X$ is J. R. Smith. But this is absurd. Furthermore, there does not seem to be any way of distinguishing uninstantiated essences of individual persons. What would differentiate the essence of the uncreated Smith from the essence of another uncreated person who shared all of Smith's essential properties except the property of being J. R. Smith?

In the next section we advance the view that a human being is an immaterial soul but we do not assume that such a soul is a deliberate instantiation of some proper noun concept like 'being Catherine'. On our view, it is not possible to have two human beings who are really just two tokens of the same unique person. Moreover, we shall claim that, since it is immaterial, the soul is indivisible, and hence there is no danger that a soul split up into two souls, each of whom might have equal claim to be the original person. According to our view, God creates a soul and gives it control over a body which is properly suited to it. If, as Carl Jung held, the structure of a woman's psyche differs from that of a man's psyche then God would be unlikely to create a female soul in conjunction with a male body. However, God's choice of a body is not tied in any rigid way to a particular zygote or genotype.

## II

In this section I argue that Smith is an immaterial soul that (1) exists in time, (2) normally has a body, (3) normally thinks, and (4) has a conscience. I begin by giving some reasons for thinking that Smith is an immaterial soul.

## (1) Counterfactual considerations

The counterfactual

> If Smith had white skin, he would have better job opportunities

is a perfectly sound utterance. It does not merely mean 'whites have better job opportunities'. It means, more specifically, that if *Smith* were white, *Smith* would have better job opportunities. The speaker is imagining *Smith's* being white. Since skin colour is hereditary, this suggests that the same person might have had a different genotype, or different parents. The personal identity of the job-hunter is not tied in any essential way to his actual body, or to his actual parents. The same point is suggested by counterfactuals such as the following.

> If Smith were a woman, he would join the infantry.
>
> If Smith were a genius, he would have a Ph.D.
>
> If Smith had been born in 1985, he would still be at school.

All these counterfactuals suggest that who Smith is is not linked in any necessary way to his body or genotype. He is, rather, a non-physical entity, a soul.

## (2) Possibility of possession

Smith goes to the bathroom to shave but when he looks in the mirror he sees that he looks just like Marilyn. A few more observations and he realises that he has a body just like Marilyn's. He rushes back into the bedroom where he finds someone who looks just the way he used to look. This person says, 'what are you doing with my body?'. Marilyn and Smith realise that they have switched bodies.

Fairy-tale possibility is not the same as logical possibility. None the less, because it is conceivable, the above story does give us a prima-facie reason for thinking that a person is not his body but something which preserves its identity regardless of its relation to physical objects.

## (3)  Out-of-body experiences

While he is unconscious, a person leaves his body and looks down on the team of doctors operating on his heart. After regaining consciousness, he correctly describes all the details of the operation. He reports that the doctor seated behind him was biting a toothpick. Given the position of his head and eyes during the operation, he could not possibly have seen this in the normal way.

Examples of out-of-body experiences are not hard to find. Swinburne, for example, mentions some that would be similar to the case we have just described.[4] For mystics like Saint Paul out-of-body experiences are commonplace.[5] Explaining these experiences in terms of an immaterial soul is simpler than trying to explain them in terms of a purely physical reality.

## (4)  The recycled zygote

A team of scientists takes a collection of elementary particles (say, protons, electrons, and neutrons) and assembles them to form an ovum and a spermatozoon. These are joined in a test-tube and, a few months later, the scientists have a human infant. The scientists then track down all the elementary particles they used to form the ovum and the spermatozoon. (Some of them are still in the child's body; others are in its excrements.) They take these particles (which are numerically identical to the original particles) and assemble them in exactly the same way as before to form a new ovum and spermatozoon. The new test-tube baby therefore has the same genotype as the first test-tube baby. Indeed, both babies grow from the very same zygote. Proton for proton, electron for electron, neutron for neutron, the second zygote is a perfect reconstruction of the first. It is as if you took a watch apart and then, without changing any of the parts, you put it back together in the same way.

---

[4]  Swinburne, *The Evolution of the Soul*, pp. 301–5.
[5]  2 Corinthians 12: 1–4.

It would be the same watch. Hence the two babies grow from the numerically same zygote. Indeed, we can imagine a whole series of these infants being produced. When they grow up and go their separate ways—assuming the scientists do not kill the baby in recovering the particles in its zygote—there is no reason they should consider themselves to be just one person. On the view we associated with Catherine of Siena we might regard them all as instantiations of, say, Smith-hood. However, we saw that this view is problematic. The more natural conclusion is that who a person is is not determined by which zygote he grew from.

Note that we cannot conclude from this argument that a human being is a soul. The scientists can play the same trick with dogs or houseflies and, unless we are inveterate Pythagoreans, we do not want to say that a dog or housefly is really a soul. None the less, our argument does suggest the soul as a metaphysical basis for answers to questions like, 'are these two test-tube babies the same person?'

## (5) Dividing

Identical twins are formed when, very shortly after conception, the union of ovum and spermatozoon splits in two. For those who believe that a human being begins to exist at the moment of conception, this poses a philosophical riddle. Nor is this a newly discovered riddle. Augustine was pondering the same conundrum in AD 387. In 'The Greatness of the Soul' he considers the case of a worm being cut in two.[6] Both halves survive, and Augustine wants to understand this in terms of the following assumptions:

(*a*) worms have souls;
(*b*) the same worm always has the same soul;
(*c*) a worm's soul is located in its body;
(*d*) a worm is dead if its soul is not in its body;
(*e*) a worm soul, being indivisible, cannot be in two places at once.

Given these assumptions we cannot say that the original worm survives in the two new worms. Perhaps it simply dies and two new

---

[6] Augustine, *De Quantitate Animae*, 31–2.

souls are provided for the two half-worms, or perhaps it survives in one of the half-worms (as chosen by God?) and a new soul is provided for the other half-worm. Augustine does not pursue the matter.

Recently, Parfit has explored a new version of this riddle.[7] Suppose that the two halves of my brain are perfect images of each other. Everything is duplicated. The left half is transplanted in the empty skull of some corpse, which then comes to life. This newly created combination thinks it is William Anglin. It has memories, intellectual skills, preferences, and vices just like mine. Moreover, the same thing happens to the right half of my brain. It is transplanted in a second empty skull belonging to a second corpse, which then comes to life, and thinks it is me.

There are three possibilities: I have died; I have survived in exactly one of the two bodies; I have survived in both bodies and there are now in some sense two of me. It seems that if only one transplant had been performed, and the other half of my brain had been destroyed, then I would have survived as that single new combination. Moreover, the fact that there is or is not a second transplant can hardly affect the fact that I survive as that first combination. But both transplants have equal claim to be me. Thus there are two of men. However, it then follows that the original William Anglin has two separate futures. It is possible that his first future consists in murdering William Anglin and going to hell, whereas his second future consists in being an innocent murder victim and going to heaven. We have the same sort of bizarre possibilities that led us to look askance at the theory suggested by Catherine of Siena.

Parfit does not think that there are two William Anglins. He tries to argue that the question raised by dividing need not have a definite answer. He tries to argue that the answer is unimportant. If, however, we take the view that a person is an immaterial soul, we can give a clean solution to the problem. For if William Anglin is an immortal soul, he cannot be divided in two. Being immaterial, a soul lacks spatial extension and hence cannot have its 'left part' cut off from its 'right part'. It is indivisible. (Of course, it may have components. On Jung's view, there is the Ego-consciousness, the Anima and the Self. On Freud's view, there is the ego, the id, and

---

[7] Parfit, *Reasons and Persons*, pp. 253–61.

the superego. The fact that a soul lacks spatial extension does not mean it is merely a geometric point, without any psychoanalytic structure.) Now God could take the original soul and put it in control of one of the two new combinations (whichever he chose), or he could take the original soul to heaven and provide two new souls for the two new combinations. We may not be in a position to know which alternative God chooses but at least there is some definite fact about the matter. Both new combinations may protest that they must be William Anglin because they have his memories, but at least one of them is wrong. Moreover, it may be that God gives souls bodies which are somehow very well-suited to those souls. If this is so, then, unless the three bodies in the puzzle are bodies of identical triplets, God would probably link two new souls to the two new combinations, and take William Anglin to the next world. In any case, assuming that a person is a soul, there is a definite answer to the riddle. Even if we do not know what happens to William Anglin, we at least know that God knows. There is a definite fact about the matter. However, if, like Parfit, we do not assume that a person is a soul then we are left with a paradox.

## (6) Affinity with immaterial things

What is not me comes to me in images. I do not have direct access to, say, physical realities but only to symbolic representations of them. Thus, as Descartes pointed out, I have no completely sure way of knowing whether or not I am dreaming. The things most immediately related to me are symbols and forms. These are what I have 'in my mind'. Certain emotions and intellectual insights characterise my 'inmost self'. These are not, it seems, physical in nature.

On the other hand, I am not merely a series of perceived images or memories. Another person could experience the same images or memories, and yet not be me. Besides, I can *decide* to a certain extent what images I perceive and what memories I have. I can think about them and I can choose to like the things they represent. A mere set of immaterial things would not have that kind of control over the contents of that set. Thus, although I have an affinity with immaterial things, I am not just a set or sequence of such things. I am an immaterial thing which governs a set of immaterial things. I also govern some material things, such as my right arm.

Since he is not contingent, the divine being is neither a physical object nor an ephemeral sequence of images. The divine being created me in order that we might love each other. Now just as a rock cannot have an emotional relationship with a dog, so a purely physical person cannot have a genuine love relationship with a divine being. For us to love God, we must have an affinity with God. In particular, since he is immaterial, we must be immaterial too.

## (7) Libertarian free will

Suppose Marilyn decides to do X. If Marilyn is merely a physical object then this decision is a physical event and, as such, it is governed by the laws of nature. If the relevant laws are deterministic then the decision is not made with libertarian free will. If they are statistical then the decision is a matter of chance rather than being a human action. Since, as we argued in Chapter 1, Marilyn has libertarian free will, she cannot be a mere physical object.

When a person decides to do something, they sometimes make this decision against a number of physical and psychological factors tending to make them choose otherwise. For example, a person may resist the temptation to commit adultery in spite of a desire which is stronger than any other desire he has. (The 'strength' of a desire can be measured independently of the decision made in response to it—for example, by means of a Jungian word-association test.) Moreover, a person is properly identified with 'the thing that decides' and, in this case, the thing that decides is deciding against the easiest course, against the physical and psychological tendencies. Hence a person is not a physical object but some immaterial entity which can transcend the laws of physics.

The seven preceding considerations are not so much arguments for the conclusion that a human person is a soul as incomplete sketches of arguments. As we conceded at the beginning of this chapter, this is not a book about dualism and it does not contain the definitive treatment of the nature of human beings. However, I do think that the above considerations at least tend to make it more plausible that a person is a soul. In what follows we shall assume that this is so—and in the next section we defend this view against some objections raised by Parfit. Note, however, that our arguments for the immortality of human beings will not depend on the assumption that a human person is a soul.

Smith, I claim, is a temporal being as well as an immaterial soul. Indeed, I do not think he could be otherwise. God himself may live above Time. Certainly, God has given Smith the capacity to understand timeless truths, such as the truths of Number Theory. Smith can commune with God in timeless, mystical moments. He can step back from history and, like God, grasp the threads in it which transcend the days and years, which are not dependent on time for their reality. Moreover, Smith can love with a love that does not grow old or fade but which completely surpasses the limitations of past, present, and future. Yet in spite of his atemporal dimension, Smith is a creature who, to be fully himself, needs the dimension of time. When he does mathematics, the enjoyment he gets is partly from going from start to finish, one bit at a time, and only then seeing the truth of the theorem in its entirety. When he prays, it is often in the context of a 'liturgy of hours', one song and then another, the rhythm and pace of the psalms building up to a long, rolling alleluia. When he loves, Smith does so with a sequence of words and gifts, touches and laughter, persevering through time, always seeking the other's joy. Were Smith to lose his temporal aspect for ever, he would be but half his self, that is, not really Smith at all but something else and no longer him. Thus, for example, if it is *Smith* whom God makes immortal then it is a partly temporal immortality he makes for him. Unlike a timeless God, who never grows older, Smith shall attain an age as large as you might care to mention.

Smith is also a being with a body. He is not just his body but his body is an important part of him. Now by 'Smith's body', I do not mean these particular atoms which happen to be in Smith's body now. When, by means of natural biological processes, all of these atoms have been replaced by others, the result will still be Smith's body. His future bodily existence in heaven does not, therefore, depend on 'atom chasing'. God does not have to reassemble the exact atoms which made up Smith's body on the day of his death in order to 'resurrect' his body. Chemically similar atoms will do just as well. Some of the early Church Fathers—like Athenagoras—

were avid atom chasers.[8] They thought the existence of cannibals posed a serious threat to the doctrine of the resurrection of the body. On the Last Day, they wondered, how would God resurrect both cannibals and victims when their bodies had shared many of the same atoms? Nowadays we find this question somewhat puerile. None the less, we should give the atom chasers their due. What they said was fully in line with the fact that if it is *Smith* that will live for ever—and not just some ghost of Smith—then he must have a body, at least for most of the time. Of course, just as Smith has an atemporal side, he has an immaterial side. We are assuming that, as a typical human being, he is a soul. However, there are also many things, important to Smith's being Smith, which do require a body. He runs and dances; he sings and listens to singing; he climbs mountains; he swims and sails and, perhaps best of all, he sees. He sees the oceans and the stars and the snowflakes. He sees the human form. In this way Athenagoras is right: if there is some good news about a future life for us—and not merely for some Platonic shadow of humanity—then it will sooner or later include our bodies. They will be healed of any defects; they will be imperishable, glorious, and powerful, but they will none the less be bodies, and our own bodies they will be.

Smith is also a thinking being. By nature as well as preference, he is a philosopher. Thus if he is going to be immortal, he will not only exist in time and have, almost always, a body but he will also continue to reason and question and learn. Smith does have an emotional side and he does have a mystical side. Clearly to be human is not just to reason. A being who did nothing but logical deductions would be a conscious computer, perhaps, but certainly not human. On the other hand, human beings do have the capacity to reason and they would not be human without it. Those who drug themselves with nonsense chanting in religions designed to help you part with your sanity do not achieve happiness. On the contrary, they are trying to commit suicide in favour of some flower-selling zombie, some mantra-mouthing robot. This is not life after death

[8] Athenagoras, 'The Resurrection of the Dead', in vol. ii of *The Ante-Nicene Fathers*, ed. Alexander Roberts and James Donaldson (New York: Charles Scribner's Sons, 1925), 149–62. See also Gregory of Nyssa, 'On the Soul and the Resurrection', in vol. v of the second series of *A Select Library of Nicene and Post-Nicene Fathers of the Christian Church*, ed. Philip Schaff and Henry Wace (New York: The Christian Literature Company, 1893), 430–68.

but death before the end of life. It is the bad news of psychic collapse, not the good news of personal immortality. No, if it is Smith's own identity or immortality that is at issue—a future *Smith*—then the being who lives on must be at least as much a reasoner, a questioner, and a philosopher as Smith is now. That is his nature as a human being and that he could not relinquish and survive.

Smith is also a being who has a conscience. That is, he has the capacity to see the value of things. He can imagine ways in which something could be better—or worse. Since he has libertarian free will, he can choose between the better and the worse. If he goes to heaven, he will no longer have the opportunity to choose anything really bad but he will still be able to choose among various good things. If he goes to hell, he will no longer have the opportunity to choose anything really good but he will still be able to choose among various bad things, some worse than others. In either case, if it is to be *Smith* who survives into the next life, then it will be Smith with his conscience. It is an essential part of who he is.

Sometimes we talk about a person who 'has no conscience', meaning that he is not bothered by, say, the fact that he is a professional killer. A person who literally has no conscience, however, would not be bothered by anything. He would not feel the slightest obligation to his friends, his spouse, or his children. No military, political, economic, or religious ideals would move him. He would have no standard by which to judge himself or others. Someone who believes it is his duty to rid the earth of black people is obviously twisted. None the less, he has an ideal, no matter how perverse, and he has a concept of better and worse, no matter how badly applied. The person with literally no conscience, however, does not even have twisted ideals. He has no ideals at all. He is pathological to the point of being non-human. Thus no human being survives death unless he survives it with his conscience.

## III

Parfit begins the section on personal identity in his *Reasons and Persons* with the following thought experiment.[9] A human being

---

[9] Parfit, *Reasons and Persons*, p. 200.

on earth enters a 'scanner' which (1) records the exact state of all his cells; (2) destroys his body; and (3) beams the record of the exact state of all his cells to Mars. On Mars there is a 'replicator' which uses this information to create, out of new matter, a living body just like the body that the scanner has destroyed. Parfit has a variation of this thought experiment in which a 'new scanner' omits step (2) so that the human being remains alive on earth as well as being 'replicated' on Mars.

On the view of personal identity we presented in the previous section, the new person on Mars is the same as the original person on earth only if a soul has travelled from earth to Mars. Given (2), the person on earth dies. His soul goes to the 'next world'. Now God *could* put this same soul in the newly created body on Mars. This would be a case of reincarnation. However, God has no reason to incarnate that same soul a second time, and he may well choose to create a new soul for the new body—just as he creates a new soul for a new zygote.[10] Of course, with the new scanner, God leaves the original soul in the original body. On my view, the fact that there is a 'replica' of a person (i.e. someone with the same genotype and memories) has no special relevance to his life, death, or non-existence. Parfit, however, claims that if the person on earth is going to die, he ought to 'regard having a Replica as being about as good as ordinary survival'.[11] (Parfit assumes that dying and ceasing to exist are the same. This leads him to think that dying is usually a bad thing.) Although the replica is not temporally or physically continuous with the 'original', it has the same memories, abilities, and appearance as the original, and, for Parfit, whether the replica is the same person or not, these similarities are what matters. (Parfit assumes that memories are 'carried' by brain cells.) The original can 'live on' in the replica somewhat in the way that a parent can 'live on' in his children. Thus it should not be important to the original person if he is going to cease to exist.

Parfit would label my view of personal identity 'non-reductionist' because I do not want to 'reduce' personal identity to the existence of a brain or a series of mental events. On the contrary, I hold that a person is a separately existing spiritual substance, a kind of Jungian psyche.[12] This substance does not have spatial extension but it does

---

[10] Hebrews 9: 27 seems to rule out reincarnation.
[11] Parfit, *Reasons and Persons*, p. 201.
[12] Ibid., p. 210.

have 'psychic parts' (e.g. the Anima, the Self, and so on) and may therefore have more than one stream of consciousness. Parfit argues against such non-reductionist views.

First, Parfit claims that we have no evidence for the thesis that we are separately existing spiritual substances.[13] Parfit thinks that we *might* have such evidence but, in fact, we do not. However, he says nothing about accounts of (1) astral travel, (2) out-of-body experiences, (3) people 'remembering' past lives, or (4) possession of one person's body by another person. These accounts may be inconclusive. They may not 'hold up in court'. However, they do exist and they do incline a number of people to believe in the independent existence of the soul. Parfit might have mentioned them if only to say why he doubts their credibility.

Second, Parfit considers the possibility of replacing $x$ per cent of someone's brain and memory with new matter and new recollections.[14] If $x$ is very small, we still have the same person. If $x$ is large and if, moreover, the replacing does not occur gradually (via very small changes), the person is replaced by a different person. (For example, if (1) my body is destroyed except for 0.1 grams of brain cells, and (2) my memory is erased except for one recollection of eating fish soup, and (3) a completely new body and set of memories are then added to that tiny residue of me, then I have died.) Now, on my non-reductionist view, I am committed to holding that below some critical value of $x$, the soul of the person remains, whereas above some critical value, it is replaced by another soul (one more suited to the new body or memory). There is a 'borderline' between the two cases. Parfit thinks that this borderline must be a sharp borderline.[15] I disagree. Within certain limits, God is free to decide whether or not to replace the given soul with another soul more suited to controlling the entity in question. Thus the difference between 'life and death' does not consist in a very small change. Parfit thinks that non-reductionists are committed to holding the allegedly ridiculous view that a very small change can make all the difference—but they are not. Parfit also claims, against the non-reductionist view, that we 'could never have any evidence where the borderline would be'.[16] Unless God chose to tell us, we could not, I grant, always know exactly when he replaced the old soul with a new soul. However, we could have

---

[13] Ibid., p. 228.   [14] Ibid., pp. 236–7.
[15] Ibid., pp. 238–9.   [16] Ibid., p. 239.

evidence as to where, approximately, the borderline is. Suppose that we perform this 'surgery' on 1,000 thin, introverted mathematicians in an attempt to produce 1,000 fat, extraverted sailors. We find that when $x$ exceeds 60, the resulting person is usually best described as bulky, extraverted, bored by mathematics, and interested in ships. However, when $x$ is less than 30, the resulting person is usually best described as slender, introverted, amused by mathematics, and keen on the ocean. For values between 30 and 60, we do not obtain any significant results. Since the physical appearance and psychology of a person are to some extent expressions of his soul (at least on my view), and since the difference between the less than 30 per cent and more than 60 per cent cases is quite marked, we have some evidence that, for the change from thin, introverted mathematician to fat, extraverted sailor, the borderline is roughly at 45 per cent with a margin of 15 per cent on either side. Parfit's borderline objection is thus not as sharp as he thought it was.

Parfit's third argument for the reductionist and against the non-reductionist view turns on the idea of a divided person. Parfit asks us to imagine a student 'splitting' his mind into two centres of consciousness in order to work through two approaches to the same physics problem simultaneously.[17] This is like a case of schizophrenia. On my view, the soul itself remains intact. It is just that there is a lack of the normal kind of communication between psychic parts. Just as a schizophrenic's various 'personalities' think their separate thoughts, so the student's two 'egos' work on separate approaches to the problem. Moreover, just as we say that a schizophrenic is only one person, so we should say that the student is only one person—even though, for awhile, he has two streams of consciousness. The unity of the student consists not in his streams of consciousness, of course, but in the spiritual substance which is his soul. This structure is not in its normal state, but it is sufficiently intact that it remains the same entity. There may be a long crack down the centre of a bridge without the bridge ceasing to exist. Parfit finds it difficult to believe that 'the life of a *person* could involve subjects of experiences that are not persons'.[18] He therefore thinks that his example undermines a non-reductionist view such as mine. However, one need only read Carl Jung (or other psychoanalysts) to learn that, at least in certain cases of

---

[17] Parfit, *Reasons and Persons*, p. 246–7.  [18] Ibid., p. 250.

schizophrenia, there are subjects of experiences that are not persons. Jung calls them 'psychic complexes'. Thus Parfit's example does not threaten the non-reductionist position. It is unfortunate, moreover, that Parfit nowhere discusses the relation between his view of 'person' and a psychoanalytic view of 'person'.

Finally, Parfit considers another version of division, namely, that which I discussed in the previous section. Recall that in this example a person's left brain is joined to one brainless body, and his right brain is joined to a second brainless body. The two combinations then 'come to life' and have all the same memories of the original person. On Parfit's view it is impossible, even in principle, to decide whether one or both of the new persons are the same as the original person. In any case, it does not matter. For example, if the original person committed a crime, it does not matter, says Parfit, if you cannot decide who (if anyone) still bears responsibility for that crime. There is no definite answer to such questions and, anyway, they are unimportant. On my view, however, there is a definite answer to such questions. God, at any rate, knows what has happened to the soul of the original person. As I showed in the previous section, one reason for holding a non-reductionist view is that it offers a metaphysical basis for resolving puzzles raised by dividing, rather than dismissing them as 'empty' or 'unimportant'.

In the previous section I advanced the view that a human person is an immaterial soul. In this section I have defended that view against Parfit. In the next section I advance some arguments for immortality. These arguments do not depend on my particular 'philosophy of souls'.

## IV

Suppose for the moment that a human being is a soul. Although a soul may have psychic parts (e.g. Ego-consciousness, Anima, Self), it cannot have any spatial extension—since it is immaterial—and thus it cannot have any spatial parts. As a result, it is indivisible or 'unbreakable'. Physical forces may be able to influence it (via the human body with which it interacts) but they cannot destroy it by reducing it to small pieces. The worst that can happen is that they induce schizophrenia. In that case the various psychic parts of the soul are not in proper communication with each other. There may be separate streams of consciousness. The soul itself, however, remains intact. We say that Smith is mad. We do not say that he has died and now two new persons exist inside what used to be Smith's brain.

It does *not*, however, follow from the above that human beings are immortal. Like other contingent things, the soul was created by God and it can be destroyed by God. God has made the soul so that it cannot be destroyed by being 'broken apart' but he has not made it utterly indestructible. He can simply choose not to sustain it in existence and, if he does so, it will cease to exist. That much is implied by the fact that souls are contingent and God is a divine being. Because of this, a human person is immortal if and only if God wills that he be immortal. To prove that a human being is immortal, we must prove something about God's will. For example, we must show that destroying a soul is inconsistent with God's purpose in creating that soul. The following arguments for immortality turn on the idea of a goal for human life. This goal presupposes the existence of someone whose goal it is, namely, the divine being. The arguments do not turn on my view that a human being is a soul.

> The ultimate goal of human life is perfect love.
> There is no perfect love unless it lasts for ever.
> If love lasts for ever, life is everlasting.
> If life is everlasting, we are immortal.
> Either the ultimate goal of human life is achieved, or life is meaningless.
> Life is not meaningless.
> If the ultimate goal of human life is achieved and this goal is perfect love, there is perfect love.
> Hence we are immortal.

In logical symbols:

$$U$$
$$P \Rightarrow F$$
$$F \Rightarrow E$$
$$E \Rightarrow I$$
$$G \text{ or } M$$
$$\neg M$$
$$\underline{G \,\&\, U \Rightarrow P}$$
$$I$$

Another argument is the following;

> God created Smith (or any other human) in order that he and
> Smith love each other for ever.
> Since this is so and since God is omnipotent, God will sustain
> Smith in existence for ever.
> Hence Smith is immortal.

In logical symbols:

$$G$$
$$G \,\&\, O \,\&\, (G \,\&\, O \Rightarrow S)$$
$$S \Rightarrow I$$
$$\overline{\qquad\qquad\qquad\qquad}$$
$$I$$

Neither of these arguments says anything about a particular
theory of personal identity. What counts is God's purpose and
God's power. Of course, as we argued in the chapter on
omnipotence, God's powers extend only to what is logically
possible. Thus the second argument, at least, presupposes that there
is *some* theory of personal identity according to which it is logically
possible that a human being exist for ever. Of course, there is such a
theory. If I am a spiritual substance the possibilities of death,
memory loss, dividing, and so on create no problems.

Let us consider an argument against immortality.

> God does not make someone immortal unless there is a reason
> for it.
> God created Smith so that they might live together in love.
> Smith chooses to hate God and will always choose to hate
> God.
> If God created Smith so that they might live together in love
> and if, moreover, Smith chooses to hate God and will
> always choose to hate God then there is no reason for God
> to make Smith immortal.
> Thus Smith is not immortal.

This argument, however, overlooks the possibility that God may
have reasons other than mutual love for creating Smith or for
maintaining him in existence. God's purposes may also include
'respecting Smith's decisions' or 'giving Smith what he wants'. In
Section IV we shall try to say why God would choose to send
sinners to hell rather than simply annihilating them.

To conclude this section, let us consider an objection to the thesis that human beings live for ever. Over a very long period of time, a person will undergo too much change to remain the same person. Even if we discount changes as radical as death and bodily resurrection, how can we imagine that a person will be the same person after, say, twenty trillion years of psychological development? Can a person be immortal if, with so much time, he is certain to evolve into a virtual stranger?

I reply that a person is who he is not merely as a lonely metaphysical substance in some unnumbered possible world but as a member of a community. At the very least, he is loved by God. Who we are is partly determined by those we love and how we love them, and also by those who love us and how they express their love. I shall remain me if it is me God continues to love. And I shall remain me if my friends keep calling me by my name, if we together recall our good times and maintain our common ideals. The soul as a continually existing substance with certain almost indelible characteristics does, I believe, provide a sufficient 'identity link' for immortality. More to the point, however, is love. I am affirmed as the person I am by you, my fellow saint, since you love me as I am, and you I affirm as the person you are, since I love you as you are. When a person arrives in heaven, he is greeted by some of his friends and he, in turn greets some of his friends when they die. For all the years of eternity, these friends discuss the wonders of God both in heaven and in their mortal lives. Always sharing their memories and always accepting each other's eccentricities, the members of this community make of their immortality a practical and felt continuity of individual persons.

## V

For those philosophers who accept the possibility of temporally discontinuous personal existence, defining 'immortality' is an interesting exercise in the mathematics of Lebesgue measure theory. Is someone immortal if he lives one minute the first year, half a minute the second year, a third a minute the third year, and so on? Is he immortal if his existence corresponds to a set of points on the real line which, although it has Lebesgue measure infinity, is totally disconnected (like some variants of the Cantor set)?

If a human being is an instantiation of a previously given proper name concept like 'Catherine-hood' then discontinuous immortality is possible. However, as we saw in the first section of this chapter, that view is problematic. Suppose, then, that it is wrong. Suppose, moreover, that God creates a person just like Aristotle and drops him off in New York City in 1990. This person will think and act like Aristotle. He may claim (in perfect Greek) that he *is* Aristotle. But the original Aristotle would, I think, take little comfort in this sort of 'resurrection'. Even if God created the new Aristotle using the same atoms that were in the original Aristotle on the day of his death, we would still have no reason to suppose that the original Aristotle had come back. The key question, on my view, is whether the new Aristotle has the same soul as the original one. If God has taken the original, continuously existing soul and put it in the body in New York then, yes, this is Aristotle, now in 1990. However, if God has merely created a new soul like the soul of Aristotle, then it is not. A new soul can be an instantiation of many concepts which Aristotle himself instantiated but, assuming Catherine of Siena is wrong, it would not be an instantiation of the proper noun concept 'Aristotle'. Indeed, if resurrection consists merely in God making someone just like you then he could resurrect you before you died. God could introduce you to your resurrected self and your resurrected self could come to your death-bed and try to console you by telling you that because he would live on, you would live on too. This you might find difficult to appreciate.

Let us assume, then, that no one is immortal unless he exists continuously throughout time. This is certainly the more natural view. Note, however, that what counts for immortality is not the fact that one lives throughout the rest of an endless history. For one might have a machine for backwards time travel. (Recently, some physicists argued that this is a physical possibility.[19]) As the year 5000 approached, one could journey back to the year 1. Each time the year 5000 approached, one could do the same. In this way, one's 'personal time' could be infinite even if the universe's time was finite. The fact that someone is immortal does not imply that the universe will last for ever.

Needless to say, the above view is a bit awkward. If someone

[19] See Michael S. Morris, Kip S. Thorne, and Ulvi Yurtsever, 'Wormholes, Time Machines, and the Weak Energy Condition', *Physical Review Letters*, 61 (1988), 1446–9.

lived through the twentieth century an infinite number of times then there would be infinitely many versions of that person in existence at any given moment in the twentieth century. The more natural view is that a temporal person is immortal just in case time extends infinitely far into the future, and there is some moment $t_0$ (e.g. 18 billion years after the Big Bang) such that for all moments $t > t_0$, the person exists at $t$. It is, I believe, in this sense that we normally think of someone being immortal.

## VI

In this section and the next, I deal with heaven and hell. I give a picture of heaven and hell which is at once logically coherent and also compatible with orthodox Christianity. However, I must stress that much of the material in these sections is not itself part of orthodox Christianity. Much of what I claim is speculative and tentative.

Let us assume that human beings are immortal. Some of them may return God's love not only now but from some point on. Let us call the set of persons who do this 'heaven'. Some human beings may refuse God's love, not just for a while, but for ever. Let us call the set of persons who do this 'hell'. We can also use the words 'heaven' and 'hell' to refer to the geographical locations, if any, where the respective sets of persons usually live. A person 'goes to hell' if there is some moment of time after which he consistently refuses God's love.

Short of divine revelation, we do not know if there is anyone in hell. In this section, however, let us assume that there are some persons (e.g. Lucifer) in hell, and let us investigate whether this is consistent with God's goodness. We first rebut the positions of the universalist and the annihilationist. We then ask about different classes of people whether they are likely to 'go to hell'.[20]

On one view, everyone sooner or later goes to heaven. For God continues to pester the sinners in hell until they repent. 'Look, God,' they complain, 'we know it isn't so pleasant here but it's a lot

---

[20] See also Richard Swinburne, 'A Theodicy of Heaven and Hell', in *The Existence and Nature of God*, ed. Alfred J. Freddoso (Notre Dame: University of Notre Dame Press, 1983), 37–54. The last two books of Augustine's *De Civitate Dei* also contain an illuminating discussion of heaven and hell.

better than kowtowing to you. We spent our whole earthly lives rejecting you and we don't want to have to keep on and on saying no. So get lost!' According to the universalist, however, God persists. What if the sinners are just as persistent? God eventually wears them down. But *how*, assuming that the sinners' rejection of God is an exercise of libertarian free will, how does God wear them down? On the universalist view, God does not respect the free decisions of human beings. He refuses to take no for an answer. If necessary, he will compel the sinner to accept him. And, in that case, God will have saved not the sinner but some subhuman replacement for the sinner, a being without libertarian free will. The universalist does not see that genuine love and co-operation presuppose an exercise of libertarian free will. The universalist denies the dignity of free human beings. For the universalist, one does not have the right always to refuse God's love.

Then there is the annihilationist. If God is good, he says, God will annihilate those who choose to remain in hell so that they will no longer suffer. The annihilationist thus denies to human persons the dignity of free will. Has the annihilationist consulted the persons in hell about their annihilation? No. He has, with condescending paternalism, made the decision for them. No doubt they are unhappy in hell but perhaps they would still prefer to exist. 'Of course, it isn't all roses here,' say the sinners, 'but we are living out our selfish lives just as we always wanted to. *We* don't have to bow and scrape and listen to dreary hymns. We can shout and curse and hate and feel sorry for ourselves all we damn well want to! Whether we are right or wrong, we want to go on existing, if only to put a big black blotch on God's creation.' The annihilationist assumes that hell is far worse than non-existence. In a way, he is right, for what is a life without love? On the other hand, the annihilationist is, perhaps, taking too seriously the images of fire and brimstone. Perhaps hell is unpleasant in a more sophisticated way. Perhaps God gives the damned just the sort of godless life they want. Their punishment may be no more or less than those illusions of happiness which the sinners have so often preferred to God's will. For those who loved luxury, there will be nauseating quantities of good food, enervating doses of sexual release, voluminous cupfuls of sedating drugs, and centuries of second-rate television. For those who loved to strive against others, there will be months of violent sports, and gruelling, ulcer-causing competitions for job promotions.

For those who took excessive pride in their learning, there will be reams of partially true theories to memorise and reruns of every boring lecture they ever gave. For those who dabbled in the occult and put their hope in astrology, the devil himself will be there to tell them all the details of their totally monotonous future. Now if this picture is true, God is merely respecting the choices made by the damned. The annihilationist, however, does not respect their choices but imposes on the damned his own idea of that would be better for them.

As to who goes to heaven and who goes to hell, let us consider the following questions. In each case the answer will have to do with a libertarian free choice.

(1) Can a person go to hell if he follows his conscience?

No, not unless he has deliberately chosen to twist his conscience to value what he believes is wrong. The negative answer to (1) means, for example, that if a person's conscience tells him to join religion X then he will not go to hell by joining religion X, even if religion X contains much less truth than, say, Christianity. Of course, it is a person's duty to make a reasonable effort to discover which religion is the best.

(2) Can a person go to hell if he refrains from serious evil-doing?

Yes, for his conscience may always have exhorted him to be better than lukewarm. Someone with a great aptitude for love and truth who chooses to repress his 'good side' in favour of a minimal 'staying out of trouble' may be in danger of going to hell. Jesus says

Anyone who is not with me is against me, and anyone who does not gather in with me throws away.[21]

(3) Can a person go to hell because he has never heard of Jesus?

No, not unless he has deliberately contrived not to hear about Jesus, and has done so against his conscience. However, a person who has never heard about Jesus can go to hell for other reasons. Then, on the contrary, there are people who have heard about Jesus from 'missionaries' who give such a bad example that it is as though *they* had never really heard about Jesus.

[21] Matthew 12: 30.

(4) Can a person who is mentally deficient or insane go to hell?

No—unless it is his own fault that he is in such a state. For example, suppose a normal, healthy person chooses to hate God and shoots out part of his own brain in order to express that hatred. He survives the shooting but becomes mentally deficient. Such a person might go to hell.

(5) Can a poor person go to hell?

Yes, if he chooses to act against his conscience. However, hell is mainly for rich people. Their riches entangle them in a world of corruption. They are subject to far greater temptations—such as the temptation not to think about sharing half their wealth with the poor. Jesus says

> Alas for you who are rich:
> you are having your consolation now.[22]

(6) Can a person in hell choose to remain in hell?

Yes, it is like a person who chooses to eat some noxious dainty by himself rather than join in a feast. Perhaps he regrets his decision but he sticks to it none the less, out of pride. This is irrational but, precisely, the damned are those who choose to make an irrational response to God's love.

The answer I have given to each of the six questions turns on the assumption that 'going to hell' means freely choosing to reject God, and freely choosing to reject God involves going against one's vision of God, one's concept of goodness. Thus 'going to hell' is not a possibility that should be considered in terms of a single religion or a single set of good deeds. Rather, it has to do with the relation between one's will and one's conscience.

Since God is good, he gives everyone a decent chance to go to heaven. Indeed, he expends a great deal of love and energy encouraging us to use our free will to do what is right. One might even say that he woos us as a lover woos his beloved, hoping that she will finally cast aside all pride and throw herself into his arms. None the less, we should not take God's love for granted. People should not be excluded from heaven because they cannot stomach a doctrine which says that some people will be excluded from heaven, but nor should they think they can go on destroying themselves and

[22] Luke 6: 24.

others and then, with all impunity, go and sit at the right hand of God.

Those who believe in God and know something about his love for us are in an excellent position to return that love. Anyone can 'love God' by loving what is right and true but someone who knows God personally can love him more easily. None the less, if we ask whether a religious person can go to hell, the answer is yes. As long as a person is alive, he has libertarian free will which extends to evil.[23]

## VII

Some people confuse their future existence with that of some other being. They tell you, for example, how pleasant it will be for them when they have been absorbed by God. However, if they are really going to be 'absorbed by God', they themselves will no longer exist: only God will exist. Other people express the hope that they will be reincarnated as a higher, non-human being, without realising that such a reincarnation would mean that they would be *replaced* by the higher being, they themselves ceasing to exist. Again, there is sometimes talk about a future existence which is so thin and ghost-like that nothing in it could reasonably be called human, so that any human who became a ghost in this sense would no more be his former self than the dirt and water which become a carrot remain dirt and water. To survive death as a medium's mist is not to survive at all but merely to provide something useful for the survival of some other being. The ghost will live because I have ceased to live.

To start with, then, let us be clear that for, say, Smith's immortality, it is Smith's own future self which is at stake, not something else's. Since Smith is a being who is temporal, normally has a body, thinks and has a conscience, and since it is *Smith* (not someone else) who, I claim, is immortal, it follows that Smith's immortal life will be temporal, he will normally have a body, he will think, and he will be able to discern good and evil.

Assuming, then, that Smith (and not someone else) will go to

[23] Hebrews 6: 4–8.

heaven, we can make some reasonable conjectures about what he will do there. Having always delighted in the mountains and the stars, Smith will have his mansion in the hills by a long, thin waterfall which he will name 'Grace'. There he will have a fresher, more intimate friendship with God, free from the confusion and obscurity of this fallen world. He will 'see God', and that will be his greatest joy. Moreover, Smith will not only see God: he will also talk and sing and dance with him—and the other saints. For the second greatest joy in heaven will be the friendship with those who love God. With Abraham, Smith can recall his travels in the Middle East; with Daniel he can discuss the difficulties of finding the truth in an academic environment which rejects God; with Justin Martyr he can find new expression for the one true philosophy; with Clare and Francis, he will go for rambles, picking flowers; with John of the Cross he will contemplate the fiery majesty of God; with Mary he will find beauty in the smallest grains of dust.

Perhaps there will be saints whom Smith will have to forgive, and those who will have to forgive him. This he will do graciously, knowing the sad constraints of our past. If his ex-wife is in heaven, she will be a saint like other saints, worthy of all his respect and love. She will be as he dreamed she was when he first fell in love with her. If his son, whom he has not seen for so long, chooses the life of Christ then he will once again hug his father, and they will once again play together—although they may both be the same eternal age!

What of those who are not in heaven? If certain friends or relatives are not there, will Smith miss them? God himself would prefer that these friends and relatives had chosen to accept his love. Even in his infinite joy, God regrets that they chose to put their own view of the world above what they once knew was right. But God is not unhappy that they now have what they chose to have. He created them to respect their decisions and if they decide to live without the truth then the misery of its absence is justly theirs. Smith, too, will accept their sentence, the consequence of their deeds, for such is the nature of love—on a libertarian view—that it is freely given or freely withheld, and those who withhold it are to be left to their liberty.

Perhaps Smith's third greatest joy in heaven will be doing mathematics! Smith always had a passion for the subject, and since he will still be Smith in heaven, he may still carry on with it.

Against this idea, one may object that Smith will soon enough become bored with mathematics. For any mathematical proof of any interest is less than, say, 1000 pages long. Given at most 1000 different letters and mathematical symbols and at most 10 000 spaces for them on a printed page, there is an upper limit of $1000^{10^7}$ proofs one could print in 1000 pages. And they could all be discovered in a finite amount of time simply by writing out all the possible things one could write in 1000 pages and then throwing away the jibberish, retaining only what makes mathematical sense. Thus in, say, a mere $1000^{10^7}$ years all that is of interest in mathematics can be done. For the rest of eternity, mathematics will be trivial or boring.

The above argument rests on two premisses which may be questioned. The first is that there is an upper limit on the number of pages in a proof of interest. The second is that once we have discovered all the proofs in mathematics capable of being written down in 1000 or fewer printed pages, we shall never forget them. To the first premiss one can object that in heaven our minds will be clearer and more powerful, so that there will be no limit on the size of a proof we might find worthwhile knowing. The mathematics can become as long and complicated as you like, and it will still bring Smith joy. To the second premiss, one can object that, if it brings us joy to do so, it may well be possible to forget certain things, even in heaven. Forgetting mathematical proofs and then rediscovering them would be pointless if the object of mathematics were simply to build up a collection of proofs but, precisely, the object of mathematics is not this but rather to touch a kind of transcendent beauty, to experience in the surprise discovery of some theorem the truth who is God. Discovering a mathematical proof for the second time need not be pointless, any more than being kind to someone for the second time is pointless. There is no reason, therefore, to think that mathematics will ever cease to give Smith joy. And the same may be said of music, dance, games, or poetry.

I may be accused of being too much of a concretist in regard to heaven. Heaven, it may be objected, will be much more splendid than we mortals can ever hope to imagine. All of the good things of earth will be replaced by inconceivably better things.

I disagree. God promises not only to create a new heaven but also a new earth. His original creation is a good one—a *very* good one—

and, although it must be freed of sin, God is not going to do away with it but remake it. We human beings, created in his image, are splendid beings and the universe would lack a distinct beauty without us. Thus it is that we shall exist with our new bodies on the new earth, not as different creatures but as ourselves and hence with the good things of this world which go with us. To say that everything will be replaced by what is much better is to say that God's original creation is only second-rate, that the good things which we now admire and hold precious are really not worth so much. But God created this world good, and he has redeemed it from evil. He has taught us that there are many things in it which must be valued: sun and stars, art and icons, song and human smiles. In the Bible, at any rate, we are taught that there is a resurrection of the body, a future new earth, a jewel-studded city, and a river of life. To replace our wicked 'hearts of stone', God will give us not 'invisible hearts' but 'hearts of flesh'.[24] Besides, if the future were so radically different from this present life, so much more 'spiritual', how should we say that it was *our* future life? If I am going to do and experience things that are unimaginably higher than those I now do and experience, how will it really be me who is doing them? For I am a human being, not an angel, and if I became an angel, I would cease to exist, just as wood ceases to exist when it becomes fire and ashes. Of course, I shall be different in heaven: I shall be pure and kind and free of worry. But I shall still be me, valuing the things which God teaches me to value, and therefore, since it *is* heaven, having those things which I now value, thanks to God's teaching. Perhaps there will not really be a 'banquet of rich food, a banquet of fine wines', but there will be hands to hold, feet to dance, lips to kiss, brains to think, and many other good things which God has already given to us in this present world.

[24] Ezekiel 11: 19.

# 8

# Revelation

A WOMAN went travelling in a far distant country. At home was a man who wanted to marry her. Finally, she decided to call him up and propose. The man was delighted, and they set a date for the wedding. She promised to return as soon as possible.

Unfortunately, the telephone operator was a clever sadist. He noted the man's number and, disguising his voice to sound like the woman, he called him and told him the wedding was off. The man sensed there was something queer about the call but it threw him into torment.

The above story is meant to suggest some of the difficulties God has in communicating with us. In this chapter we assume that there is a wholly good, omnipotent God who created us human beings and wishes to have a personal relationship with us. In particular, he wishes to communicate with us, and he wishes us to know that it is he who is communicating. We shall explore some of the obstacles God faces in this project, and we shall consider some of the strategies he may adopt to overcome them. We shall also consider the problem of what we ought to do to increase our chances of identifying God as the author of those communications which really stem from him.

From the outset, we should note that God's communicating with humanity has to do with libertarian free will. As we shall explain, this is because the purpose of his communicating is to establish a personal love relationship with us. If God were merely trying to impart information, he could accomplish his goal by simply implanting that information in us. If what he wanted us to know was some proposition $p$ then he could easily cause us to view $p$ as a self-evident truth. If he liked, he could also make us know that some other truth $q$ was a good reason for $p$'s being true. The object of God's communicating, however, is not primarily to teach us facts. It is to enter into a personal relationship with us. Hence, to achieve his end, God must allow us to receive his communications in such a way that we shall become friends with him. In particular, he must show the sort of respect for our reason that will allow us to evaluate these communications in a libertarian mode, and to respond to them with a freely given gratitude and intimacy. It is sometimes said that God does not simply show us the whole truth because that would leave no room for faith. To this remark it should be added that the faith is important because it is an essential ingredient in the love relationship. Part of loving someone is trusting in what they say, and trusting them. In the first chapter we argued that 'genuine' reason and love involve a libertarian free will which extends to evil. One of the corollaries of this is that if God is to 'talk' with us as one friend to another, he must leave us the option of taking what he says in a careless or even perverse manner. Because God wishes to converse with us in order to love and be loved, he must leave us free to evaluate his messages as we would those of any lover. When a lover sends a message to his beloved there is a risk. This is especially true if they do not yet know each other well. For the beloved may misinterpret the message, or he may show it to his friend to laugh at, or he may simply imagine that it was written by some friend for a joke. This is true of human love-letters and it is also true of divine love-letters.

In the first section of this chapter we describe the problem of communication from God's point of view. In the second section we assume that there is a devil, and we look at some stratagems he might employ to defeat the proposed communication. In the third section we ask what we humans might do to increase the probability of correctly identifying divine communications. Finally, in the fourth section, we examine an example of revelation. In all this we assume that the communications are subject to libertarian free will: the 'rules' preclude the possibility of it being determined that a particular communication succeed.

I

It is only thanks to his omnipotence that God might possibly succeed in building a love relationship with someone like Professor Smith. God is infinite. God is enthusiastically finite. God is a spirit. Smith finds it hard to love anyone without firm young flesh. God is perfectly good. Smith's only goodness is that he occasionally ceases to resist God's grace. Indeed, the differences between God and Smith are so vast that it would be a wonder if God could get as far as convincing Smith that he would *like* to have a friendship with him. How, then, is God to set out some plan whereby—unless Smith uses his free will to resist God's love for ever—God can eventually bring Smith to enjoy a love relationship with him? In particular, how can God reveal himself to Smith in such a way that Smith will come to love and trust God, and to become a loving and trustworthy human being? I suggest that God might adopt any or all of the following strategies in order to communicate with human beings.

## (1) Build communication aids into creation

If one of God's ends in creating the universe is to build love relationships with human beings then one thing he might do is to design human beings, in particular, and the universe, in general, so that human beings would more easily come to a knowledge of their creator. For example, God might give human beings a conscience that would not merely help them lead a rational, social existence but would also help them glimpse something of the divine beauty. As another example, God might fill the universe with countless types of creatures, each inspiring wonder in human beings, and leading human beings to consider the idea that such creatures must have a creator. It would not be surprising if, as Calvin says, God

not only sowed in men's minds that seed of religion of which we have spoken but revealed himself and daily discloses himself in the whole workmanship of the universe.[1]

In the words of Ben Sira, 'he put his own light in their hearts to show them the magnificence of his works'.[2]

Of course, there are limits as to how much God can reveal himself through nature. First, nature is finite but God is infinite. Second, guilt and fear may cause human beings to repress any sense of the divine beauty around them. Third, the universe shows forth the glory of God especially in so far as it is ordered; yet the more it

---

[1] John Calvin, *Institutes of the Christian Religion*, trans. Ford Lewis Battles (Philadelphia: The Westminster Press, 1960), 51–2.
[2] Ecclesiasticus 17: 8. See also Romans 1: 20.

is ordered, the more human beings can appreciate it merely in terms of 'laws of nature'—without lifting their minds to God.

## (2) Raise up prophets

If someone chooses to seek God and to become his servant then it does not violate their free will if God reveals himself to them in such a way that they are convinced that he exists and they can no longer doubt the nature of his intentions. For although that person may no longer be able to exercise libertarian free will seriously to question a 'word from God', this is only on account of their own original, freely made decision. In certain cases, then, without ceasing to respect libertarian free will and the good things for which it is a prerequisite, God can reveal very specific truths to people—and have them repeat those truths to others.[3]

Of course, free will is only one of several possible obstacles to such revelations. Even if the potential prophet is fully willing to come to know God and to share his knowledge with others, there is still, for example, the question of whether it is *appropriate* for God to use 'supernatural' means to reveal himself. Being omnipotent, God could easily produce, say, audible Hebrew sentences, and say the sort of things that would convince the willing seeker of God that it was God himself who spoke. God could tell the seeker some secret details of people's lives, or give an exact description of a political event that would occur in the near future. These things might not *entail* that the invisible Hebrew speaker was God—a sceptic could reasonably challenge this—but they could well suffice to lead the seeker in question to the correct conclusion that it was God who was talking. One might, however, judge that God, although he *could* produce audible Hebrew, simply should *not* do so. For if God creates a natural order then his providence should uphold this order. God should not undermine his creation with petty miracles. If God 'raises up prophets' then he should do so merely by arranging his creation in such a way that the potential prophet is somehow 'influenced' to believe and to say the right things. Any direct intervention on God's part would be in-appropriate. Moreover, if God did speak to prophets in audible

[3] See George Mavrodes, *Revelation in Religious Belief* (Philadelphia: Temple University Press, 1988), 125–6.

Hebrew, he would merely cause confusion. The mentally ill, the machiavellian prince, the intolerant heresiarch, the wandering mountebank, and the simple rogue can all *say* that God speaks audible words to them, and so, if that is to be the nature of God's revelation to prophets, the prophets would be competing with a farrago of falsehood, and their listeners would not know who to believe.

The question, then, is this: in raising up prophets, should God use 'supernatural' communication tools—such as audible Hebrew, visions, or burning bushes—or should he confine himself to a more subtle approach which, out of respect for nature, does not rely on specially caused 'signs and wonders'? I claim that if God wishes to communicate fairly specific information to a prophet then the first alternative is the only one. For example, suppose God wishes to tell the prophet, 'I forgive you for having committed adultery. You have repented of this and now is the time to stop grieving over the damage you caused that person and pay more attention to your children.' We shall designate this communication by the letter '$q$'. Now if God is to communicate $q$ without disturbing the natural order of things then he must subtly arrange the circumstances so that the prophet comes to believe that God is telling him $q$. Assuming that what God does can be expressed in a proposition, there must be a proposition $p$ such that

> (i) without violating any law of nature, God can make it the case that $p$

and

> (ii) if $p$ were the case then the prophet would be likely to believe that God was communicating $q$.

However, it is not clear that there is such a proposition $p$. Even if, thanks to the statistical aspect of natural laws, God can occasionally intervene in such a way that they are not actually violated, it is not at all obvious that he could do this in such a way as to set up a situation in which our prophet would be likely to believe that God was communicating $q$. Moreover, even if God could set up such a situation, the prophet might simply choose not to believe that God was, in those circumstances, communicating $q$. For although our prophet is open to God, he knows that not every communication which apparently comes from God really comes from God. Perhaps the prophet responds by saying, 'this is the sort of situation that God, or the devil, or my unconscious might bring about if any of them wanted me to forget my sin and pay more attention to my children—and it would be rash for me to conclude that it is God who is the author of this situation.' Part of the problem is that, since the situation is so 'natural', it is ambiguous. In a supernatural conversation with God, the prophet could ask questions and be reassured in various ways that $q$ was really God's message to him. However, if the regular pattern of nature is maintained the prophet may well wonder if the situation is not just some coincidence. In short, if God wants to build a relationship with a prophet by means of sharing specific information, it will be more efficient to make use of certain 'signs and wonders'.

On the other hand, God will not have an easy time communicating with us even if he does use signs and wonders (e.g. audible Hebrew, visions, burning bushes). For, as everyone knows, these may well come from an active imagination or from a clever enemy. To some extent this possibility is a good thing. If a sign-and-wonder approach left no room for anyone to doubt then it would violate the free will of those who, unlike the prophet, were not yet open to God's love. Because of this possibility, however, a signs-and-wonders approach will not work unless God produces signs and wonders that cannot easily be replicated. He must work 'miracles' which would be very hard or even impossible to bring about by natural means. Nor is this the end of it. As the prophet realises, an enemy might perform a wonder which everyone (incorrectly) believes can only be performed by God, and God might perform a wonder which some people (incorrectly) believe non-divine beings can perform. The fact that a communication is backed by an alleged wonder does not have any precise implications for its authorship.

In spite of the above difficulties, I think that God still has good reasons to adopt a striking (but not overwhelming) signs-and-wonders strategy in raising up prophets and having them convey his message to others: (i) people would expect an omnipotent creator to use signs and wonders, and so they would be less likely to identify him as the author of his messages if he did not; (ii) since it is difficult to perform wonders, the use of wonders as a partial guarantee of divine communications would discourage at least a few of the would-be false prophets; (iii) using supernatural means,

God would be able to reveal himself to the prophet in all the detail allowed by human language.

Finally, in reply to the objection that in performing signs and wonders God would violate the patterns which he himself instilled in nature, we may point out that if the whole purpose of creation is to build a love relationship between God and his rational creatures then there is a higher 'law' at work—the 'law' of love—in harmony with which God can fittingly interrupt the usual workings of the universe. The patterns we normally observe are a mere means to an end.

### (3) Produce a book containing revelation

Another way God might reveal himself in such a way as to befriend human beings would be to write them a love-letter. Since a more lengthy love-letter would tend to reduce the chances of misunderstanding, God might actually stretch his love-letter out into a book.

This book might be published in any number of ways. God might simply create it *ex nihilo*. Copies would suddenly appear on the desks of all the rulers of the world, each in the language of that ruler. A second possibility would be to dictate the book to a prophet who would then preach and proclaim it. God would presumably have the prophet correct any spelling mistakes, and the book would certainly not contain any grammatical errors. A third possibility would be for God to act in history in such a way that a whole collection of prophets, poets, editors, translators, and copyists would eventually produce a book containing what God wanted it to contain. If, along the way, some editor or copyist had added something God did not want then God would act so that a future editor or copyist would be inclined to change the text, making it more to God's liking. If the change was made, God would then arrange the loss of the earlier versions of the text. After a few centuries, in spite of a number of misuses of free will on the part of various editors or copyists, the desired book would be produced, and God would then set about conserving it. Note that such a book might change a little over time and still say what God wanted to say. Finally, a fourth way in which God might publish his book would be to delegate the task to various prophets, editors, and translators. Although in some sense inspired, the work would be a human product. As such, it might contain much error but, hopefully, it would more or less convey the message of God's love.

Before we try to decide which of the above four publishing tactics God would be likely to adopt, we should consider how God might not only publish his book but also convince people that he was its author or originator. It is not enough that he write, 'this book is by God', for any book can claim that it is written by God. Indeed, there are many 'holy books' in the world, each claiming a divine origin, and, to add to the confusion, some even contain parts of others. There is a dispute among Christians as to whether the Bible contains sixty-six or seventy-three books.

To ensure that many of us accept God's book as really coming from God, there are a number of things he might do: (i) he could centre his book on prophecy, the prophets having already manifested divine signs and wonders; (ii) he could make any open-minded person who read the book experience a 'feeling that can be born only of heavenly revelation';[4] (iii) he could designate a succession of prophets who would each proclaim that this and this alone was God's book; (iv) he could give his book a consistency and accuracy which would stand up to any scientific or historical test imposed upon it by scholars; (v) he could include in his book some information which would not be accessible to any human being at the time at which the book was written, but which human beings could verify later on (e.g. a detailed account of a future contingent event); (vi) he could include moral teachings which, although exalted, would accord with the conscience of many human beings. No doubt there are other possibilities too—but in every case God must not actually impose the knowledge of his authorship upon people in such a way as would violate their free will. Respecting their autonomy, God must not overwhelm them with the truth but confine himself to giving them evidence for it.

Since the object of his book would be to build up a personal love relationship with the reader, we may suppose that God would be likely to use that method of publication most conducive to this end. For example, it is unlikely that he would simply make his book appear on the desks of all the rulers of the world. First, that would take away from free will: we would almost *have* to believe in the

[4] Calvin, *Institutes of the Christian Religion*, p. 80.

supernatural. Second, it would seem like an imposition: 'read, know and obey this, the absolute truth!' In order to build up a love relationship with humanity, God might be better off adopting a strategy whereby human beings participate in the production of the book. He and they would come to a close communion of ideas if God could consult with them about the text, and if he could express his ideas in terms of their experiences. A greater intimacy could be achieved if they were brought in as co-authors. Better than a single love-letter would be a whole series of love-letters back and forth from God to humanity. Thus in writing the book God should not use dictation—as if the accuracy of the information were the only important thing—but participation—because the goal of the book is a partnership.[5] Again, for the same reason, it will not do if God leaves the writing of his book wholly up to us. Just as dictation is too one-sidedly divine, so delegation is too one-sidedly human. If this book is to build up a real friendship between God and man, it should be co-authored. It is, of course, God's book rather than, say, a mystic's book about God, and so it is appropriate if God has a veto over what goes in it but, none the less, human beings should contribute to its writing in such a way that its purpose is furthered, namely, the friendship of God and humanity. God would thus be advised to use the third option for publishing his book.

There are, of course, limits as to how much God can reveal himself in a book. For one thing, many people will write books which other people will (mistakenly) think come from God. Some people will hold that God has written more than one book, and they will hold this whether or not the allegedly divine books are inconsistent with each other. Other people will claim that God's book is now scattered in many books, that it consists of their favourite chapter from Plato, their favourite verse from Wordsworth, and so on. If God does not limit his book to statements actually preached by prophets, people will wonder how much of the accompanying 'poetry' is really 'inspired'. If God sets up a chain of bishops to tell people which book is his, then there may be some people who will argue from that very book that the bishops are demons in disguise. A book can function as part of God's revelation but it will not by itself resolve the 'communication gap' between God and sinful humanity.

[5] See 1 Corinthians 1: 9.

## (4) Incarnate

Another way in which God might reveal himself in such a manner as to draw us to accept his love would be to participate in our history. He might find a way of playing a role in key historical events which, although it did not undermine our free will, none the less enabled us to identify and relate to him. Indeed, if it is possible, he might open the way to intimacy with us by himself becoming a human being and living among us.

There are difficulties with this idea. Even if it is not actually impossible for God to become a human being, many people will quite naturally think it is, and they will reject any prophet who claims to be divine. Again, many people will hold that God could not be a human being unless it was as a mighty king; however, if God comes as a mighty king, he will undermine our dignity as the forgers of our own destiny. Another problem is that some people will misunderstand the lofty ideas God will express in his ordinary life and speech—and they will dismiss him as a conceited visionary.

If God chooses to reveal himself via an incarnation, he will have to accept the risks and limitations involved. On the other hand, an incarnation would create unique possibilities for divine-human friendship, and thus God might be well advised to try it.

## II

Having looked at the problem of revelation from God's point of view, let us now assume that there is a devil, and let us ask what strategies he ought to adopt to defeat God's revelation, and thus to defeat its primary goal, namely, a fellowship with human beings.

First, the devil might try to distract people from God's revelation. This can be done by providing enticing 'pomps and vanities'. If people might reflect on God in the quiet darkness of their rooms, the devil can prevent this with the help of glamorous television shows, frenetic rock music, or alcoholic anodynes. Of course, he should be careful that human beings do not have so much of these amusements that they simply become bored by them.

Second, the devil might attempt to block God's revelation by main force. If people are drawn to God by meditating on the stars, the devil can fill the skies with neon light and smog. If people listen to a prophet, the devil can arrange to have him killed. Of course, if the prophet is God himself, strange and dreadful things might occur if the devil had him killed. Perhaps in that case the devil would be advised to send dreams in hopes of preventing the prophet's death.[6]

Third, the devil might create counterfeits. He can raise up false prophets or write misleading holy books. He must, however, be careful not to make his counterfeits so like God's true revelation that those who are deluded by them will actually come to know a great deal about God. It would be dreadful for the devil if his false religion F was actually such a good copy of the true religion T that sincere adherents of F could achieve almost as much insight and holiness as sincere adherents of T.

Fourth, the devil might inspire certain academics to attack God's revelation. There will be sceptics to question it, wits to ridicule it, and savants to claim it is outdated. Here the devil must be careful lest these academics provoke equally clever friends of God to write intellectually superior refutations.

Fifth, the devil might advertise in such a way that people associate God with pain or boredom. The devil would be wise to obtain good television coverage for 'Christian' preachers who emphasise dutiful suffering, sexual repression, or hell fire. Here the danger is that the preachers will rebel against their gloomy religions, seek relief with prostitutes, and discredit their ministries.

Sixth, the devil might undermine revelation by watering down or destroying the very concepts in which it is expressed. He might try to have people associate 'love' with pleasure, 'authority' with repression, 'retribution' with revenge, or 'sin' with error. The devil might consider the possibility of keeping people illiterate, but a more sophisticated tactic would be to have them read just well enough to fill their minds with second-rate romances or science-fiction stories filled with vague ideas about luck, karma, or moral relativism.

If God really is trying to reveal himself to us in such a way as to befriend us, and if there really is a devil trying to prevent this, then we might expect the devil to adopt some or all of the above tactics.

---

[6] Matthew 27: 19.

## III

From the human point of view, the problem is to know when something really is a revelation from God and when it is a trick of the unconscious or an error made by another human being or a deception of the devil. No doubt God can find a way of communicating with anyone who sincerely desires to know God, but part of this sincere desire ·includes a willingness to examine purported revelation and judge upon its origin.

In *Divine Revelation and the Limits of Historical Criticism*, Abraham argues that theologians need not rule out the possibility of God's direct intervention in history.[7] Dealing with revelation in connection with prophecy, he suggests seven criteria for judging whether an alleged prophecy really is a message from God. According to Abraham, we should examine

(1) the moral and spiritual character of the putative agent of God;
(2) the effect for good that the experience of receiving revelation brings about, e.g. an increase in penitence, peace, humility, spiritual power, and authority;
(3) the inner certainty and conviction disclosed by the prophet as to the origin of his message;
(4) the inner consistency and overall coherence of the prophet's message;
(5) the degree of continuity between what is agreed to be known already about God and the content of the prophet's message;
(6) the capacity of the putative revelation to illuminate and deepen what is known of God from elsewhere;
(7) the degree of harmony between the content of the message and the course of events that are its context.[8]

Abraham also mentions miracles. He does not think that they are foolproof warrants for revelation but they can function to create a context harmonious with 'the content of the message'.[9]

Abraham's (4), (5), and (6) have to do with consistency. If the prophet is speaking truly then his message does not contradict itself and it does not contradict any known facts. For example, if the

---

[7] William Abraham, *Divine Revelation and the Limits of Historical Criticism* (Oxford: Oxford University Press, 1982), 187.

[8] Ibid., p. 38. See also John Locke, *An Essay Concerning Human Understanding*, 37th edn. (London: William Tegg, 1875), book iv, ch. 18, sect. 8.

[9] Abraham, *Divine Revelation and the Limits of Historical Criticism*, p. 38.

prophet 'reveals' that event $E$ will occur within $t$ years and it does not, then he is not a true prophet. As we read in Deuteronomy:

When a prophet speaks in the name of Yahweh and the thing does not happen and the word is not fulfilled, then it has not been said by Yahweh. The prophet has spoken presumptuously.[10]

Again—even if the prophet has correctly prophesied the future (or worked some other wonder)—if he contradicts some previously revealed truth (e.g. he says that some God other than Yahweh should be worshipped) then he is not a true prophet.[11] The underlying presupposition here is that God will communicate only true things. Since no two true things contradict each other, a message that is really from God will not contradict itself or anything known to be true.

An interesting corollary to the consistency criteria is the view that God's book of revelation (if any) will be entirely self-consistent and consistent with known scientific truths. It is not a far jump from Abraham's (4), (5), and (6) to the view that, properly understood, God's book is inerrant. However, it may not be wise for a human being to reject as God's revelation every book with any inconsistency or falsehood in it. For the devil would know that we put a great deal of stock in the consistency criteria, and he would do his utmost to corrupt the text of any divine book. For example, he might try to distract copyists or translators in such a way that they would make at least a few minor mistakes, mistakes which would introduce error or inconsistency into the text.

A related danger is the danger of too readily accepting an apparent inconsistency as a real logical contradiction. Suppose that the Bible really is God's book. Suppose that Smith notices that, according to Matthew 26: 34, Jesus told Peter, 'before the cock crows, you will have disowned me three times'. From this Smith infers that the third disowning cannot occur after the first cock crow (assuming the prophecy is correct). However, in Mark 14: 71–2, Smith learns that the third disowning occurs immediately before the *second* cock crow. The passage reads

he started cursing and swearing, 'I do not know the man you speak of.' And at once the cock crowed for the second time.

[10] Deuteronomy 18: 22.
[11] Deuteronomy 13: 2–4.

If Smith immediately concludes that there is an inconsistency and throws the Bible in the dustbin, he is being a bit hasty. A prophecy is not always easy to understand. Jonah proclaimed that Nineveh would be overthrown in forty days and it was not.[12] However, this does not imply that Jonah was a false prophet because the prophecy meant, and was understood by the Ninevites to mean, that their city would be overthrown in forty days *if they did not repent*. The consistency criteria must not be applied in a completely wooden manner—as if prophets gave instructions to computers rather than putting people in touch with the living God. The consistency criteria should not be understood in such a way that the prophecy taken in a completely unintelligent, literal manner must match the facts; rather they should be understood to mean that the prophecy taken in the way in which an intelligent hearer of the prophecy would take it must match the facts.

As for Jesus' prophecy of the three denials, one can show that there was no real contradiction by displaying the following 'consistency model'. Peter was bragging to Jesus about his fidelity. Jesus contradicted him. Jesus said:

> No, Peter, your so-called fidelity will not last you until lunchtime tomorrow. It will not even last until breakfast. In truth I tell you, this very night, before the cock crows, you will have disowned me three times. I can give you a precise prophecy: this very night, before the cock crows twice, you will have disowned me three times. You think you are so faithful! But I tell you, Peter, by the time the cock crows today you will have denied three times that you know me.

The fact that Jesus might well have said this shows that there is no contradiction. Smith should not assume that Jesus would always speak in an evenly precise manner. There is no reason why Jesus, speaking roughly, should not use the expression 'before the cock crows' to mean, say, 'before the cock has finished crowing'. Smith should recall that Jesus was fond of a poetical way of expressing himself. Jesus did not talk to his disciples with the sort of exactness needed to give information to a computer.

When presented with some allegedly divine revelation, a human being would do best by evaluating it according to a number of

---

[12] Jonah 3.

different criteria—and not taking any one criterion too narrowly. Relying on more than one criterion would make the conclusion more solid. Not taking any one criterion too narrowly would prevent him from rejecting something hastily. The criteria provided by Abraham would no doubt serve well. Moreover, if the human being knew that God himself had come as a certain prophet then that human being might especially examine

> (8) the degree of harmony between the message and the teaching of the divine prophet;
> (9) the degree of harmony between the message and the teaching of any religious body set up by the divine prophet to safeguard and promulgate his teaching.

Finally, we should note that if the prophet reveals something about God himself, we human beings need not expect that the message can be checked—or even understood—in the usual, objective, 'scientific' manner by any normal adult. As Alston has pointed out, it may well be the case that

(A) God is too different from created beings, too "wholly other", for us to be able to grasp any regularities in His behaviour.
(B) We can only attain the faintest, sketchiest, and most insecure grasp of what God is like.
(C) God has decreed that a human being will be aware of His presence in any clear and unmistakable fashion only when certain special and difficult conditions are satisfied.[13]

## IV

In this section we look at an alleged revelation, namely, the Christian doctrine of the Trinity. According to this doctrine, the unique divine person is, in some sense, three 'persons'. The 'Son' is 'eternally begotten' of the 'Father', and the 'Holy Spirit' 'proceeds from' the 'Father'. According to most thinkers (e.g. Aquinas) this

---

[13] William P. Alston, 'Christian Experience and Christian Belief', in *Faith and Rationality*, ed. Alvin Plantinga and Nicholas Wolterstorff (Notre Dame: University of Notre Dame Press, 1983), 129.

doctrine is not meant to imply that there are three divine beings but according to some (e.g. Swinburne) it does.[14]

How is one to react to this alleged revelation? There are at least four possibilities.

## (1) Treat the Trinity as incomprehensible

If something is a revelation from God it may well be startling or difficult to understand. God is transcendent and human beings will likely find him overwhelming or unimaginable. The doctrine of the Trinity is a good illustration of this point, one might say. If it is, strictly speaking, logically incoherent, that simply means that the logic with which we conceive the universe is inadequate. If it sounds like nonsense to us, that simply means that we have an opportunity for submitting our reason to God by means of affirming this apparent nonsense in our creeds.

To this approach I object that if God is really behind the doctrine of the Trinity, thus understood—that is, if God has really revealed what we can only take as a piece of nonsense—then he favours shibboleths over reason, and enjoys creating occasions for bitter logomachies. If God respects the reason he gave us then we cannot suppose that incomprehensible mysteries constitute part of his revelation. If the doctrine of the Trinity really is incomprehensible, then it is at best not a revelation from God but some garbled copy of a divine communication.

## (2) Treat the Trinity as a human invention

The doctrine of the Trinity may serve all sorts of psychological, sociological, or philosophical functions.[15] There are probably many ways of explaining how it might have emerged whether or not God revealed it. Its logic is not in what it says but in what it

---

[14] Aquinas, *Summa Contra Gentiles*, book IV, ch. 8, sect. 1, and book IV, ch. 9, sect. 6; Richard Swinburne, 'Could there be More than One God?', *Faith and Philosophy*, 5 (1988), 234.

[15] See, for example, C. G. Jung, 'A Psychological Approach to the Dogma of the Trinity', in vol. 11 of *The Collected Works of C. G. Jung*, trans. R. F. C. Hull (New York: Pantheon Books, 1958), 107–200.

helps people accomplish when, say, they *try* to understand what it says.

One might object to this that God is not behaving in a very loving manner if he allows a large number of his worshippers to mistake a purely human symbol for an objective description of his nature. If God helps those who believe in him then, surely, he guides their leaders in such a way that what they take to be 'core' revelations really contain messages from God about how he or the universe really is.

Perhaps a better point to make is that the fact that a doctrine is human, revealing something of humanity, does not exclude its also being of divine origin. God made man in his image, and the doctrine of the Trinity may reveal human as well as divine attributes. Indeed, Augustine and others have often taken it that way, finding three components of the human soul to mirror the three 'persons'.[16]

## (3) Treat the Trinity as a revelation of tritheism

Let $D$ be the predicate 'is a divine being'. Perhaps what God is trying to tell us in the various New Testament passages hinting at the Trinity is that there are exactly three divine beings. In logic:

$$\exists x \, \exists y \, \exists z \, (Dx \,\&\, Dy \,\&\, Dz \,\&\, x \neq y \,\&\, x \neq z \,\&\, y \neq z \\ \&\, \forall w \, (Dw \Rightarrow w = x \text{ V } w = y \text{ V } w = z) \,).$$

God does not come right out and say this lest people who are inclined to polytheism think that they can worship any god of their choosing. None the less, on this view, this is the real truth, and Muslims are right when they say that Christianity is not a kind of monotheism.

There are a number of objections to this intepretation of the Trinity. In the Old Testament (which Christians take to be part of God's revelation), someone called 'Yahweh' reveals that he is the one and only divine being. For example, in Isaiah 44: 6 we read:

Thus says Yahweh, Israel's king, Yahweh Sabaoth, his redeemer: I am the first and the last; there is no God except me.

---

[16] Augustine, *De Trinitate*, ix. 3–5.

Again, in Deuteronomy 4: 39 we read:

Yahweh is the true God, in heaven above as on earth beneath, he and no other.

Throughout the Old Testament, moreover, Yahweh is referred to as the 'Most High'.[17] He is not just one of several equally high Gods but rather a unique absolute sovereign.

This point of view is continued in the New Testament, where Yahweh is referred to by the title 'the Father'. In Ephesians 4: 5, Yahweh is called the 'one God and Father of all, over all'. In 1 Corinthians 8: 6 we read:

there is only one God, the Father from whom all things come.

In Romans 3: 29–30 Paul writes:

Do you think God is the God only of the Jews, and not of gentiles too? Most certainly of gentiles too, since there is only one God.

Thus the Bible does say that there is exactly one God, and one of his proper names is 'Yahweh', and one of his titles is 'the Father'.

The tritheist positions is different. According to the tritheist, there is a second divine being whose proper name is not 'Yahweh' but 'Jesus', and whose title is not 'the Father' but 'the Son'. Moreover, there is also a third God whose title is 'the Holy Spirit'.

Drawing on verses such as those I quoted above, I would conclude that if Jesus is divine then 'Jesus' is a second proper name for the same divine being who is also called 'Yahweh', and if the Son is God then 'the Son' is a second title for the same divine being who also has the title 'the Father'. The different titles may express different aspects of the same entity (the unique God) but they both refer to that one entity, namely, God. The tritheist, however, maintains that there are three divine individuals, one for each of the three titles 'Father', 'Son', and 'Holy Spirit'.

The tritheist position is not consistent with the strict monotheism emphasised in the Old and New Testaments. The tritheist, however, can point to a number of scripture verses which seem to be inconsistent with the position of the strict monotheist. For example, Jesus, who is said to be divine, has a conversation with the Father, also divine, in the Garden of Gethsemane. They seem to be

[17] Genesis 14: 22; Psalms 9: 1–2; Daniel 3: 26; Luke 1: 76. Note that Jesus is called the 'Most High' in the *Gloria*.

in less than perfect agreement about the crucifixion. Now how can this be if 'Jesus' and 'the Father' are just two expressions referring to a single entity? It would make more sense, says the tritheist, to suppose that there are at least two divine beings.[18]

At this point there are two moves one might make. First, one can stand with strict monotheism, and find some way of interpreting passages which may seem to suggest tritheism—interpreting them in such a way as they would be consistent with strict monotheism. For example, one might say that Jesus spoke as he did in the Garden of Gethsemane because his human mind was struggling to give in to his divine mind, or because he wished to teach us how to pray when we are tempted to take the easier but less noble way. Second, one can stand with the tritheist. However, in that case, one is committed to holding that the Bible is inconsistent: it says that there is one God only, and it also says (in passages such as the Garden of Gethsemane passage) that there is more than one God. However, if the Bible says both that there is one God only, and also that there is more than one God, then it fails on the consistency criteria proposed by Abraham. In any case, we showed in Chapter 2 that God is unique.


### (4) Treat the Trinity as a revelation of three divine aspects or roles

If we take a strictly monotheistic stance, we may wish to understand certain dogmas about the Trinity as poetic ways of describing the one God's nature or activity. For example, we may wish to understand a formula like

> The Father is not the Son

to mean that God acts differently in his role as the producer of love and receiver of knowledge than he does in his role as the receiver of love and producer of knowledge. As another example, Christians say that

> The Son was in Mary's womb

but they resist saying

> The Father was in Mary's womb.

---

[18] See C. Stephan Layman, 'Tritheism and the Trinity', *Faith and Philosophy*, 5 (1988), 293. Bible verses ascribing divinity to Jesus are John 1: 1–2: 34; Romans 9: 5; Titus 2: 13; Hebrews 1: 10–12; 1 Peter 4: 11, and 1 John 5: 20.

This may be because they take the first statement to mean

> God, in his role as bringer of truth to humanity, was in Mary's womb

and they take the second statement to mean

> God, in his role as transcendent source of being, was in Mary's womb.

Understood in these ways, the first statement is acceptable but the second is awkward. For 'being in a womb' connotes dependency, whereas 'being the transcendent source of being' connotes the opposite. The associations clash.

On this view, each 'person' of the Trinity is associated with certain aspects or activities of God, perhaps roughly as follows:

1. The Father is God loving himself and being known by himself. The Father is God as the utterly transcendent source of being. When we use 'the Father' as the subject of a sentence, we are to think of God as invisible aseity, source of love, transcendent creator. Thus the predicate of the sentence should not connote anything which clashes with these ideas.

2. The Son (or Word) is God knowing himself and being loved by himself. The Son is God as knower, as producer of truth. When we use 'the Son' as the subject of a sentence, we are to think of God as beloved of God, preacher, light. Thus the predicate of the sentence should not connote anything which clashes with these ideas.

3. The Holy Spirit is God rejoicing in himself, in his love and in his self-knowledge. The Holy Spirit is God the illuminating, God the loved, known, and thereby empowered by God. When we use 'the Holy Spirit' as the subject of a sentence, we are to think of God as spirit, as beloved lover, as empowered power, as illuminated illuminator. Thus the predicate of the sentence should not connote anything which clashes with these ideas.[19]

For a trinitarian formula to be acceptable, it is not enough that it make a true assertion about the being who is the one and only God: it must also 'get the roles right'. It must not predicate of a divine 'person' some property which clashes with the role associated with that 'person'. For example,

> The Father was crucified

---

[19] Aquinas, *Summa Contra Gentiles*, Book IV, chapter 19.

is not acceptable—not because it is false that the Romans crucified the one and only being who is, in fact, God and hence who is, in fact, the Father—but because it was in his role as teacher or revealer of truth that the one and only God was crucified. Hence the acceptable statement is

The Son was crucified.

Note that the fact that the acceptability of a trinitarian statement has to do with a 'harmony of the symbols' does not imply that the Trinity exists only on the level of human imagination. These symbols are tied to a deep, ontological reality. They exist in the mind of God. Even if God had never created the universe, there would still have been a Trinity. God himself would have called himself 'Father', 'Son', and 'Holy Spirit'.[20]

V

We did not, in this chapter, advance a specific position about how God actually does reveal himself to human beings. We did not, for example, argue that Isaiah really was a prophet of God. What we did was to consider various ways in which a personal God who respects our free will *might* reveal himself. We also considered ways in which we humans might react to various alleged revelations (e.g. the doctrine of the Trinity). Our aim was not to show, for example, that Christianity is the one religion God has given to humanity. However, we did show that it would make sense, that it would not be surprising, if God did, in fact, reveal himself in the way Christians claim he has.

[20] Note that my position is not 'Sabellian' since Sabellius held that the three 'persons' are distinguished merely on the basis of salvation history.

# Afterword

ASSUMING that there is a divine being as I have described him and assuming that an important part of our immortal lives turns on our relationship to this divine being, a natural question to ask is 'what religion, if any, should I join?' The answer to this question may be simple but the justification for it is not. The problem of the logical consistency of doctrine is one a philosopher might tackle, but there are many equally pressing problems that lie beyond his scope. To evaluate historical data, one would want a team of historians and statisticians. To evaluate the 'psychological truth' of a religion, its benefits to persons of different cultures, and so forth, one would want a team of psychoanalysts, sociologists, and anthropologists. Since much depends on ancient events recorded in dead languages, a team of archaeologists and linguists would also be useful.

A question like 'which human beings, if any, were also divine?' requires an answer that sifts through the scriptures and histories of many cultures. It is important to know, as a historical fact, whether Jesus or Confucius really claimed to be divine. A statistician is needed to help analyse the significance of miracles or reports of wonders. A theologian is wanted to reflect on whether God incarnate would be likely to proclaim his divinity.

There are many levels at which one can do Philosophy of Religion. One can work at the level where the sceptic tries to undermine all of human language and reason. Here one can criticise, defend, or refine various conceptual systems. One can ask how or if they relate to an external world at all. If there is no external objective reality then, of course, there is no 'God' as we understand that person in the Judeo-Christian tradition.

At a second level, one can argue about the truth of 'naturalism'. Is there agent causation, as seems to be presupposed by many religious teachings (e.g. that God created the world, or that Peter repented of his sin)? Is there a human self which would at least leave open the possibility of personal immortality? Or is it the case that at the most fundamental ontological level there are merely atoms acting out some necessary causality?

At a third level, one can explore the political aspects of religious thought. Is any Bible-based religion intrinsically hostile to an equal sharing of power among all human beings, women and men alike? Does a commitment to a just economic progress imply the use of concepts in which the Christian message cannot be expressed?

And one could mention other 'levels' as well, including the 'level' of this book where we presuppose a two-valued logic realism, adopt a libertarian perspective and, working within the Anglo-American 'analytic tradition', try to see what sense we can make of standard Christian teachings.

# Bibliography

*Books*

Abraham, William, *Divine Revelation and the Limits of Historical Criticism* (Oxford: Oxford University Press, 1982).

Anselm, *Basic Writings*, 2nd edn., trans. S. N. Deane, ed. Charles Hartshorne (La Salle: Open Court, 1962).

—— *Truth, Freedom and Evil: Three Philosophical Dialogues*, trans. and ed. Jasper Hopkins and Herbert Richardson (New York: Harper and Row, 1967).

Aquinas, *Basic Writings of St. Thomas Aquinas*, ed. Anton C. Pegis (New York: Random House, 1945).

—— *Summa Contra Gentiles*, 4 vols., trans. Anton C. Pegis *et al.* 1955 (rpt. London: University of Notre Dame Press, 1975).

Augustine, *Confessions*, trans. F. J. Sheed (London: Sheed and Ward, 1944).

—— *The Problem of Free Choice*, trans. Dom Mark Pontifex (New York: Newman Press, 1955).

—— *The Trinity*, trans. Stephen McKenna (Washington: Catholic University of America Press, 1963).

—— *The Greatness of the Soul*, trans. Joseph M. Colleran (Westminster, Maryland: Newman Press, 1964).

—— *St. Augustin: The Writings against the Manichaeans and against the Donatists*, trans. Richard Stothert *et al.*, vol. iv of *A Select Library of the Nicene and Post-Nicene Fathers of the Christian Church*, 1st ser., ed. Philip Schaff, 1887 (rpt. Grand Rapids, Michigan: Eerdmans, 1979).

—— *Saint Augustin: Anti-Pelagian Writings*, trans. Peter Holmes *et al.*, vol. v of *A Select Library of the Nicene and Post-Nicene Fathers of the Christian Church*, 1st ser., ed. Philip Schaff, 1887 (rpt. Grand Rapids, Michigan: Eerdmans, 1971).

—— *The City of God*, trans. Henry Bettenson, ed. David Knowles (New York: Penguin Books, 1972).

Austin, J. L., *Philosophical Papers*, 3rd edn. (Oxford: Oxford University Press, 1979).

Beauchamp, Tom L., and Childress, James F., *Principles of Biomedical Ethics* (Oxford: Oxford University Press, 1979).

Broderick, John F., *Documents of Vatican Council I* (Collegeville, Minnesota: The Liturgical Press, 1971).

Boyle, Joseph M., *et al.*, *Free Choice* (Notre Dame: University of Notre Dame Press, 1976).

Calvin, John, *Institutes of the Christian Religion*, 2 vols., trans. Ford Lewis Battles, ed. John T. McNeill (London: SCM Press, 1961).

Catherine of Siena, *The Dialogue*, trans. Suzanne Noffke (New York: Paulist Press, 1980).

Denzinger, (ed.), *The Sources of Catholic Dogma*, trans. Roy J. Deferrari (London: B. Herder, 1957).

Fischer, John Martin (ed.), *Moral Responsibility* (Ithaca: Cornell University Press, 1986).

Flood, Raymond, and Lockwood, Michael, *The Nature of Time* (Oxford: Basil Blackwell, 1986).

Foot, Philippa, *Virtues and Vices and Other Essays in Moral Philosophy* (Oxford: Basil Blackwell, 1978).

Freddoso, Alfred J. (ed.), *The Existence and Nature of God* (Notre Dame: University of Notre Dame Press, 1983).

Gardner, Martin, *The Whys of a Philosophical Scrivener* (New York: Quill, 1983).

Geach, Peter, *Providence and Evil* (Cambridge: Cambridge University Press, 1977).

Goodman, Nelson, *Fact, Fiction and Forecast* (London: Athlone Press, 1954).

Gregory of Nyssa, *On the Soul and the Resurrection*, trans. W. Moore, in vol. v of *A Select Library of Nicene and Post-Nicene Fathers of the Christian Church*, 2nd ser., ed. Philip Schaff and Henry Wace (New York: The Christian Literature Company, 1893).

Harré, R., and Madden, E. H., *Causal Powers: A Theory of Natural Necessity* (Oxford: Basil Blackwell, 1975).

Hick, John, *Death and Eternal Life* (Glasgow: William Collins Sons, 1976).

—— *Evil and the God of Love*, 1966 (rpt. Glasgow: William Collins Sons, 1979).

Hintikka, Jaakko, *Knowledge and Belief* (Ithaca: Cornell University Press, 1962).

John of Damascus, 'An Exact Exposition of the Orthodox Faith', in *A Select Library of the Nicene and Post-Nicene Fathers of the Christian Church*, 2nd ser., vol. ix, ed. Philip Schaff (New York: Charles Scribner's Sons, 1899).

Jung, C. G., *The Collected Works of C. G. Jung*, trans. R. F. C. Hull (New York: Pantheon Books, 1960).

Kant, Immanuel, *Critique of Judgment*, trans. Weiner S, Pluhar (Indianapolis: Hackett, 1987).

—— *Critique of Pure Reason*, trans. Norman Kemp Smith (London, Macmillan, 1929).

Kenny, Anthony (ed.), *Aquinas: A Collection of Critical Essays* (London: Macmillan, 1969).

—— *The God of the Philosophers* (Oxford: Clarendon Press, 1979).

—— *Will, Freedom and Power* (Oxford: Basil Blackwell, 1975).

Lewis, C. S., *Voyage to Venus* (London: Pan Books, 1953).

Lewis, David, *Counterfactuals* (Oxford: Basil Blackwell, 1973).

Locke, John, *An Essay Concerning Human Understanding*, 37th edn. (London: William Tegg, 1875).

Lucas, J. R., *The Freedom of the Will* (Oxford: Clarendon Press, 1970).

Mackie, J. L., *The Cement of the Universe* (Oxford: Clarendon Press, 1974).

Mavrodes, George, *Revelation in Religious Belief* (Philadelphia: Temple University Press, 1988).

Molina, Luis de, *On Divine Foreknowledge*, trans. Alfred J. Freddoso (Ithaca: Cornell University Press, 1988).

Morris, Thomas V., *Anselmian Explorations* (Notre Dame: University of Notre Dame Press, 1987).

O'Connor, D. J., *Free Will* (London: Macmillan, 1971).

Parfit, Derek, *Reasons and Persons* (Oxford: Oxford University Press, 1986).

Pike, Nelson, *God and Timelesssness* (New York: Schocken Books, 1970).

Plantinga, Alvin, *God and Other Minds* (Ithaca: Cornell University Press, 1967).

—— *The Nature of Necessity* (Oxford: Oxford University Press, 1974).

Plato, *The Collected Dialogues of Plato*, ed. Edith Hamilton and Huntington Cairns. Bollinger Series LXXI. (New York: Random House, 1961).

Prior, Arthur, N., *Past, Present and Future* (Oxford: Clarendon Press, 1967).

Ross, James F., *Philosophical Theology* (New York: Bobbs-Merrill, 1969).

Shestov, Lev, *Athens and Jerusalem*, trans. Bernard Martin (Athens: Ohio University Press, 1966).

Sorabji, Richard, *Necessity, Cause and Blame* (London: Duckworth, 1980).

Strawson, Galen, *Freedom and Belief* (Oxford: Clarendon Press, 1986).

Swinburne, Richard, *The Coherence of Theism* (Oxford: Clarendon Press, 1977).

—— *The Evolution of the Soul* (Oxford: Clarendon Press, 1986).

—— *The Existence of God* (Oxford: Clarendon Press, 1979).

Thorp, John, *Free Will* (London: Routledge and Kegan Paul, 1980).

Urban, Linwood, and Walton, Douglas N. (eds.), *The Power of God* (New York: Oxford University Press, 1978).

Wansbrough, Henry (gen. ed.), *The New Jerusalem Bible* (New York: Doubleday, 1985).

Wierenga, Edward R., *The Nature of God*, forthcoming.

Wiggins, David, *Sameness and Substance* (Oxford: Basil Blackwell, 1980).
Wilson, Edgar, *The Mental as Physical* (London: Routledge and Kegan Paul, 1979).


*Articles*


Ahern, M. B., 'The Nature of Evil', *Sophia*, 5 (1966), 40–2.
Alston, William P., 'Christian Experience and Christian Belief', in *Faith and Rationality*, ed. Alvin Plantinga and Nicholas Wolterstorff (Notre Dame: University of Notre Dame Press, 1983), 103–34.
Anglin, W. S., 'Backwards Causation', *Analysis*, 41 (1981), 86–91.
—— 'Can God Create a Being He Cannot Control?', *Analysis*, 40 (1980), 220–3.
—— and Goetz, S., 'Evil is Privation', *International Journal for Philosophy of Religion*, 13 (1982), 3–12.
Athenagoras, 'The Resurrection of the Dead', trans. B. P. Pratten, in vol. ii of *The Ante-Nicene Fathers*, ed. Alexander Roberts and James Donaldson (New York: Charles Scribner's Sons, 1925).
Chisholm, Roderick, and Taylor, Richard, 'Making Things to Have Happened', *Analysis*, 20 (1960), 73–8.
Chrzan, Keith, 'Linear Programming and Utilitarian Theodicy', *International Journal for Philosophy of Religion*, 20 (1986), 147–57.
Connell, F. J., 'Double Effect, Principle of', in *New Catholic Encyclopedia*, iv, ed. William J. McDonald (New York: McGraw-Hill, 1967).
Costa, Michael J., 'The Trolley Problem Revisited', *Southern Journal of Philosophy*, 24 (1986), 439–49.
Craig, William Lane, 'Tachyons, Time Travel, and Divine Omniscience', *Journal of Philosophy*, 85 (1988), 135–50.
Dore, Clement, 'Plantinga on the Free Will Defence', *Review of Metaphysics*, 24 (1971), 690–706.
Dummett, Michael, 'Bringing about the Past', *Philosophical Review*, 73 (1964), 338–59.
—— and Flew, A., 'Can an Effect Precede Its Clause?', *Aristotelian Society Supplementary Volume*, 28 (1954), 27–62.
Dunstan, G. R., 'Double Effect', in *Dictionary of Medical Ethics*, ed. A. S. Duncan, G. R. Dunstan, and R. B. Welbourn (London: Darton, Longman & Todd, 1981), 145.
Ehring, Douglas, 'Causal Asymmetry', *Journal of Philosophy*, 79 (1982), 761–74.
Gallois, André, 'Van Inwagen on Free Will and Determinism', *Philosophical Studies*, 32 (1977), 99–105.
—— 'Locke on Causation, Compatibilism and Newcomb's Problem', *Analysis*, 41 (1981), 42–6.

Geach, P. T., 'An Irrelevance of Omnipotence', *Philosophy*, 48 (1973), 327–33.

—— 'Omnipotence', *Philosophy*, 48 (1973), 7–20.

Gödel, K., 'A Remark about the Relationship between Relativity Theory and Idealistic Philosophy', in *Albert Einstein: Philosopher-Scientist*, vol. ii, ed. Paul Arthur Schipp (New York: Harper and Brothers, 1959), 557–62.

Hanink, James G., 'Some Light on Double Effect', *Analysis*, 35 (1975), 147–51.

Harrison, Jonathan, 'Dr. Who and the Philosophers of Time-Travel for Beginners', *Aristotelian Society Supplementary Volume*, 45 (1971), 1–24.

Hasker, W., 'A Refutation of Middle Knowledge', *Nous*, 20 (1986), 545–57.

Helm, Paul, 'Timelessness and Foreknowledge', *Mind*, 84 (1975), 516–27.

—— 'God and Whatever Comes to Pass', *Religious Studies*, 14 (1978), 315–23.

Hoffman, Robert, 'Intention, Double Effect and Single Result', *Philosophy and Phenomenological Research*, 44 (1984), 389–94.

Kane, G. Stanley, 'Evil and Privation', *International Journal for Philosophy of Religion*, 11 (1980), 44.

Layman, C. Stephan, 'Tritheism and the Trinity', *Faith and Philosophy*, 5 (1988), 293.

Locke, Don, 'How to Make a Newcomb Choice', *Analysis*, 38 (1978), 17–23.

Maker, William, 'Augustine on Evil: The Dilemma of the Philosophers', *International Journal for Philosophy of Religion*, 15 (1984), 149–60.

Mangan, Joseph T., 'An Historical Analysis of the Principle of Double Effect', *Theological Studies*, 10 (1949), 41–61.

Mann, William E., 'Ross on Omnipotence', *International Journal for Philosophy of Religion*, 8 (1977), 142–7.

McCall, Storrs, 'Objective Time Flow', *Philosophy of Science*, 43 (1976), 337–62.

McKim, Robert, 'Worlds Without Evil', *International Journal for Philosophy of Religion*, 15 (1984), 161–70.

Micallef, Paul J., 'A Critique of Bernard Haring's Application of the Double Effect Principle', *Laval Theologique et Philosophique*, 38 (1982), 259–63.

Morris, Michael S., Thorne, Kip S., and Yurtsever, Ulvi, 'Wormholes, Time Machines, and the Weak Energy Condition', *Physical Review Letters*, 61 (1988), 1446–9.

Nozick, Robert, 'Newcomb's Problem and Two Principles of Choice', in *Essays in Honor of Carl G. Hempel*, Nicholas Rescher (ed.) (Dordrecht-Holland: D. Reidel, 1969), 114–46.

Pike, Nelson, 'Plantinga on Free Will and Evil', *Religious Studies*, 15 (1979), 449–73.

Quinn, Philip L., 'Divine Foreknowledge and Divine Freedom', *International Journal for Philosophy of Religion*, 9 (1978), 219–40.

Scriven, Michael, 'Randomness and Causal Order', *Analysis*, 17 (1956), 5–9.

Swinburne, Richard, 'Could there be More than One God?', *Faith and Philosophy*, 5 (1988), 234.

Talbott, Thomas B., 'On Divine Foreknowledge and Bringing About the Past', *Philosophy and Phenomenological Research*, 46 (1986), 455–69.

Van den Beld, A., 'Romans 7: 14–25 and the Problem of Akrasia', *Religious Studies*, 21 (1985), 495–515.

Walls, Jerry L., 'A Fable of Foreknowledge and Freedom', *Philosophy*, 62 (1987), 67–75.

Wierenga, Edward, 'Omnipotence Defined', *Philosophy and Phenomenological Research*, 43 (1983), 363–76.

Zeis, John, and Jacobs, J., 'Omnipotence and Concurrence', *International Journal for Philosophy of Religion*, 14 (1983), 17–24.

# Index